D1116804

POLICE SELECTION

POLICE SELECTION

Compiled and Edited by

RICHARD H. BLUM, Ph.D.
Lecturer in the School of Criminology
University of California
Berkeley, California

With Contributions by

Richard H. Blum	B. Earl Lewis
Edward Comber	Wesley Pomeroy
John Guidici	Jewell Ross
Joseph Kimble	David Wilson

With a Foreword by

Earl Warren
Chief Justice
United States Supreme Court

CHARLES C THOMAS · PUBLISHER
Springfield · Illinois · U.S.A.

Published and Distributed Throughout the World by
CHARLES C THOMAS • PUBLISHER
BANNERSTONE HOUSE
301-327 East Lawrence Avenue, Springfield, Illinois, U.S.A.
NATCHEZ PLANTATION HOUSE
735 North Atlantic Boulevard, Fort Lauderdale, Florida, U.S.A.

© *1964, by* CHARLES C THOMAS • PUBLISHER
Library of Congress Catalog Card Number: 64-18707

*With THOMAS BOOKS careful attention is given to all details of manu-
facturing and design. It is the Publisher's desire to present books that are
satisfactory as to their physical qualities and artistic possibilities and
appropriate for their particular use. THOMAS BOOKS will be true to those
laws of quality that assure a good name and good will.*

Printed in the United States of America
N-1

ABOUT THE CONTRIBUTORS

RICHARD BLUM is a Lecturer in the School of Criminology of the University of California at Berkeley and a member of the faculty of the Center for Training in Community Psychiatry of the California Department of Mental Hygiene. He is a Consultant to the Sheriff's Department of San Mateo County (California) and in the past has been Consultant to both the San Francisco and San Jose Police Departments. He has conducted research in a variety of medical, university, military and industrial settings. He is the author of several scientific books and a number of articles, including several on police problems and police selection which have appeared in law enforcement publications. He holds the Ph.D. degree from Stanford University.

EDWARD COMBER is a Lecturer in the School of Criminology of the University of California and is Director of the Bureau of Criminal Information of the San Francisco Police Department. A member of the Research Committee of the International Association of Chiefs of Police, and of several committees of the California Peace Officers' Association, he is Chairman of the Electronic Data Processing Advisory Committee of that Association. He has served as State Secretary for the Peace Officers Research Association. He is an Instructor for the Institute in Training in Municipal Administration. He holds the M.A. degree in Political Science from the University of California.

JOHN GUIDICI is a Captain in the Oakland (California) Police Department. He has served as Assistant Director, Police Division, of the Northwestern University Traffic Institute and was a Kempee Fellow at Northwestern. He is an Instructor in Police Services at Oakland City College and holds a Certificate in Public Administration from the University of California. He is a member of the International Association of Chiefs of Police and of various state and national peace officer organizations.

JOSEPH KIMBLE is a Captain in the San Mateo County Sheriff's Department and an Instructor in Police Science at the College of San Mateo. He holds certificates in Police Administration and Jail Management. He is a Consultant to the Delinquency Education project of the School of Criminology at the University of California, and is the author of instructional materials on race relations in use by the State of California Department of Justice. His articles have appeared in several law enforcement journals.

B. EARL LEWIS is Coordinator of the Law Enforcement Training Program at Foothill College (California) and was formerly Captain in the Sheriff's Department of Santa Clara County (California). He has been a Consultant in Law Enforcement to the Attorney General of the State of California. His graduate studies have been in the fields of Public Administration and Political Science.

WESLEY POMEROY is the Undersheriff of San Mateo County (California). Holder of the LLB degree, he is also a member of the American Bar Association and the California Bar Association. He is a member of the Training and Research Committee of the California Peace Officers' Association and is Secretary to the Juvenile Committee of the California State Sheriff's Association. He is an Instructor in Criminal Law and Evidence at Foothill College.

JEWELL ROSS is Captain in the Berkeley Police Department (California) and has been an Instructor in the Administration of Criminal Justice for Oakland Junior College. He is an Instructor for the Institute for Training in Municipal Administration and has taught in U. S. Army and in Navy Intelligence Schools. He is a member of the F.B.I. National Academy Associates for California and is a past president of a chapter of the honorary police fraternity, Lambda Alpha Epsilon.

DAVID WILSON is a psychiatrist (M.D.) certified by the Board of Examiners in Neurology and Psychiatry. He is also an attorney. He has served as Lecturer in the School of Criminology of the University of California and as a Consultant to the Berkeley Police Department. He is a member of the American Psychiatric Association, the American Bar Association, the California Bar Association, and the American Medical Association. He has served as Chief of the Psychiatric Service at the City and County Hospital of San Francisco and has been a Lecturer in the Center for Training in Community Psychiatry of the State of California Department of Mental Hygiene. During the Korean War, he served as Commanding Officer for the well-known 212th Psychiatric Evacuation Hospital in the Korean combat zone.

FOREWORD

THE INDIVIDUAL officer of the local police department is basic to the system of law enforcement in use in the United States today and the sound administration of criminal justice depends to a high degree upon his courage, skill and intelligent self-restraint in the performance of his duties.

Too often, much too often, it has been necessary for the courts to refuse to accept or to set aside the results of his work. There are those who would relax some or all of the curbs presently enforced against police excesses, believing that a reduction in crime justifies the use of methods that may violate personal rights guaranteed to all citizens, while there are others who would abandon the local organization of our police forces in favor of a more disciplined state or even national police organization.

We should indeed be dismayed if these were the only alternatives. There have been and there are in our country many local police organizations that are well administered and well trained, who perform their duties with intelligence and with scrupulous regard for the rights of individuals as well as for the protection of the community. The example of these departments I believe shows how we can develop a sound administration of criminal justice without either crushing individual rights or running the serious risks of a great concentration of police power. Most people concerned with law enforcement agree that police selection is important. But helpful suggestions are rare. Perhaps this is because the police administrator with practical experience is too often so engrossed in his day to day duties that he has no time to develop and explain his experience for the benefit of others.

The contributors to this book are an exception. They all have wide but varied experience in the practicalities of police work. Yet they have also studied what they have been and are doing. They have met together over a period of some years, analyzing and examining their own work and each others, and each has made his appropriate contribution to this publication.

The value of this book is not to be measured by the extent to which the reader agrees with the ideas and recommendations that it contains concerning police selection. The real value of the book is in the open-minded approach of the contributing authors, their constant questioning of basic assumptions, their willingness to test any dogma, however hoary, and their invitation to all the sciences to make their contribution to the always human and very difficult problem of police selection.

This book is intended for police administrators, and the thoughtful, experienced treatment of their problems which the book contains should be of great value.

EARL WARREN
Chief Justice
United States Supreme Court

INTRODUCTION

THIS BOOK IS for police administrators and for those who would become police administrators. It is for people in governmental agencies, civic groups, and other organizations who work with the police and would benefit from an understanding of the problems and methods of police selection. Finally the book is for personnel workers, psychologists, criminologists and others who have an interest in the techniques of police personnel selection and who wish to learn the latest about the findings from research and practice in this most important area of endeavor.

The book is about police selection. It describes what the latest methods of selection are, it discusses their advantages and disadvantages, it presents new findings from scientific studies and practical administration, and it reviews the relevant literature of police work, public administration, psychology and psychiatry. It is a book of questions as well as techniques, for each of the authors has set himself the task of asking "Why?" as well as "Why not?" It is a book which sees police personnel problems in the perspective of recent history, current social problems, evolving management practices, and developing psychological science and particular police technology.

The authors have tried to be helpful and hopeful as well as critical and skeptical. The implication of their work is that police personnel selection methods can benefit immensely from the wise application of recently developed knowledge. Another implication of what the authors say is that police management is an high-level, challenging and complex affair and that to be done well, the police manager must be a high-level fellow capable of meeting challenge and understanding complexity. There is another implication to be found in these chapters; it is that police personnel work can be effective only if its practitioners know a considerable amount about the society in which they live; its directions, its resources, its stresses and strains, and its ethical and moral base.

It is an unusual fellow who agrees with himself on every issue from one day to the next. No wonder that a group of men working together on a book may not always agree with one another. The men who wrote this book *are* in agreement on the fundamentals; they are in less agreement on the state of present practice, on nuances in assessing scientific or administrative evidence, or on the desirability of all the changes in policy which one or the other recommend. They hope the readers will disagree too, for in the ferment of disagreement lie the seeds of progress. On the weighty matters of morals, knowledge, technique and major directions the authors are agreed.

The authors have been working together as a dedicated informal group over the past four years. It is a group which has no rules, no officers, no purpose but one; to explore police problems and to consider solutions. In exploring common problems one appeared again and again; personnel. Out of their own concern, their own experience, and their desire to assist the police and the community this book has arisen.

The group itself is a rather remarkable one. As far as we know it is the only one like it in the police business. Its members are police officers, criminologists, psychologists, political scientists, public administrators, lawyers, sociologists, and psychiatrists. Oddly enough there are fewer people than professions in the group. That is because all of the members are in at least two and sometimes three professions at once. Wearing more hats than one, they value the broad view and avoid, as the plague, narrow professional provincialism. Another thing about the group; its members are all working in or for police or sheriff's departments. They are practical people. But at the same time all are, or have recently been, professors in universities or colleges or teachers in special institutes and training centers. That means that they are also scholars and academicians. The combination in each author of several professional interests, of practical orientation and of scholarly bent has been, we believe, a fruitful one. As for experience, their total accumulated time in police work or closely related concerns is 145 years; an average of eighteen years each.

Each of the authors approaches his topic from the standpoint of his own special experience and point of view. The chapters are so designed that the reader may approach each as an independent unit. This means the chapters can be understood by themselves without the reader having to go over all material prior to a given chapter. On the other hand this is not to stress selective chapter reading; we hope that the book in its entirety is worthy of the reader's attention.

What will the reader find herein? In Chapter I, Director Comber reviews the development of civil service, discusses the differences which characterize selection and operation in private enterprise as opposed to the public service, speaks of the relationships between police and public which affect both recruiting and the "public image" of the police and, finally, sets forth some of the characteristics of our society and of police service which operate on selection standards to make the rational evaluation and setting of those standards a matter of crucial importance to the commonweal. His comments on the wise approach to standards establishment will set the stage for the reader as they have for the authors.

Undersheriff Pomeroy, in a hard-hitting analysis, discusses typical administrative failings as they affect personnel selection, in Chapter II. He shows how the fundamental processes of reality appraisal, policy setting, power deployment, and communication must operate, and how great is the need for feedback, for flexibility and for an understanding of human relations and management techniques. His chapter, which will twist the tails of some among the mighty, demonstrates how intimately related are community sociological processes, local values and the individual strength of character of the police administrator. His approach combines frankness and simplicity with an understanding of the latest studies in management psychology and police-community relations.

Chapter III, by Captain Lewis and Dr. Blum, is a critical analysis of selection standards. They point to some of the unexamined assumptions which lie behind standards which are now in use or are being proposed. It is something of an "unholy" chapter, for no standard is so sacred as to escape their searching questions of "Why?" and "What happens as a consequence?" Their discussion includes some intriguing proposals for flexibility and concept reexamination. It brings to bear on the standards problem some of the recent scientific data of psychology and anthropology. It is unlikely that the thinking reader will leave this chapter without having come to examine some of his own ideas; a not undesirable event for, as Socrates said, "an un-examined life is not worth living" and so it is with ideas, the un-examined ones are not worth having.

Captain Kimble, in Chapter IV, stimulates the reader to con-sider a whole range of new techniques which can be employed in the recruitment of men. He does so while at the same time evaluating present recruitment methods and stressing the poten-tial of each of a variety of information sources and communication methods which are available to the concerned administrator and imaginative personnel man. His approach, not without humor and occasional ironic sallies aimed at conventional procedures, shows how recruitment can be linked to college and university programs, and, in so doing, he points out the necessarily intimate relationship between training, degrees of professionalization, standards, and recruitment procedures.

Dr. Blum's chapter on psychological testing does four things. It sets forth the basis for scientific studies of police personnel work. It describes the kinds of tests which can be used and reviews the literature on test use in police selection. It goes on to compare some departments which have not used tests in the selection pro-cess and those that have. Finally it presents the results of his own studies in four departments, in one, a study of seven years dura-tion; research reported here for the first time. His findings show what aspects of police performance can be predicted by psycho-logical tests at the time of hiring and how accurate such predic-tions can be. He concludes by suggesting how testing and research programs can be put to work to make police selection a more efficient business; one with beneficial consequences for both the police and the public.

A mystery is solved in Dr. Wilson's chapter. The mystery, or so it has been for many police administrators, has been what a psychiatrist can and should do in a selection program and what results can reasonably be expected from his work. Neither under-selling nor overselling the psychiatric contribution, careful to take the magic out of medicine, the chapter goes on to point out how best the psychiatrist can fit in a rational program. It points out not only the psychiatrist's responsibilities to an agency, but also the personal characteristics most desirable in a psychiatrist when a department head takes on the task of selecting *him*. And in that way the chapter returns to a basic theme in the book; the crucial role of the chief or sheriff in managing personnel selection programs.

Captain Ross writes about the background investigation. His chapter is rich with techniques and practical suggestions. There are few who will read it without learning a good deal about how investigations should be conducted and how the results can be used carefully and sensibly as part of the larger selection effort. But it is not only technique which is discussed; important assumptions are brought into the open and implications which one cannot escape are faced head on. The reader of this chapter should emerge not only better able to direct investigations, but more thoughtful about the values and preconceptions which may guide those efforts.

One of the most widely used tools in selection is the oral board. It is also one which is often little thought about and prepared for even less. Captain Guidici would change that, and in his chapter tells how the oral board can be transformed into a sharp, hard-hitting device. Like other good tools it is best used by craftsmen and its considered employment is called "work." The chapter makes it clear that neither craftsmanship nor work can be escaped, and if one is but willing to raise the oral board to its high potentials, its use will be rewarding. A number of specific suggestions are made and, in addition, some questions asked. Like questions asked in each chapter, present knowledge may provide no answers. The mature reader knows that he must live with ambiguity and uncertainty despite his understandable wish that things were otherwise. As Einstein once observed, the most important step to new knowledge is "knowing what questions to ask." It has been one of the goals of the authors to raise questions unsettling enough to make the reader face the fact of uncertainty and be so curious—if not uneasy—in consequence, that the reader decrees for himself the need for further steps to knowledge through personal observation, reading, and research.

People who set themselves the task of writing—or reading—

technical books share a belief. The belief is that knowledge is
the key to the solution of problems and the successful control of
the environment. This is the thesis of science and of education.
It is an optimistic belief, for it holds that present circumstances
can not only be changed but improved. The authors of this book
subscribe to that belief and it is reflected in the final chapter
written by Director Comber. That chapter says that the police
service is changing, and for the better. But it is the wise man who
sets his own course rather than allowing himself to drift willy
nilly on the currents. What then *are* the general goals of police
service and how can personnel policies, selection included, implement these goals? One of the goals considered is that of professionalization. Professional stature is not seen as either desirable or
attainable for all police officers; only for the minority who hold
supervisory or staff responsibilities. In raising this issue and in
taking the position it does, the final chapter leads to a further
exploration of issues; of academic and in-service education for
police service; of promotional standards and policies, and of the
knowledge of science, technology and public administration
necessary to managerial competence. Finally the chapter turns to
the need to generate new knowledge; the necessity for self-exami-
nation, for information-providing links with the community of
scientists and citizens, and for the development of rigorous and
objective research on police operations. In a word, it asks us to
use the ideas and tools our civilization provides so that police
service can improve itself. And a major target for improvement
is in selection methods. So it is that this introduction and the final
chapter end with the same words, "Personnel selection is the key
to the future of law enforcement service."

CONTENTS

POLICE SELECTION

Chapter I

HISTORY AND PERSPECTIVES

Police administration has come of age. Some people may question this statement and declare that the activities collectively identified under this title lack the essential maturity to qualify for recognition. However, when due consideration is given to the broad scope of the police function, the numbers of persons who are actively employed in this public undertaking, the large expenditures in public funds to support the police effort, and the direct impact of police services on the well-being of the community the importance of this segment of public service cannot be denied. The police function embraces simultaneously many vital activities. The most critical focal point of administrative responsibility lies in the area of police personnel management.

In commenting upon the importance of the personnel aspect of administration, O. W. Wilson stated:[1]

> "Of all the knotty problems that confront the police executive, none transcends in complexity and importance the problems relating to the management of personnel. Personnel administration is important because the quality of police service is strongly influenced by the manner in which policemen are selected for appointment and promotion, trained in effective performance of their duties, and otherwise managed. Police service is rendered by individual policemen on a person-to-person basis. Its quality, therefore, is determined by the individual men who provide it, and obviously cannot be raised above the quality of service rendered by the individual members in the aggregate. If police service is to be of high calibre, the members must have suitable qualifications, and they must be directed and controlled.
>
> "The simple statement that the management of personnel is the most important of all police administrative tasks seems to be an entirely inadequate expression of such a tremendously important fact."

The significance of the foregoing comment assumes its real importance when it is found that over ninety per cent (90%) of the average law enforcement budget is allocated for the payment of personal services—salary. Further, with each attempt to raise the standards in personnel selection a smaller number of applicants are solicited and fewer qualified candidates are presented to the administrator for appointment.*

The analysis of police recruitment and selection techniques presented in this book is designed to stimulate further study and experimentation in this vital area of administrative responsibility. It is the thesis of this text that, through imaginative planning and objective testing, law enforcement will break through the limitations and uncertainty of existing selection methods and emerge in the near future with more precise devices for personnel evaluation and the prediction of performance. In an era marked by expanding law enforcement services, limited budgets, increasing technology and vigorous competition for qualified personnel, the police administrator must be aggressive and remain alert if he is to secure the necessary staff to build an efficient organization and maintain effective operations.

The changing patterns of group activity within the present American culture impinge upon the agencies responsible for the maintenance of law and order. The continuous variations occurring within our society demand a constant review of basic policies and procedures within the police organization if those agencies are to provide an acceptable level of services. The ability to recognize the need for change and the capacity to make timely adjustments require an enlightened approach to personnel selection. The crude and haphazard attempts to hire units of manpower practiced by many police agencies is not only inadequate—it is fraught with danger.

FACTORS IN PERSONNEL REQUIREMENTS

The generalization can be made that PERSONNEL is the key element in any business or government organization. While this statement may be true, it deserves more patient and critical attention. It can be demonstrated, rather easily, that the personnel needs of a manufacturing plant differ markedly from those encountered in retail store management. The personnel require-

*See further comments in Chapters III, IV and V.

ments of both of these activities are in turn appreciably different from those found in the fields of transportation or communication. Personnel differences relate to and are a product of:

a. Conditions of employment.
b. Education and knowledge required of an employee.
c. Technical skills needed to perform the tasks.
d. Prior work experience.
e. Physical condition.
f. Personal appearance.
g. Job attitude—ability to work with others.
h. Status level of the occupation, etc.

These same elements can be recognized in any comprehensive evaluation program established for the recruitment and selecting of law enforcement personnel. The significance of these elements and their application to each field of employment, public or private, is intimately related to the tasks that are performed, the degree of independent action exercised by the employee, the social and economic importance of the end-product or service, the competitive nature of the business or activity, and the system of employee rewards that flow from participation. It is specifically because of these latter characteristics of employment that the personnel demands of law enforcement merit particular attention.

Some police officials contend police work is so unique that the personnel problems require separate treatment. Yet, these same officials find it difficult to identify clearly the nature and extent of uniqueness. An objective analysis of the total personnel function will demonstrate that screening devices can be incorporated in the selection process that will permit measurement of individual qualities insofar as the characteristics submit to measurement. A total personnel program includes many procedures and techniques of a specialized nature which are not the normal experience of a police administrator. Therefore, the law enforcement administrator should study the personnel process and utilize the assistance of a central personnel agency to perform those functions that that agency is qualified to provide. The police administrator must make his personnel requirements known and insist that a high standard of selection is maintained. Police personnel standards will be found to differ from those found in other forms of public service; however, the variations will occur in degree of qualification rather than kind.[2]

Most people think of employment primarily in terms of opportunities offered in business and industry. The free enterprise system attracts persons to perform services by participating in specialized vocational activities or becoming identified with the professions. Only during the last few decades has government employment begun to achieve a status and stability that would invoke the interest and challenge the intellectual capacity of the younger citizens. The negative image of public employment can be traced to its early beginnings in this country and to its colorful and somewhat tainted historic development. Only in the last generation has public employment emerged as a dedicated "career service" offering a real opportunity to the young man or woman who is seeking a place in the society.

THE DEVELOPMENT OF CIVIL SERVICE

During the formative years of our nation, the number of public employees was few and their duties were limited. This was in part a reflection of the political philosophy that favored a restricted centralization of power as the best guarantee of individual liberty. Great stress and social credit was given to "private enterprise" and its counterpart, "individual initiative." Employment in government service was considered a "second-rate" occupation fit only for the less gifted or those who depended upon political preferment. The criticism was not without some measure of justification. The "spoils system" received its first major impetus as a philosophy of democratic government during the presidency of Andrew Jackson in 1829. This policy remained the dominant criteria for public employment until after the Civil War. Repeated evidence of dissatisfaction with the "spoils system" arose during the period 1865 to 1883 and was manifest in the formation and activity of reform movements. The Pendelton Act of 1883 was the first significant reform legislation and has been identified as the landmark in the establishment of federal civil service. A parallel development occurred in a number of states and resulted in passage of civil service legislation in New York

(1883) and Massachusetts (1884). A number of cities joined in this reform movement with public service regulations enacted in a New York city in 1884. By the turn of the century, eighty-five municipalities adopted some form of civil service program The trend has been progressive both in depth and scope. Hence, the chronology of public administration acknowledges the period 1883 to 1935 as the era of reform and bureaucratic evolution.[3]

The social and economic structure of the nation became more complex as it increased in geographic area and population. The great moving forces of history—urbanization, industrialization, social unrest, war and depression have made their impact upon the public and the government. The idealistic "freedom" and "individuality" of former years was not compatible with the changes in socio-economic conditions. The individual became lost in and a victim of the "free enterprise" system during times of economic stress and social evolution. As a result, the government assumed the responsibility to render economic aid and provide additional services. Each new service increased the scope of government employments. In turn, the progressive changes in the character of government services forecast a reassessment of required skills and the personal attributes of persons hired to perform these tasks.

The original structuring of civil service was designed "to keep the scoundrels out." While this negative approach served an initial purpose in the formative years of civil service, it did not encourage the full development of a public personnel program. Experience indicates that modern public personnel requirements demand a more dynamic approach to current needs. Progressive personnel administration is now oriented toward an employment system that will select the "best qualified" applicant. The change in emphasis in civil service has become quite clear in the last decade. The trend has been described by O. Glenn Stahl in the following terms:[4]

> "A competent civil service could not come just from initial employment on a competitive basis and "equal pay for equal work". The big job of personnel management was emerging as that of securing the ablest people for the public service and of maintaining a well-trained, happy, productive working force...

"It has meant making the public service attractive as a career for the cream of the graduates from that nation's schools and colleges. It has meant inclusion of in-service training for orientation, for skill improvement, for increasing employee potential for advancement, for creating a sense of "belonging" and a sense of unity and common purpose in an organization."

It is for these reasons that the present period beginning in 1935 has been referred to as the era of positive public personnel administration. The term "merit system" embraces the philosophy of civil service today. The broader identification "career service" is gaining attention and marks the mature development of a true public service structure.

PRIVATE ENTERPRISE VS PUBLIC SERVICE

While a number of the employees in private business and in government apparently perform tasks that are highly similar there are substantial distinctions in the management goals and responsibilities of the respective activities. These distinctions are real and provide the basis for variations in employment requirements. The characteristics of public service that distinguish it from private business have been identified as follows:[5]

"1. The services performed by the State are more urgent than those performed by private institutions....
2. The services of the State are generally of a monopolistic or semi-monopolistic character....
3. The supply of services by the State is not governed by the market price....
4. The conduct of public services is governed by legal provisions....and,
5. The business of government, particularly in a democracy, is conducted very much in the public eye."

The importance of these characteristics and their application to law enforcement merit fuller comment.

It is generally accepted that the quality of the end-product of any organized process cannot be higher than the potential quality of the basic ingredients that were gathered and blended in its creation. This statement could apply in many areas of human activity—the preparation of miracle drugs, the manufacture of a guided missile or an automobile, the processing of food, and even the assessment of human organizations. The individual citizens, as well as the public at large, will accept or reject a product or service in proportion to the degree of satisfaction that is attained from its use or application. In an overwhelming number of situations, the individual as consumer will determine the worth of the product or service by the value of what he is willing to exchange for it. If the level of satisfaction falls below the value of the exchange, and particularly if the deficiency persists, the individual will shift his interest and seek a substitute satisfaction. In commerce and industry, this phenomenon provides a form of economic regulation through the interplay of supply and demand. The deficient product will either be up-graded in quality, reduced in cost, or be doomed to elimination in the economic struggle of survival of the fittest.

In our culture a great variety of products and services are provided through private organizations. There are in addition other substantial sources of services that are a direct outgrowth of public responsibility and civil authority. The "public services" are of vital concern to the citizen and are essential to the well being of the nation as a whole. Public services bear a special relationship to the individual citizen inasmuch as they were created by statute, the functions have the sanction of law, and the service is usually of a type that is not satisfactorily provided under the private enterprise system. In any case, the service is intimately related to a basic responsibility of government. In each situation, the public service activity carries a symbol of authority and preemptive status that is not a common denominator in private business. Further, some public services are performed to assure the freedom and safety of the individual citizen and provide for his convenience within the practical and philosophical framework of our society.

Whereas the individual consumer may choose among competing business concerns to secure satisfaction for a personal requirement, such choice of action is not to be found if the service is provided by a public agency. The vital regulatory impact of economic factors and public acceptance common to business are not present in the public service area. The established measures of efficiency and success utilized by business and industry are not directly applicable to the field of public service. Business enterprise has shown a readiness and capacity to adjust quickly to external demands and is free to participate, associate with other organizations or remain independent, expand or contract services, etc. The business concern responds to the will of its management and is limited only by financial resources and administrative skills. In contrast, the public agency is subject to greater limitation in independent action due to the provisions of the legal statute that defines its function and area of responsibility. The expansion and contraction of a public service is not necessarily subject to current demands for its services.

The basic elements that provide motivation and substance for service producing agencies vary to a considerable extent. The variations in the directing forces cannot be divorced from the organization and they shape the nature and character of the services performed. A study of individual organizations will reveal that, while they differ widely as to purpose, structure, process, policy, etc., they do converge at a common meeting place. This meeting place is the labor market where they compete for the skills and experience of employable persons. History has shown that success has been attained in private enterprises by progressive managers who are able to attract sufficient talent and manipulate the available human and physical resources in such manner as to produce a functioning organization that in turn generates a satisfactory quality of service. Thus, the entrepreneur has become aware of the need to secure the services of qualified personnel to staff his organization. Personnel classification, recruitment, and selection have been subject to the attention of aggressive management in the business field for many years. The development of civil service has not been stimulated by the same self-interest. Public services are seldom evaluated on the basis of profit realized through operations. As a matter of fact, the aspect of "profit" is an anomally in the field of public administration.*[3] While the private institution reflects the positive stimulus of profits, the public agency experiences the negative caution of a tax rate. The objective in public administration is to provide a maximum level

---

*The author recognizes the existence of public utilities operated by governmental entities; however, these represent a special situation.

of satisfactory services in return for each tax dollar allocated to the agency. Therefore, public service in the modern era demands that critical attention be given the elements of a personnel program to attract and hold qualified persons who will respond adequately and continuously without the compelling drives common to the private enterprise profit oriented organizations.

LAW ENFORCEMENT SERVICE AND THE PUBLIC

In the early history of American law enforcement the police officer was primarily in contact with the criminal element rather than with the orderly members of society. In sharp contrast, the modern law enforcement agency has many service responsibilities that promote a high rate of contact with the non-criminal segment of the community. This situation has been the natural outgrowth of the increasing number of regulatory measures that society has enacted to promote its own safety and convenience. It is a cruel commentary that the specific agency that society has created and charged with responsibility for the maintenance of security and public order is, in turn, subject to apathetic support and frequent irrational criticism. The reasons for this paradox are many and varied. Some factors can be readily identified, others are obscure and intangible.

The public tends to accept the law enforcement agency as a "necessary evil" and does not assess it as a positive personal service that protects the individual and the social order. This attitude might be closely related to the general public resentment of regulation as an infringement on individual liberty. Much of this resentment is baseless. The fact that it exists is evidence of the extent by which many individuals and groups view the democratic concept as a license to take liberty, rather than the privilege to share a mutual benefit through the exercise of responsible restraint. This is exemplified best by the many instances wherein an individual will violate a law knowingly yet seek refuge in questionable rationalization when confronted by a peace officer who is attempting to carry out his sworn duty.

The performance of law enforcement services in the United States has not been uniform nor of a consistently high order. Police conduct has merited criticism on a number of occasions.

The public is quick to identify any current defect or irregularity with corruption and misconduct that prevailed during prior periods of administrative failure. Law enforcement has the dubious distinction of being subject to public and official scrutiny more than any other service agency. The police officer lives literally in a "fish bowl." This high visibility pertains to all segments of the service and extends into the private life of the individual member.

Many of the past failings of the police can be identified with "the system" that prevailed when the irregularities occurred. Police power has always suffered as the step-child of local political power. When the local political power is used wisely and fosters sound police administration, the community is the fortunate beneficiary. On the other hand, when political manipulators prostitute the police service for selfish ends, the community must contend with confusion, uncertainty, and a double standard of enforcement. The police agency that is compelled to operate in this environment cannot function effectively and lacks the fundamental basis upon which it may build or attain self-respect. It cannot portray its own image but must live with and by the image drawn by the local political power structure.*

Fortunately, the modern police administrator has acquired an enlightened view of his responsibility and is concerned about the image of the department. Not only is it a measure of public acceptance of the service, but it is also an indirect gauge of the public attitude towards the total government structure. The public's image of the police service is a prime factor in the attraction the service holds for potential candidates for recruitment. The police image is important because membership in a law enforcement agency presents some handicaps to those who seek participation. The many hours of night duty are out of harmony with the normal working periods of a major segment of society, thus the service imposes a social barrier in the life of the officer. The semi-military character of police organization, the discipline, and the customary use of a uniform set the officer apart from the public. Department rules regarding personal conduct follow the member on or off duty and restrict his personal freedom. The

*See aditional comments on this subject in Chapter II.

law enforcement officer is also subject to recall to duty at any time. The recall may only occur infrequently: however, because of this contingency the member is seldom completely at ease. When an officer is off-duty in the home setting he risks the possibility of becoming involved in neighborhood disputes just because he is known to be a "cop" and is therefore subject to the entreaty of his neighbors.

The public is quick to call the police when an incident occurs. The officer is expected to take command of the situation regardless of the circumstances or the odds. If the subsequent action of the officer does not satisfy one or more of the participants, or a bystander, the officer and the department share the resulting criticism. The person voicing the complaint may not know all of the facts, he may not be able to distinguish whether or not the incident was a police matter or a dispute that comes within the purview of the civil court, in all probability he does not know the laws of arrest, etc., yet these deficiencies of knowledge do not restrain his comdemnation of the police.

The police service has made mistakes of judgment and tactics over the years. Many of these events have come to the public attention. Until these deficiencies are corrected or reduced to a minimum the police image will never achieve the status that commands public respect and acceptance. Many of these defects are being eliminated in the more progressive departments. Reference is made specifically to such unjustifiable practices as:

    a. Continued use of illegal and inhumane tactics with respect
       to arrest and interrogation.
    b. Tolerance of vice and lotteries.
    c. Double standard in the enforcement of laws.
    d. Cover-up of personnel wrong-doing.
    e. Falsification of records.
    f. Lack of discipline within the organization.
    g. Lack of cooperation with allied agencies, etc..

The existence and continuation of these practices can culminate only in public disrespect for the local police agency. The public will become suspicious of every police act; attempts at routine enforcement will produce resentment; the public will become uncooperative.

The standards for a police officer in this generation are not
the same as those that existed at the turn of the century. The
police officer that was hired and retained in those days was a
product of his time. He was qualified within the requirements of
the service of that era. In all probability, he would not be acceptable as a recruit for law enforcement today. Modern police
service is markedly different from that which prevailed a few
generations ago. The change in standards reflects the trend in our
culture as a whole during the intervening years. Each change has
been an adjustment to meet growing police responsibility. As the
nature and scope of law enforcement has expanded the demands
upon the members of the service have become more exacting.
The adequate policeman who pounded a "beat" in the Bowery
in the early days had only a whistle and club as a means of communication in contrast to the modern officer who patrols in a
radio equipped motor vehicle. Modern police service with its
specialized communications and variety of transportation, with
its crime laboratory staff and canine corps, with its planning and
research unit and juvenile aid bureau, with its community relations unit and its traffic education detail has moved into an operations area where effective service can evolve only if the personnel
of the department is highly qualified, adequately trained, and
properly supervised. Lest the reader be of the opinion that police
recruitment standards are already too high, it may be observed
that the trend of history is quite clear and consistent. The highest
standards that we could devise today will probably be judged
inadequate by our successors within the span of a generation.

WHY SELECTION STANDARDS IN LAW ENFORCEMENT MUST BE RAISED

The justification for high personnel standards in law enforcement can be expressed in many ways. Following are the principal
reasons why no compromise with excellence can be made in police
personnel selection.

1. *The complexity of our social setting demands police competence.* The urban community has become increasingly more
congested and the social inter-relations more complex. These
centers of humanity generate political and socio-economic prob-

lems of a magnitude that is unique in world history. These mix-
tures of culture, education, skills, and status offer unprecedented
opportunities for conflict. Those charged with responsibility for
the maintenance of justice, peace and order must be of high
caliber.

2. *The educational achievement level of the average citizen
is rising steadily.* A few generations ago the person with a high
school diploma was in a preferred status and could command employment opportunities that were above the average. The high
school graduate was in demand by those who sought quality in
their employees. Today this status is reserved for persons who have
completed a college education. Business and industry are cognizant of the need to up-grade employment standards in order to
compete successfully. The law enforcement officer who must work
with and for members of the community will not command respect or perform his task satisfactorily unless his educational
achievements are at least equal to the average citizen with whom
he will be in contact. When we consider that the officer will be
called upon to assist and advise the citizen who is in difficulty, we
can logically conclude that the officer's level of intelligence and
store of knowledge must be of a higher order than the average.

3. *Our society is governed by a growing multiplicity of laws
and legal rulings.* One of the basic tenants of our culture is that
"we are a society governed by law not by man." As our social
system became more complex, laws were enacted to provide
guidelines for individual and group conduct. Regulations have
multiplied until we find that the present era is marked by legal
confusion and uncertainty. The police officer is called upon to act
quickly and precisely under adverse circumstances. He is expected
to "know the law" and act accordingly without fear or favor. This
is an ideal that will be difficult to achieve. However, any hope
for the attainment of this goal will rest upon the employment of
law enforcement personnel who have qualifications that are above
those possessed by the average citizen.

4. *Police service is a highly personal service.* Of all the public
services the police function stands in sharp relief in view of its
potential and actual impact on the life and convenience of the
individual citizen. The police officer may, under proper sanction

of law, stop a person on the street, inquire as to his identity and purpose, search his person, enter his residence, seize property, arrest and detain the individual. The action of a police officer may require that the person arrested appear before a magistrate, stand trial for a public offense, serve a penal term and even, under particular circumstances, lose certain rights of citizenship. The social and economic results of such incidents can be readily understood without elaboration. Among the many public services, law enforcement allows the broadest exercise of discretionary action on the part of the individual members of the agency. This latitude in public contact is a necessary condition of the service if it is to be effective and responsive to the needs of the individual citizen.

5. *Modern police duty covers a broad scope of activities.* The variety and detail of functions involved in police duty has acquired new dimensions. Each day additional responsibilities are placed upon the law enforcement services. Each change brings with it concurrent demands for particular knowledge and associated skills. This trend has promoted "specialization" in the services which complicate the administrative processes. The great need is to develop qualified generalists who can function adequately in all areas of police responsibility. This cannot become a reality unless the service attracts and holds persons of exceptional ability.

6. *The law enforcement services have shown persistent tendency to grow from within.* Historically, police agencies have demonstrated a resistance to influences that are external to the service. This self-isolation can be detected in the many provincial attitudes and policies that exist between these agencies and which separate the individual agencies from the public they are sworn to serve. One of the outstanding marks of this in-breeding can be seen in the promotional practices which discourage open examinations and impose severe limitations upon any inter-agency transfer of personnel. This self-regenerating atmosphere needs imaginative stimulation if the hazard of stagnation is to be avoided. New concepts and new strength must be continually drawn into the law enforcement services if they are to meet the challenge of the day. This problem directs attention once again to PERSONNEL. If the service is to produce high quality management personnel in

the future, it must consider this need when initial selection programs are established.

7. *The goal of law enforcement is to attain recognition as a profession.* High qualification for entrance into an activity is one of the elements common to a profession. These high entrance standards invoke a sense of pride and dedication that are effective in the execution of responsibilities.

8. *There is an imperative need to build a proper "image" of the police service.* The standards within the law enforcement services must be raised to such a level that the public will recognize the value of the standard in terms of satisfactory service experience. It may be many years before the public fully accepts the police services as a positive element in the society, yet acceptance of quality service dispensed by skilled practicioners who are dedicated to public service will result in acceptance and status.

9. *Modern police service requires a high level of inter-agency cooperation and coordination.* Although the police agencies are organized primarily on a local basis, their activity requires extensive intercourse with other law enforcement agencies in other jurisdictions. The local organization must maintain a trained staff that is capable of working with the police employees in other departments. They must possess at least the same level of skills and technical knowledge.

10. *There is an impelling need to find a practical solution to the crime problem.* Crime represents a blight upon society. It has existed in all eras, in all cultures and in all localities. Crime represents a needless waste of human and physical resources that begs for correction. The solution of this problem will require the combined talent of all segments of society. The police services form the first line of defense and are in a unique position to observe crime and the criminal in action. The police agencies provide access to a great wealth of source data which may hold the key to any practical remedy. Therefore, it seems logical that society would be the direct beneficiary in any move to assure that law enforcement personnel were selected on the basis of high standards.

Each author who contributed to this book directed his attention to a specific aspect of the personnel selection process. He undertook the evaluation of the particular selection device to identify its characteristics, describe its contribution to the personnel program, and assess its limitations based upon current knowledge and experience. The authors will express strong views with respect to the values of these selection devices where the evidence warrants such conviction. The reader will also note that some uncertainty exists as to the present validity of other techniques. This is a reflection of the true status of the practice of selection today.

The selection techniques have been developed to measure objectively the qualifications and potentiality of an applicant. However, many of the personal attributes of interest to the employer do not submit to ready measurement. Testing devices are only formalized procedures of assessment based upon certain empirical standards. While some tests are classified as "scientific," even these elite tests are founded upon certain assumptions, all of which cannot be proved or demonstrated. This does not mean that these tests have no value. They are useful and powerful methods of sampling the personal qualities and attitudes of an individual and permit comparison of the results with the characteristics possessed by standard populations subject to the same test. The significance of these testing devices lies in their use as an aid to the administrator who must exercise final judgment on the qualification of each applicant. The tests are offered to provide an objective basis for the decision to hire rather than depend on a hunch or the personal recommendation of a local politician. The selection process properly conceived and implemented can be used by the police administrator to avoid improper influences in the selection of personnel. These devices are administrative tools and are essential implements in a sound personnel program.

BIBLIOGRAPHY

1. Address delivered by O.W. Wilson before the International Association Chiefs of Police in Los Angeles, California, September 25th, 1952.
2. *Municipal Police Administration.* International City Managers' Association, Chicago, Ill., Fifth Ed, 1961, page 121.
3. *Municipal Personnel Administration.* International City Managers' Association, Chicago, Ill., Sixth Edition, 1960, pages 3-17.

4. Mosher, W.E., Kingsley, J.D., and Stahl, O.G.: *Public Personnel Administration,* Third Edition. Harper and Brothers, New York, 1950, page 39.
5. Stahl, O.G.: *Public Personnel Administration,* Fifth Edition, Harper & Row, New York, 1962, pages 7, 29-47.

Additional References

6. Germann, A.C.: *Police Personnel Management.* Springfield, Thomas, 1958.
7. Leonard, V.A.: *Police Organization and Management.* Police Science Series, The Foundation Press Inc., Brooklyn, New York, 1951.

Chapter II

THE ADMINISTRATIVE SETTING

W HAT KIND OF AN administrative setting is needed to allow a good personnel selection program to flourish? The answer is simple. A good personnel selection program or any other sound program will be successful in any department whose administrator practices the widely-accepted and well-written-about valid principles of administration and management with intelligence and imagination. The only reason that there needs to be any further discussion on the matter beyond this point is the sad fact that very few law enforcement administrators really do this. Some sincerely try, and some of these come close, but the vast majority perfunctorily practice those principles or ignore them altogether.

Although it is quite easy to see how this situation could be corrected, there isn't much hope that it will be. All that would have to be done is to remove the incumbent heads of many of the law enforcement agencies in the United States and replace them with men who have the intellectual ability and the guts to run a police business as well as most private businesses are run. Since this will never happen, it seems that it might be reasonable to discuss a few factors in the administrative process that have some relationship to the success or failure of a good personnel selection program.

The administrative considerations that will be discussed in this chapter are:

1. Be sure you know what you want.
2. Say what you mean.
3. Be willing to back policy with power.
4. Be realistic—know your environment.
5. Check results.
6. Be willing to change.
7. Use your "human materials" well.

The major influence on any departmental program is the chief, sheriff, or director and his *real* attitudes. If he does not wholly support a program and demonstrate that he does, the program won't be worth a tinker's dam. Even though he doesn't really "buy" everything he has read (or someone has read to him) about good administration, it behooves him to recognize and accept certain concepts of administrative theory if he expects successfully to hire and to keep good, competent individuals in his department. This chapter and those following are, of course, for anyone in any law enforcement agency to read (and to accept or reject), but the hope of the authors is that department heads will read and be influenced in someway. If they are not, very little in this book will ever be translated into any part of a working procedure. The head of the law enforcement agency is the one person who most nearly determines whether that agency is good or bad. What this author has to say is primarily for him.

KNOW WHAT YOU WANT

Before you can begin a personnel selection program, you must decide what you want that program to do for you. What kind of department is desired? What kind of people must you recruit into the department to build such a department? What should the relationship of the department be to the community it serves?

Probably the latter question is the one that should be considered first. What the relationship should be to the community depends to some extent on whether the community is primarily residential or commercial, or somewhere in between; whether it is metropolitan or rural in character; and what type of service should be given to the community ("type" of service, here, does not refer to quality).

It seems apparent that the type of services that would be appropriate for town A of 5000 population made up solely of residences situated on lots of 2-acre minimum size would not be wholly suitable for city B, a seacoast city of 500,000 population. It seems reasonable that a personnel selection program for town A should be designed to recruit men whose interests and qualifications indicate that they probably would make good generalists, while the hiring process in city B should develop candidates who are interested in a livelier job situation and in eventually becoming specialists.

The chiefs of both town A and city B should organize their

departments so that those departments can offer the most appropriate services to their communities. Then they can determine what kind of personnel should be recruited into their departments and what testing procedures should be used to do this. A man who does an excellent job in the slum district of a good-sized city may do very poorly in a setting such as town A. Conversely, a man who is highly efficient in a small, residential town may fail miserably in city B.

Once the law enforcement administrator has determined what sort of relationship should exist between his department and the community it serves, he will find that he has defined the aims and goals for that department and the type of men he must recruit in order to attain those goals. This follows, since he necessarily must have considered those areas in defining the relationship of his department to the community.

After the administrator has decided what type of individuals he needs in order to achieve departmental goals, he should design a personnel selection process that will give him the type of people he wants. This involves the choosing of testing techniques, and the employment of specialists who can best administer and evaluate the tests.

If psychological tests are used, and they certainly should be, the services of a psychologist will be required. Care should be used in selecting a psychologist to make sure that he has the skills that are suitable for selecting law enforcement officers or agents. Even though he is otherwise competent, he should be oriented to the problems of law enforcement personnel selection and should be sympathetic to them. If he is not, his evaluations may not suit your purpose. In addition, there is a strong likelihood that staff resistance may develop because of his attitudes. The same principles apply in the selection of a psychiatrist, if psychiatric interviews are used.

SAY WHAT YOU MEAN

Police Officers, by training and experience, have learned that they must deal with things as they actually are. They have found that truth does not always coincide with what it is represented to be. They have learned that this is the case even in the matter of departmental policy. Whenever a new policy is prepared and issued by the administration of a law enforcement agency, the personnel in that agency may be inclined to adopt a "wait and see" attitude until it is made known to them by the administration exactly what was meant by the stated policy.

The stated policy may actually mean one of several things.

1. It may mean that it is to be interpreted literally—that it means exactly what has been said in the order, or rule or other formal method of presenting policy.

2. It may mean something approximating the formally stated policy, but somewhat different from what it says literally.

3. It may mean nothing at all in terms of getting something done. The policy may have been prepared and issued for the sole and expedient purpose of quieting criticism of the department in some area of general, public concern—an area, perhaps, such as the hiring and retaining of competent personnel. Until such time as the administrator makes known in other ways what his *true* intent regarding the issued policy is, the personnel in the department may not actually put it fully into practice.

A rough analogy might be drawn to the relationship between statutory law and case law. Statutes can be enacted into law by the legislature in what seem to be clearly understandable terms. When these statutes are tested in the courts, however, and interpreted by them, they may take on different meanings from what seemed to have been intended by the legislature.

Similarly, a written policy of a law enforcement agency can acquire a different meaning by the interpretation given to it by the agency head. As a matter of fact, since he is dealing with his own policy, he has much greater power to alter it by interpretation than has a court of law with a legislative enactment. The job of effectively communicating policy is not completed until the agency head *does* interpret it. This interpretation can be effected in several ways.

1. It can be done by issuing additional, consistent orders or rules—although this is not too effective, since it doesn't really represent meaningful interpretation. It merely serves to reiterate what has already been said in the same terms.

2. It can be done by establishing an on-going program that

puts into effect the policies and procedures contained in the written orders or rules.

3. It can be done most effectively through informal methods of communication—methods that may not even be considered to be communication by the administrator. These informal methods usually will involve either action or inaction on the part of the agency head.

An obvious example would be a situation where a stated policy is openly flaunted and nothing is done about it. In such a case, if the basic organization of the department is sound and the chain of command operates well, and there is therefore no reason for the agency head to be uninformed, he communicates quite clearly to those working under him that the policy doesn't mean what it says, and, is in fact, no policy at all.

Another example could be stated hypothetically by supposing an instance where a young man with only a grammar school education is permitted to take an entrance level examination for the position of patrolman, even though departmental policy states that the minimum educational requirement for the position is high school graduation. The reason he is allowed to take the examination is because he comes from a family that represents political influence in the community. The administrator may justify his action by saying that the applicant has experience that is of as much worth to the department as a high school education, when, in fact, he does not have such experience.

By failing to follow his own stated policy, the head of the department has communicated in plain terms, not only to the members of his department, but to the public, as well, that the policy is of no value. The inevitable effect will be to mar the image of the department, and to cause the public to hold the department in low esteem. It probably will have the further effect of discouraging qualified men and women from applying for positions in that department through regular channels, and will encourage the use of political influence to place people in the department who may or may not be qualified to do the job. It will also cause members of the department to feel shame and resentment for a shoddy course of action over which they can exert little control, with a subsequent drop in morale.

If, on the other hand, the administrator refuses to make an exception for the young man in question, he will retain the respect of the personnel in his department, of the general public, and even of the political sponsors of the applicant. The latter may not like the decision too well, but they will have to respect the man who made it.

There is another aspect to the subject of communication that is germane to the matter of personnel selection and should be mentioned. No matter how well a communicator may express himself, no matter how clearly he may demonstrate that he means what he says, he will be ineffective if the persons to whom he is communicating haven't the ability to understand. Communication needs to have a communicator and a communicatee, and there has to be some basic understanding between them in order for intelligence to be transmitted between them. As with a radio transmitter and receiver, both must be tuned to the same frequency.

It is basic that the police administrator not only must try to upgrade existing personnel in this department, but that he must also design his personnel selection program so that it is most likely to bring into the department men and women who are capable of understanding departmental policy and of implementing it. For this reason, if for no other, a written test that can measure intelligence should be administered to all applicants.

BACK POLICY WITH POWER

This is an extension of the maxim that you must "say what you mean." Here, the law enforcement administrator "says" it with whatever power he has in such a way that it creates and maintains high departmental morale by giving support to his personnel. Once the administrator has set policy and the men and women in his department follow it, he must make sure that he, himself, consistently follows it so that he doesn't leave his employees "out on a limb" by cutting the support out from under them. This is not to say that policy shouldn't be changed, but that it shouldn't be changed unexpectedly in such a way that an honest, well-motivated employee is humiliated.

Let's use an example to illustrate. This example should be familiar since it has occurred innumerable times in many departments. It may be happening right now in your department. It is an example often used by oral boards in interviewing candidates for promotion because it "has no correct solution."

The chief of a municipal police department has established a policy that the year long probationary period is to be used as a meaningful tool in the selection process. During this period, new employees are to be carefully evaluated and only those who have performed well are to be certified to a permanent position at the end of the probationary period.

After several months of his probationary status, it becomes apparent to his supervising sergeant that a new officer is performing quite poorly. He has reported to duty late a number of times, several substantiated complaints that he is rude and tactless have been made about him, he consistently has been careless in his personal appearance. Although the sergeant has discussed these matters with him, he has maintained a flippant attitude toward the sergeant's advice and has made no effort to modify his ways. The sergeant therefore recommends that the officer's employment be terminated.

The chief does not follow the sergeant's recommendations, although he agrees that the sergeant's evaluations and conclusions are correct and that the officer should be terminated. The reason for the chief's action is that the officer needs the job because he has several children and is badly in debt.

Although there can be no question that the chief's motives toward the officer are kind and humane, the effect on his personnel policy and the men in his department will be very destructive. You can be sure that the sergeant involved will hesitate a good long while before he again tries to make an honest evaluation of a probationary employee's performance. One such incident could result in destroying the initiative in a supervisor that has taken years to develop. In addition, the chief has demonstrated that he doesn't really intend to use his power in a consistent manner for the good of the personnel in the department. He has said, by his actions, that the probationary period is worthless and that every rookie has a de facto permanent status in the department from the first day he dons his uniform.

Every law enforcement administrator has power, whether he

likes it or not, and if he uses it properly, it will contribute substantially to the smooth running of his department. If he uses it badly or fails to use it when he should, the personnel in his department will never know where they stand and their morale will suffer as a result.

BE REALISTIC

It is a practical fact that, for various reasons, the actual power of the administrative heads of many police organizations has been considerably watered down. This serves to dilute the ability of the department head to effectively determine all policy, but it doesn't, in any case totally negate it. He is, at least, left with the power of persuasion. Whatever power he may have, he has the solemn obligation to create as fine a department as he can within the limits of practical political reality. If policy changes are indicated, he must try to make them, stopping short only of the point where he stimulates opposition to the degree that his ability to do business is impaired.

It is essential that a good police administrator is aware of the realities of the political sphere in which he operates. He must objectively analyze the role he fills and its relationship to those persons and groups around him who can strengthen or weaken his policy making power, either directly or indirectly. He should then determine how he can function with optimum efficiency within this political culture without compromising principle for the sake of expediency. He must know when it is appropriate for him to sacrifice a small gain, if by doing so he increases the probability of ultimately attaining a larger and more important goal.

Temporary, reasoned withdrawal can be a perfectly legitimate tactic if it enables an administrator to maintain a strong policy making position. Very little is gained if an agency head takes such a strong position on a relatively minor issue that he is removed or rendered powerless as a result. Just how strong a position should be taken on a given issue is a determination that can be made only by the administrator at the time when an issue arises. No clearly definitive rules for such a determination can be set down by anyone else. This area of administration is an art, not a science. How well that art is practiced depends almost entirely upon the subjective, personal skills of the particular administrator involved.

How well the administrator does in this area must necessarily be measured in terms of ultimate results. One must here apply the rule used in the military service, that is, the true test of the worth of a particular tactic is how well it actually works.

Every law enforcement administrator must assemble data and prepare justification in support of any departmental program he presents to those who control the budget within his jurisdiction. In order to do this well, he must consider the political reality of selling his program in terms of economic savings. He must show that a program that costs more than the old way of doing business will actually result eventually in a saving of money for the jurisdiction.

A good personnel selection program is going to seem expensive if measured in terms of the cost of the testing process alone, without taking into consideration the savings that will be realized by recruiting men and women who will perform their tasks with greater skill and efficiency. A poor selection procedure is actually much more costly since it results in hiring people who can operate less efficiently with a resultant loss of prestige and public acceptance. As prestige is lost, fewer qualified applicants will apply, further depressing the quality of personnel coming into the department.

A good, apparently expensive selection program is actually the most economical in the long run. It increases the probability that well motivated, emotionally stable, healthy, intelligent candidates will apply and be hired. It decreases the likelihood that personnel in whom the department has an investment both in time and money will have to be suspended or terminated for disciplinary reasons. It will almost surely guarantee that the department will be respected by the members of the community it serves.

If an administrator heads a law enforcement agency in a political atmosphere that permits him to use the power and exercise the discretion that he should have, he has a good chance of establishing a good personnel selection program. If he is in a political milieu, however, where the law enforcement agency is not much more than a political tool, his position is almost untenable. Let us consider a situation where an administrator finds himself in such a culture.

In a city where this type of political environment exists, the chief finds that he has very little or no control over the personnel selection process. Things are so bad that it is only by pure chance that well qualified applicants have found their way into the department, since they are hired solely on the basis of political expediency. It is the department wherein the saying "it's not what you know but who you know" has real meaning.

The chief is only the nominal head of the department. He doesn't really make policy because it is actually dictated by the political forces in power through the mayor or police commission. The policy is shaped to further political ends, not to satisfy law enforcement needs.

Personnel policy is designed so that it can be used to pay off political debts, not to select the best qualified candidates for openings in the department. This is done in many ways. Several of them are:

1. Appointing to the department individuals who have rendered valuable service to the party.

2. Appointing relatives of those who are politically important.

3. Rewarding party's subalterns by allowing them to sell appointments to the department.

There are many other political reasons for passing out jobs in the police department. Their number is limited only by the imagination of the political hacks who determine who is to be allowed to dip his hand into the employment pork barrel.

Although a civil service system exists, it functions only as a front, providing a facade behind which valid personnel selection practices are callously subverted. Actually, the facade fools no one unless he really wants to be deceived. The system exists because the public either actively supports it or simply doesn't care.

There are several courses of action open to the chief in this city, all of which have built into them limited rewards and small satisfaction.

He can stay and try to upgrade the department as best he can. If he does, he must be satisfied with only small gains and live with almost constant frustration. If the chief decides to take this course of action, he should reconcile himself to certain facts of life. First of all, he will be the head of a department composed of individuals over whom he has very little disciplinary control. Since everybody knows that political influence is the key to getting whatever you want in the department, political influence will be used and the chain of command will be ignored in every case where it is more expedient to do so.

Since a law enforcement agency is primarily concerned in giving service, and since the quality of a service is directly related to the quality of the person rendering the service, it follows that in order for this chief to make his department more effective, he must increase the effectiveness of his personnel.

He can do this by training departmental personnel, no matter how unqualified they may seem to be, to do as good a job as their capabilities will permit. Once it is assumed that a good **training program can** be productive and is worthwhile, it will become apparent that the law of averages has supplied some really competent people in the groups of political appointees.

The chief will have to accept the fact that there can be only unequal enforcement of the law in this city, since politically important persons (or their friends) will escape prosecution from many types of offenses. Those residents of the city who have no political connections will be the only ones who can be routinely processed through regular channels.

The chief will have to accept the fact that his tenure in office will be uncertain. He will be able to stay only as long as he offends no one who is important in the political machine. He will have to realize that he is going to have to live with frustration, and that he cannot afford to show it for fear that he will offend someone politically important and thereby render himself ineffective.

He must accept the fact that progress in improving personnel standards will have to be measured in almost minute gains over a long period of time. In order to make these gains he must be willing to compromise. He must be willing to give up progress on many fronts in order to establish a permanent gain on another.

The only real hope he has is that he will be able to develop the full potential of those who are already within the department, who demonstrate the ability to understand and to accept concepts of professionalism. He must continue to attempt to recruit good potential applicants as though there were no political considerations involved. He will have to "play the game" by pretending that the hiring procedures through civil service are really fair and objective. By doing this he will at least get some people in the department who are there because they have some ability.

Another alternative that the chief can take is to leave quietly. By doing this he should not lose any self-respect, because if the department is, in truth, dominated by a political machine and there is no foreseeable hope for a change, he should not be condemned for abandoning a lost cause. He should not be asked to sacrifice himself for the benefit of a community that obviously enjoys living in its own political pig sty. For make no mistake about it—bad political environments and resulting deficient public agencies exist only because the people within those environments want them. The public in such a community may occasionally righteously upbraid its law enforcement agency when some glaring fault is exposed, but it will only be using the police department as a whipping boy for its own irresponsible lack of social conscience. If the people really want changes to be made, they can make them by creating a community setting within which honest, professional public administrators can function properly.

There is still another alternative the chief can take. If he feels strongly enough about the principles involved, and he has an affinity for lost causes, he can fight for those principles until he is thrown out. Before he does, however, he should thoroughly assess the consequences of such a stand before he takes it. Not only he, but his family as well, will be subjected to harrassment and ridicule. He may suffer financial losses from which it will be difficult to recover. He probably will either have to move to another community or change his line of professional endeavor after he has almost inevitably lost his fight.

However, if he has taken a valid stand on real issues and if he conducts his fight well, he will gain in stature within the law enforcement profession. He will have demonstrated that he is the type of man who is able to give real leadership to some other progressive and enlightened community that really wants a good police department.

Every political jurisdiction in the United States has its own unique characteristics. It would be impossible to discuss each of them here, and to comment on the alternative courses of administrative action within each. The key point is that the law enforcement agency head must be realistic enough to define for himself what political forces he has to deal with and what his relationship to them is. This is essential if he is to make any progress at all.

CHECK RESULTS

Once a personnel selection program is begun, the job is only half done, as far as the administrator is concerned, even after the program is going in full swing. Unless he takes the trouble to check the results of the program, he will never be able to tell if it is doing the job it was designed to do. There will be no way to determine what changes should be made, to make the program more effective. Changes almost surely should be made from time to time no matter how well the program was originally conceived.

One way in which an administrator can judge the value of the selection process is by examining existing departmental records. They should give an indication, at least, as to whether the people being hired under the new procedure are doing a better job than those who were not. Some questions that could be asked in this regard are:

1. Is the number of arrests increasing, even though the crime rate remains about the same?

2. Are "better" arrests being made—arrests that are most likely to result in successful prosecution?

3. Do the newer men have fewer automobile accidents?

4. Do they have fewer lost-time personal injury accidents?

5. Are fewer complaints being made by citizens about the new men?

6. Is less sick time being taken by the new men than was taken by men hired under the old selection process when they were the same ages and had the same amount of time in the department?

If the answers to the above questions are "no" instead of "yes," it would seem to indicate that the new program is not doing what it is expected to do, and that it should be re-examined.

One measuring device that can be very useful is a good, *working* rating system. Although many law enforcement agencies have some sort of rating system, there are very few who use them effectively. As a consequence, there is a great deal of dissatisfaction with rating systems, because "they don't work." The truth is that almost any rating system will work and will give a pretty good picture of an individual employee's worth to the organization if the administrator is honest in his ratings of the subordinates he evaluates, and if he makes sure that supervisors all the way down the line make honest appraisals of those they rate.

Another indication of whether or not the selection process is a good one is the rate of turnover in departmental personnel, considered along with each employee's reason for leaving when he does. Of course, there are a number of reasons why an employee might leave that have nothing to do with the factors that surround his recruitment into the department, but there are several factors that are relevant.

Motivation for entering the field of law enforcement is certainly one thing that should be considered in testing a new applicant. This can be done through psychological tests, psychiatric interviews, oral examinations, etc., which will be discussed by the other authors. If the reason for an employee's leaving is that he really wasn't too interested in the job in the first place, you either are not using the right kinds of tests to measure motivation or you are not paying enough attention to this particular attitude of the applicant.

Another reason an employee might leave, either voluntarily or otherwise, is that he didn't have the intelligence or common sense to handle the job in the first place. If this is so, it is obvious that these qualities were not measured well enough in the pre-employment testing.

The same is true of personality traits that interfere with an employee's doing his job well. This part of the testing procedure is one of the most important to any law enforcement agency, and it is the one most often ignored or, if not ignored, poorly done. Many departments, even though they incorporate some type of psychological testing in their selection process, don't really examine the worth of the tests used or the competency of whomever administers them. It is the administrator's responsibility to make sure that the tests measure what they purport to measure and that the psychologists who give the tests are capable enough to interpret them. The law enforcement administrator, himself, need not be an expert in this field in order to tell whether a good job is being done or not, any more than he needs to be an expert criminalist in order to determine whether or not his laboratory personnel are handling their assignments properly. He need only check results in terms of the employee's performance, and if those results show a good correlation with the test results that measured what one would expect the performance to be, he can be reassured that a good job of testing is being done. If there is not such a correlation, it is time either to use different tests or to change psychologists, or both.

One important aid in checking results is the exit interview. After the employee has decided to leave (or the department has made the decision for him), he is more likely to be honest in his criticism of the department than at any other time, since he now has "nothing to lose." His observations in the exit interview can be of a great deal of value in determining not only where the selection process may have been faulty in selecting him, but also in other areas of departmental concern, such as the effectiveness of his supervisors, the fairness of administrative decisions, and the efficiency of various systems in the organization.

If the law enforcement administrator does not check the results of his department's entrance-level testing to make sure that it is doing what it is supposed to do, he is ignoring one of his most important obligations to the community he serves. The law enforcement profession deals in a service, and the most important instrument through which this service is rendered is the individual officer who actually deals with those he serves. *Everything* else in the department exists for just one reason—to aid him in doing his job. If the individual line officer is second-rate, the service he renders will be second-rate also, no matter how bright and shiny and new the automobiles, the radios and the emergency equipment may be. The record system may be excellent, the laboratory may be topnotch and the training program may be comprehensive, but if line officers are not basically competent, competent work cannot be done by them.

It is essential, then, that only the very best men be taken into every law enforcement agency at every level of government. There is no other single individual in our free society who is given as much raw power as the individual law enforcement officer or agent. He literally has the power of life and death over the people with whom he deals. In certain situations, our laws explicitly give him the right to act as executioner, bypassing the whole system of the administration of criminal justice (escape of prisoner, arrest of a felon). In addition, he has the right and the power to deprive citizens of their freedom on the basis of his decision alone, before those citizens are given the opportunity to be examined by a magistrate.

It seems elementary that such individuals must possess the highest degree of integrity and competence. If this is so (and I believe it is), many law enforcement administrators in the United States are criminally negligent in the casual way in which they confer this awesome power on stupid, psychotic, morally bankrupt incompetents. The kindest thing that can be said of such administrators is that some of them do not know that the men they hire have these disabilities. But they *should* know, and their failure to know constitutes a sad dereliction of duty.

BE WILLING TO CHANGE

One of the vital essences of a creative, progressive administrative approach is flexibility—the willingness to change when good reason for doing so is indicated. The corollary to this is knowing when change should occur, because simply changing for no good reason is disruptive rather than beneficial.

In order to know when to change, a law enforcement administrator must become and remain sensitive to the needs of the community he serves and to the needs of the department he heads. He must feel the professional responsibility to adapt to new knowledge and new techniques. He cannot afford the lazy luxury of being suspicious of new ideas, simply because they are new.

A law enforcement agency is an action-oriented organization, designed to deal with symptoms of sociological problems. In dealing with these symptoms of anti-social behavior, the law enforcement administrator must have some understanding of the reasons underlying such behavior. To do this, he doesn't necessarily have to be schooled in the social sciences, but he does have to be sensitive to the social, economic and cultural dynamics of his department's jurisdiction. This is becoming more important as time goes on. The changes that are occurring in the United States today are occurring more rapidly than ever before and there is every evidence that this rate of change will continue to accelerate. Traditional ways of doing things no longer constitute a valid standard by which to measure the probable worth of future programs in law enforcement agencies.

There are so many types of changes underway that it would be impossible to attempt to deal with them in any depth in just one chapter (or book). We can briefly consider some of them, however, along with the ways they affect the selection of personnel.

Gains in Population

The simple fact that additional people move into an area, and the responsible law enforcement agency must increase in size to give them service, might indicate that a different type of service would be more appropriate, and that a different type of person should be hired to give that service. As mentioned earlier, the needs of a large city are different from the needs of a small town, and different types of line officers may have to be recruited to meet those needs. Just how different they should be has to be the subjective judgment of the administrator, who must tailor his departmental operations so that they continue to be appropriate to the changes that are occurring in his jurisdiction. Some factors that should be considered are: Are line officers to function more nearly as generalists or as specialists; should specialist positions be added to the organization; to what extent should line personnel be involved in community affairs; how aggressive or passive should the role of the officers be? All of these considerations should be weighed in determining how to modify the design of the selection process.

Increase in Size of Minority Groups

Whenever there is an increase in the size of a particular minority group in a particular area, new problems for law enforcement are certain to manifest themselves because of the fact that the members of these groups bring with them their concepts of law enforcement officers, concepts learned in the areas from where they came. The law enforcement administrator has a two-fold obligation in respect to this problem. He must enforce the law as it is, even though it may be contrary to the attitudes of the members of the minority groups. He has no alternative, since it is his sworn obligation to uphold and enforce the law as it actually exists. The other obligation he has is to understand the reasons why these attitudes exist and to make an affirmative effort to work out, with leaders within these groups, some ground rules for doing business in the best way possible.

The growing importance of minority group problems is relevant to the hiring of police personnel in at least two ways. First, men must be brought into the department who have the capacity to deal with minority groups with understanding. This is not to say that they should have no biases or prejudices, but they should be mature enough in their basic attitudes to be able to deal fairly with members of minority groups despite their personal feelings, if these feelings do, in fact, exist.

Secondly, the law enforcement administrator should make sure that members of the minority group will be given every opportunity to compete, on an equal basis, with other applicants for positions in the department. In addition, he should be certain that minority group members know and believe that equal opportunity for employment actually exists in the department. Even though the administrator may sincerely be willing to take into his department qualified personnel without regard to race or color, and even though he may have set up procedures and administrative controls designed to prevent job discrimination, he may be surprised to learn that the members of the minority group simply will not believe him until such time as he *convinces* them that he means what he says. There is a good reason for this cynicism and disbelief. The minority group member has learned from countless experiences throughout his entire life that the white authority figure hasn't really meant what he has said when he has told him that he would be treated just like everyone else. He has been humiliated and embarrassed so many times that he is not apt to apply for a police position when experience has taught him that he probably is merely being set up for another insulting rejection.

There is no need to discuss the moral issues raised in considering whether or not minority group members should be encouraged to join a law enforcement agency. There are several "non-philosophical," practical reasons that suggest that taking this course of action is wise.

For one thing, the activities of the law enforcement agency will be more acceptable to the minority group members. If the particular minority group is composed of Negroes, for instance, and Negroes have been employed by the police department in their city, the Negroes within the community are not so apt to think of the department as enforcing only the "white man's law." There will then be less reason for Negroes to resent the authority wielded by the police, since some of the policemen wielding that power are also Negroes. Making Negroes a part of that police department almost surely will make the job of law enforcement less difficult in that city.

Another benefit that should accrue to a department from the practice of hiring minority group members will be the development of a better understanding by the white members of the department of what the minority group is and what it wants. This understanding will come about in the best way possible—by working beside fellow officers who are from the minority group. When this type of understanding does develop, it is inevitable that law enforcement problems with the minority group can be handled with greater ease and less friction.

Another practical reason for hiring minority group members on the department is that by doing so, the department has provided the perfect answer to the charge that there is job discrimination against them. The administrative head of the department is not then required to spend time (and sometimes this can be a great deal of time) defending his hiring policy against spokesmen from the various social action groups.

Of course, no one should be accepted into a law enforcement agency simply because he is the member of a minority group. Just as there should be no discrimination against such a person, there should be no discrimination in his favor. It seems to be perfectly reasonable to make a special effort to let minority group members know that they are welcome to apply for positions in the department, while, at the same time, requiring those applicants to qualify in every way that every other applicant must. This is the "other side of the coin"—the obligation on the part of the minority group member to accept the responsibilities that go along with the rights he has.

Change Your Way of Doing Business when a Better Way of Getting the Job Done Appears

If a law enforcement administrator has set up controls within his department for the purpose of auditing his personnel procedures ("checking results"), he should be aware of deficiencies in those procedures as they develop. If those deficiencies have developed because changing conditions have made the procedures obsolete, or because better ways of doing the job have been devised, the administrator should be willing to bring his department's practices up to date. There is a tendency in public administration to make change much too slowly, even when change is indicated, because it is difficult for anyone who is outside a public agency to demonstrate that the agency is not really as efficient as it should be. One reason for this is that success or failure cannot usually be measured in terms of profit or loss as it is in private businesses. It must be measured in less reliable and more easily manipulated terms of statistics and philosophical approaches.

A conscientious law enforcement administrator, because there is no absolute measure of accountability, has a high personal responsibility to modify his way of doing business as the need for modification becomes apparent to him, even though no one demands it or is apt to demand it. This is very difficult to do. It is difficult to establish and maintain an attitude among the members of a law enforcement agency that will accept the idea that changes must constantly be made. Changes, even where necessary, are always somewhat disruptive to and uncomfortable for staff. If drastic changes are necessary, members of the department will accept them more readily, because the importance of making the changes is apparent to everyone, and it will seem worthwhile to staff for them to put out the extra effort to get the job done.

However, staff is not as willing to put themselves out too much in order to make smaller, "less important" changes. The reasons for making these types of changes are not nearly so dramatic to staff as the reasons for making more drastic changes. There is a strong tendency to continue to do things in the "traditional" way and to neglect getting around to making small modifications.

If the law enforcement administrator really wants to make a change, he has to do more than just issue an order implementing the change. He has to make sure that the change is actually carried out in the way it was intended to be carried out. This seems to be a pretty basic point, and it is, but it is one that is very often overlooked by administrators. As a result, although changes are ordered, they are often not made or, if made, are made improperly.

Part of "being willing to change" is making sure that a decided-upon change is carried out. Let's look at an example of where a change is not carried out as it is supposed to be. This example should be familiar to almost anyone who has been in a law enforcement agency that has used a probationary period for new employees, during which they are rated by their various supervisors.

A probationary period is, or should be, an integral part of the selection process. If it is not, you might as well not have it. In order for it to be a useful tool in the selection process, supervisors must honestly evaluate new employees, and if any of the new employees are unsuitable, the administrator must see that they are terminated before the end of the probationary period.

Among law enforcement agencies that have a probationary period, there are very few in which that period actually serves the purpose for which it was designed. It is much more comfortable for a supervisor to rate every new employee as "satisfactory" than it is for him to face up to his responsibility constructively to criticize and correct. Administrators, also, don't like to feel uncomfortable, and it is very unpleasant to have to tell a probationary employee that he is unsuitable for law enforcement work, especially if he has gone to the expense of buying uniforms and equipment and if he has a family dependent upon him for support. Since no one wants to be the villain, the probationary period is not used to advantage in most departments. Many administrators who apparently have been willing to change haven't really meant it, since they haven't made sure that the program works the way it should.

Being willing to change also includes the responsibility of trying to look at departmental operations in new dimensions and with imagination. For instance, ask yourself why your agency has set up certain minimum standards that must be met by job applicants. The standards might be quite valid and necessary, but the administrator should know why they are, and he should know why because he has taken the trouble to think about them. Whether or not minimum standards are valid is becoming more and more important to law enforcement administrators, since it is becoming harder and harder to recruit qualified personnel for law enforcement work. If there has been a minimum standard set up for which no good reason exists, the field from which qualified candidates can be drawn has been unnecessarily made smaller. Make sure that you know *why* applicants for your agency cannot be less than a certain height, or that they must have perfect vision (how many of your older men do?), or why they must have any of the other qualifications. If you can find no reason for certain of your hiring standards, change them and increase the number of persons from the general population from which you can recruit.

"Being willing to change" does not mean that one should make changes merely for the sake of change. Changes should be made only after thorough study of a particular problem has been made and considered estimates have been made in the light of data developed by the study. If a law enforcement administrator takes such an approach to anticipated changes, and if he does change when conditions warrant it, and if he makes sure that desired changes are carried out by his staff, he can thereby make sure that his organization will remain vital and effective.

USE YOUR HUMAN MATERIALS WELL

It will do no good to recruit the most promising people into a law enforcement agency if they are not utilized properly and if they are not treated well after they are hired. It is possible for a Police Department or Sheriff's Office to have an excellent program for the recruitment and selection of the best candidates possible, and at the same time, have a very poor program of personnel management from that point onward.

Much has been written about good personnel management principles, and probably most of the readers of this book have read at least some of it. The basic premises of good personnel management are simple to declare, but, for some reason, seem to be much more complicated when one attempts to put them into practice. The complications generally appear when the administrator begins to forget the simple fundamentals underlying the stated rules.

All the principles of good personnel management are based on four requirements:

1. That the structure of the regular chain of command must actually represent the real power structure of the organization
2. That every employee is presumed to be a mature human being whose feelings and dignity must be respected
3. That the administration must not be unreasonable, arbitrary or capricious
4. That personnel must be supplied the knowledge and tools necessary for them to do their required tasks well.

The administrator needs to have competent persons under him in order to do his job effectively. If they are not competent, he cannot be effective. He is very foolish and self destructive if he does not do everything possible to attract the best people into his organization and then use them to their best advantage after they are hired.

He can do this best in a good administrative setting. It is to his advantage to do everything he can to create such a setting. Outside factors may prevent the administrator from having "the best of all possible worlds," but they should not prevent him from doing his job with imagination and vitality. No matter where he is, it is up to the administrator to use what he has and to fashion himself into an effective tool for excellence in personnel management.

Chapter III

SELECTION STANDARDS

OUR INTENTION, in this chapter, is to examine the minimum standards used in selection for law enforcement. Our question about each asks, simply, is the requirement reasonable? It will be found that many of our standards are accepted "on faith," and that we lack clear evidence showing how each is related to job performance.

A basic problem will be found to underlie many of the standards in use today. Standards reflect compromises between two opposing forces. One force tends to keep standards low, that is to set up criteria for employment which do not screen out a large proportion of applicants. Behind this force is the desire of police agencies to avail themselves of as many potential recruits as possible so that openings in an agency can be filled without undue delay. In some agencies low standards are also sought because of the ease with which hiring may be done; no elaborate procedures are necessary, no painful decisions to reject need be made, and no political problems are created by the rejection of an alderman's son who failed to meet a height and weight requirement.

In conflict with the pressures toward low standards there is an increasing force toward setting higher standards, that is, establishing criteria for employment which relatively few applicants can meet, criteria which presumably will endorse as employable only those candidates for police service who are especially well endowed with physical or psychological assets. Behind this set-the-standards-higher pressure we may also discern several separate origins. For one, there is the increasing awareness of police administrators that the primary resource of a police department is its personnel and that most of the departmental assets and liabilities come in the shape of persons rather than materials. It is not surprising that the responsible and ambitious administrator wants to increase his assets and reduce his liabilities. Over the long haul he knows that his own, as well as his department's success and reputation, will rest upon how he keeps his accounts in the personnel ledger.

A second component in the higher-standards movement is the less rational decision to make a display of selectivity for public relations purposes. A department which is under pressure from the press, perhaps because of an unfortunate series of incidents involving police personnel and the public, may decide that it must "do something." What it does is announce that its employment standards have been raised. An admirable ploy to be sure, but what assurance do we have that the standards so raised are at all related to the kind of trouble the department is experiencing?

A third component in standard-raising also has its origins in public relations, but this particular component reflects the long-range desire of law enforcement people to be better thought of and more admired by the public. They want to create an image in the public eye that they belong to an admirable group of men, a group deserving of respect because of their mental and physical prowess. Regardless of how the present departmental personnel came to be hired, it is imagined that by acquainting the public with the standards of excellence required of new men, that the public will come to a high regard for the police as a whole. This same concern with a public image may also underlie some of the wishes to professionalize the service. It is pleasant to be a "professional," to have the status accorded him and to feel the skill, responsibility, and independence which are embodied in that role. Standards may be set high in order to move toward professionalization, partly because of the real complexity of police work and considerable skill demanded of police workers, but perhaps partly because professionalization is status-seeking, with all the pitfalls and advantages implied in what sociologists call "upward mobility."

In the opening paragraph we indicated that standards in use may not have been set up on the basis and understanding of job requirements. Underlying this statement are several separate problems. One problem is that job performance in police work may be a mystery even to those involved in doing and supervising it. What does a policeman do? Until we know, how can we say what qualifications he must have in order to do that job well? But there is no such thing as one police job. There are dozens of them; how many depends upon the size and situation of each department. They differ by command rank, by bureau, and by job or post assignments. They also change over the years as cities and their populations change and as technology, crime, law, and police methods are altered. Nevertheless as long as we are hiring generalists rather than specialists, line versus staff personnel, we must not only know what these jobs are, but we must find within them common denominators so that we can say what the minimum capacities of each recruit must be, the minimum capacities which will allow that recruit to work anywhere and anytime in our agency and still turn in acceptable performance. What is required is that each agency perform a job analysis for each job, that it compare and combine the results of this job analysis, and that it come up with basic capabilities and skills which every policeman will need.

No recruit—or very few of them—enter departments as full-fleged workers capable of assuming responsible duties the next day. No sensible department expects its recruits to be that good or believes its own work to be that simple. As a consequence any agency worth its salt intends to train its men; the better the agency, the better that training. But if men can be trained it is obvious that selection standards do not have to cover the whole range of skills and abilities which a department will require. Indeed, if men can be trained why have selection standards at all? It is not a foolish question. Its answer rests upon distinguishing between permanent versus modifiable human characteristics. The man who is not able to undertake police work at the time of his application, but who is capable of being trained, whose deficiencies are modifiable through learning, is certainly a desirable recruit. The man who is unable to undertake police work but whose deficiencies are permanent, and cannot be modified in training, the man who is himself not capable of learning, is not a desirable recruit. The task for the administrator who sets standards is to find which deficiencies—or which undesirable features—can be altered and which can not. This, of course, has been understood yet when we examine the elemental standards we will find that the presumption of permanence which underlies certain standards may be false.

Let us assume that our agency has done a job analysis for

each important position, that it has described what the officer is required to do, how he does it, why he does it, and the skills and abilities required to do it.[1] The next step is to derive standards based upon those skills and abilities. Now let us assume that those standards are posted and those engaged in selection are instructed to rule out unfit applicants. How are those responsible for selection to perform *their* tasks? How do they find out if a man meets or fails to meet a standard? Obviously they must evaluate the candidate; in some fashion or another they must test or measure him to find out what his characteristics are, whether these be physical, mental or moral.

A standard will be useful only if the measurements employed in evaluating its presence or absence are trustworthy. If we set a minimum weight requirement and weigh our applicants upon a broken scale we have done neither applicant nor agency any service. It may be that the likelihood of our using a broken scale is not very great; on the other hand measurements for some of the elemental standards—and certainly for the complex ones—are not as easy as mechanical scales and, in consequence, we must always be aware not just of the possibility of error when we measure, but of the *certainty* that we will make errors when we evaluate men, no matter how simple the standard is against which we are measuring. Our standard exists in writing. It is an ideal, an abstraction. When we move out into the field—or into the medical examiner's office, the psychologist's testing room, or merely sit at our own desk evaluating written reports and documents describing age, grades, marital status, criminal record, citizenship and the like, we can be sure that the ideal standard has for all intents and purposes disappeared. What we are now dealing with are ranges of error, with probabilities, and with some inevitable uncertainty.

We cannot escape from the uncertainty and error in every measure which we apply to applicants. What we can do is to know as much as we can about the selection tools we are using so that we know about what the likelihood of error is, where the measurements will be poorest, and where we need to concentrate on building new selection tools to replace faulty ones now in use. The task is not greatly different from that encountered in criminal investigation, except that in this instance it is our own methods of evaluation which are being investigated. One wants to gather as much information as one can, one wants to be sure of the accuracy of the information one gets. To do this one uses as many sources of information as one can find, one checks on the consistency of all reports received, and one is skeptical of the veracity of any single witness or any single criminalistics test unless corroborating evidence is compiled. So it is with selection method; one is grateful for the information they provide, but one wants to know what the chances are that faulty information has been given. As the police administrator reviews the use of the contemporary selection methods; written examinations, medical examinations, supporting documents, psychological tests, psychiatric evaluations, background checks and the findings of the oral board he must remember his own obligation to know what the range of error of each device will be.

There is an oddity in selection standards as they are now employed. Let us grant that reasonable standards derived from job analysis have been set up and that moderately accurate assessment tools have been used to screen candidates. The recruit class will consist of a number of highly selected men, each endowed with desirable qualities. Will they maintain those high qualifications while serving the department? Or will they, as is common, improve in some ways and decline in others? Insofar as they do decline, their assets will become liabilities. Thin agile men become fat slow men. Honest and ambitious men become slothful and corrupt men. Enthusiastic lads turn into sour-faced critics. It is very embarrassing. All the effort that has gone into selection seems wasted. If the whole department is going downhill it may well be that the only persons qualified to perform police work, at least according to the standards, are the newest men, while the others, no longer fit, cannot meet the standards which they themselves—for now some of them have become command personnel—require the new men to meet. In some ways it is inevitable. A man once hired does grow older and so the majority of a department's personnel must be considerably over twenty-one or even thirty-five. Agreed. But then why require that only young men come aboard in the first place? As people grow older they do become ill more often; chronic disease is the curse of late middle age. Agreed. Why then hire only the healthy to begin with? Because the chances of their being sick later on are less if they are healthy to begin with? A plausible assumption to be sure, but what evidence do we have for such a statement? If there is evidence, all well and good. If there is not, our standard is in doubt.

MINIMUM STANDARDS

With these general problems and questions in mind, let us turn to the critical review of minimal standards currently applied. In 1960 the State of California created a "Commission on Peace Officers Standards and Training." The minimum standards it prescribed for selection are as follows:

1. Citizen of the United States.
2. Minimum age of twenty-one years.
3. Fingerprinting of applicants with a search of local, state, and national fingerprint files to disclose any record.
4. Shall not have been convicted by any state or federal government of a crime the punishment for which could have been imprisonment in a federal penitentiary or state prison.
5. Good moral character as determined by a thorough background investigation.
6. Graduation from high school or a passing of the General Education Development Test indicating high school graduation level or a score on a written test on mental ability approved by the commission and equivalent to that obtained by the average school student.
7. Examination by a licensed physician and surgeon. Only those applicants shall be eligible for an appointment who are found to be free from any physical, emotional, or mental condition which might adversely affect performance of his duty as a peace officer.... Note: This requirement is in keeping with the concept that in order to render proper service to his community a California peace officer must be mentally alert, physically sound and free from any physical defect or mental or emotional instability which might adversely affect his performance of duty. His personal safety and the safety and lives of others will be endangered if he lacks these qualifications. The applicant shall possess normal hearing and normal color vision. He must possess normal visual

functions and visual acuity not less than 20-40 vision in each eye without correction and corrective to 20-20 in the better eye and not less than 20-25 in the lesser eye.

8. All interviews shall be held by the hiring authority or his representative, or representatives, to determine such things as the recruits' appearance, background, and ability to communicate.

These standards were set after careful deliberation by experienced law enforcement personnel. They are subscribed to by 90 per cent of California's local law enforcement agencies. The excellence of their intent cannot be challenged. It is likely that these standards have made local law enforcement conscious of the importance of evaluating applicants. We may guess that the quality of employed police recruits has improved in consequence.

But what are the elements in these standards and how may we, in the service of possible improvements, examine the assumptions contained therein? The elements are legal status (citizenship, and having attained majority), chronological age, absence of felony convictions, good moral character, educational achievement, physical and mental health, and personal appearance.

CITIZENSHIP

This requirement is a general one applying to most employment with governmental agencies. It is not likely to be within the power of the police department to change it. It reflects widespread beliefs about who should be eligible to receive tax money and public employment (and may well be an extension of patronage ideas converted into broader, nationalistic terms). It reflects beliefs about loyalty and a desire to prevent any conflict of loyalties in a police officer which would involve one's nation of citizenship versus one's nation of employment, and beliefs about the likelihood of nationals being more familiar with American codes and customs, thus rendering them better able to understand and enforce laws and to deal with citizens.

These are reasonable beliefs, but there will no doubt be occasions when non-nationals, for example policemen who are here in school or on training visits or who are immigrants, might well be qualified for service in local agencies. Insofar as these visitors or immigrants come from countries with codes and customs similar to our own, the likelihood of culture-conflict is slim. In the meantime the citizenship requirement eliminates a recruitment pool which might be tapped among English-speaking immigrants or even among active policemen in nations with advanced police systems; England, Japan, Switzerland, Sweden, etc. In these days of international recruitment for trained specialists, the citizenship requirement not only restricts recruitment but prevents what might be an exceedingly constructive system of international police exchanges in which, much as with present teacher exchanges, individuals trade posts and duties for periods of one or two years.

It is up to the citizens of each town or state to determine whether the loss under the citizenship standard is worth the presumed gain. As with any inflexible criterion, there is no opportunity to take advantage of exceptional applicants so long as this standard exists. It would be well to keep in mind that the armed services do not require citizenship for service and that industries engaged in secret military projects do not hold such a requirement. It is unlikely that the national loyalties required of policemen would exceed those required for military personnel or sensitive-project worker. Over the long haul, given the increasing ties between Western nations and the excellence of other nations' police systems, knowledge of which would benefit many American agencies, it would be well to consider legislation which would provide police departments some measure of discretion in applying the citizenship standard.*

AGE

In many states the minimum age limit for police work is set by law. The law recognizes that the under-twenty-one person does not have full rights or responsibilities. It is presumed that these responsibilities must be exercised in the performance of police duties. It is also argued that men under twenty-one lack emotional

---

*One must keep in mind the legal prohibition against an alien carrying a weapon. If non-citizens are to be employed in police service, enabling legislation must be passed to allow them weapons. In the meantime it might be possible to use them in assignments for which weapons are not required.

maturity; an arbitrary cutting point having been established after which it is said to be likely that most persons will have become emotionally mature.

The twenty-one years of age standard restricts recruitment. Potential police applicants who graduate from high school find it necessary to obtain other employment and are likely to fall in career channels which take them away permanently from their original police interests and aptitudes. While it is apparent that chronological age has some relationship to emotional maturity, it is also evident that there is no one-to-one correspondence. Men are considered mature enough to fight in war at age seventeen. Some persons are obviously emotionally immature at age fifty.

It is suggested that the age twenty-one requirement is more restrictive than beneficial. Background checks, interviews, psychiatric evaluations and psychological tests should be able to establish emotional maturity with considerably more certainty than a fixed age standard does. It would appear reasonable to match age and educational requirements. In this regard Germann writes:

> "It would seem logical that educational requirements and minimum age requirements be geared together. Thus, if a high school educational level is set, the age minimum might well be placed at seventeen or eighteen years and the use of 'cadet' or 'aide' programs expanded. If a junior college education level is set, the minimum entrance age might be placed at nineteen or twenty; then if a college or University degree is required the minimum age set at twenty-one or twenty-two."[2]

Maximum age limits are usually set by personnel selection agencies and, for recruits, ordinarily range between thirty-one and thirty-nine. Justification for upper limits are sought in the consideration of retirement pensions for which a minimum number of years in service must be completed before a required retirement age is reached. It is also suggested that the sickness risk of older persons is higher so that a department which hires older men risks greater lost-time and is deprived of the earlier years of greater health. Another reason advanced for the upper age limit is that men who wish to change jobs after age thirty-five are employment risks because of their failure to have established themselves in a career; that the chances are they will be unstable job-hoppers.

Each of these reasons is plausible, although none are unanswerable. Pension rules can be revised; an older applicant might be allowed the option of waiving his pension or of contributing a proportionately greater amount of his salary to it each month. Men who are retired from military service after twenty or twenty-five years are in their early forties and, already receiving a pension, might well settle for small adjusted police pensions. As for sickness risk and job-hopping, it may be possible to estimate these risks from medical examinations and background checks. Certainly it would appear that flexibility in upper age limits accompanied by very careful evaluations would be of benefit to the department which seeks to expand its recruitment pool.

ABSENCE OF FELONY RECORD AND PRESENCE OF GOOD CHARACTER

The prohibition against the employment of anyone convicted of a felony and the requirement for good moral character are related standards. They involve at least two assumptions. One is that a department does not wish to be known as a receiving station for persons with bad reputations, regardless of how honorably they may now conduct themselves, for fear that there would be loss of public respect for the police service and increased suspiciousness of the integrity of the police. The second assumption is that persons with criminal records are likely to be recidivists while those with good moral characters are likely to continue along the path of virtue. Implicit here is the notion that criminal conduct will be detected, reported, and the reports made available to the inquiring police agency at the time of recruitment.

These assumptions appear reasonable, but there is some uncertainty involved in each. No scientific studies have been done to establish just how it is that the public develop their views of a police department. No doubt some "reality" affects public attitudes so that a department with former criminals in it may very well stimulate public apprehension. On the other hand it seems apparent that there is no one single-minded "public" but a variety of groups each with differing points of view. The attitudes of

members of these various citizen groups are no doubt shaped by
their prejudices, social background, way of life and personality as
well as by any objective knowledge of police recruitment policies.
In addition we must recognize that some departments *do* have
criminals therein without their presence producing any unusual
public concern.

A study reported in Chapter V indicates that about one fourth
of the applicants to two departments studied did have records of
arrest and conviction on other than traffic offenses. Since there
are still departments which select without fingerprinting applicants and rejecting those with records, it is not unlikely that such
departments have accumulated, over the years, at least a minority
of members with records of past offenses. In addition to prior
offenses any frank assessment must admit that some police departments are providing more than their fair share of current offenders
from among their own employees. We speak here of the painful
facts of police illegality which are of three major sorts; (a) criminal acts which occur in the process of police work itself; illegal
search and seizure, harrassment, entrapment, false arrests, assault,
etc. (b) criminal activities which are not means to legitimate
police ends, but which are part of the police-politics environment.
Here one recognizes differential law enforcement, bribery and
corruption, the oppression of minorities, tolerance for vice, etc.
(c) individual or deviant criminality in which persons or small
groups participate in crimes disapproved by the department;
burglary, rape, fraud, etc. Given the presence of all three kinds of
police criminality in some departments, it seems incongruous
that these same departments would require clean records from
their recruits.

The criminal record of the recruit is assumed to be an accurate
reflection of his conduct. Yet if we grant the fact of criminal
conduct which goes undetected—and unprotested—within some
police departments themselves, we must surely recognize that
most criminal conduct on the outside also goes undetected, or
at least unapprehended. Whether one looks at speeding, petty
larceny, adultery, burglary, rape or homicide, the fact is that many
offenses are not reported and that convictions occur in only a
small proportion of the total cases. Indeed every citizen has proba-

bly committed a felony or two—if not more—without ever having it recorded against him. As a consequence our use of the criminal record as a screening device for police applicants is hardly a complete measure of conduct. What it probably does do is to point to those citizens whose offenses have been so frequent, so extreme, and so socially disapproved that in spite of our famed American tolerance for crime they have been protested against and caught. One could also argue that these same offenders are more susceptible to being caught because they are less discreet, or more flagrantly aggressive, or neurotically seeking exposure and punishment, or less bright about planning their crimes. In any event no sensible administrator would wish to hire such men, but what the administrator should recognize is that his screening system tends to exclude the "dingbat" criminals, but is not a sensitive measure of all criminality.

Implicit within the search for men without records and with good character is the belief that criminal predispositions are permanent and that past criminality predicts to future criminality. While the studies by criminologists on parole prediction support such an assumption, these same studies also demonstrate that recidivism depends upon a variety of factors, for example, age at first offense, family background, work record, marital history and the like. Quite clearly not everyone who is convicted of juvenile offenses continues through life as an offender. To the contrary, most juvenile offenders stop getting in trouble as they grow older while, among older persons arrested for crimes, there are many who have no record of prior offenses. These are the facts as best we know them now. What they suggest is that while the present standard has a reasonable basis, its limitations and range of errors is completely unknown. What police selection needs are a series of scientific studies which relate juvenile offenses to later conduct so that, knowing what kind of a record an applicant has, one can make a prediction about his chances for getting in trouble again. The completion of such studies would reduce the difficulties which the police administrator now has when evaluating the record of an applicant with several minor offenses. Instead of guessing that these offenses are predictive of later trouble-making, or are not predictive of it, the administrator could refer to a set of tables containing research findings and read from them what the range of probabilities would be for a person of the recruit's background to become a recidivist.

In spite of the difficulties in measuring "normal" criminality, it is even harder to measure "good moral character." This definition depends completely upon the local standards for conduct and upon the adequacy of information gathered about the applicant. While the standard itself appears eminently reasonable, it is difficult to find a device capable of measuring it. We shall discuss it no further here, for Chapter VII contains an excellent summary of the problem with recommendations for its control.

EDUCATION

Most law enforcement agencies require a certain level of educational attainment. What is required varies from grade school education, in some rural jurisdictions, through high school, junior college and, for example the FBI, a college degree. There are several arguments for high educational attainments as a selection criterion. For example Frost writes:[3]

> "To accept men possessing only a fifth or sixth grade education may be inviting disaster. After all, a peace officer must be able to write an intelligent report, express himself clearly and commandingly in court and.... possess sufficient mental ability to make spontaneous rational decisions."

Others have held that regardless of the skills acquired in high school or college, the educational attainment requirement assures the social equality of the policemen in his dealings with other citizens; a fundamental need in order to secure self respect as well as citizen and community respect. A third argument deals not with acquired skills or social respect, but notes that by requiring junior college or college training the potential recruit is prevented from offering himself on the job market and is held uncommitted to other work until such time as he has attained age 21 and is legally eligible to apply for police work. A fourth argument for high educational attainment contends that a school degree is proof of desirable social and personal qualities, even if these are unrelated to acquired knowledge. In the "Columbia Roundtable" discussions it was held that:

> "College attendance is a measure of drive, ambition, and related qualities. If a man lacks these qualities he could have very high intelligence, but that is not the key point."[4]

A final argument for education rests upon what people "ought" to know and to have experienced. It says that regardless of what one does or does not learn academically in school, one should get a degree so that one learns social know-how, one comes to belong to the educated middle class. This is an argument for "acculturation," for school attendance as an initiation rite to membership in the respectable social order and to the rituals and values of "proper" society. It is the American equivalent to the British "old school tie" and implies the requirement that police officers be socially "in" rather than socially "out."

Educational achievement then is held to be a measure of intelligence, of acquired skill in judgment, writing, thinking and expression, of suitable social respectability, and of proof of ambition and perserverance. Higher education is also seen as a way to keep young men "marginal" and unemployed until police departments are ready to hire them as they reach their majority.

On the negative side, several factors must also be considered. The higher the educational requirement the greater will be the competition with other employers for the more highly skilled graduates while the large potential recruitment pool of less trained men is denied to the police service. While these less trained men no doubt include many with relatively low intelligence, it must be recognized that failure to complete high school or college is associated with social background and economic factors more often than with intellectual ones. Those who come from "culturally deprived" groups; the poor, the abandoned, the out-of-touch rural folk, the sons of recent immigrants, the slum dwellers, the Negro, Mexican and American Indian youth; these are the ones who drop out of school. One must admit that the high educational standard serves to reject the socially disadvantaged American from the opportunity to perform police service, regardless of the intelligence, interest, or other desirable personal qualities which such an individual might have.

Another problem which is encountered when high educational achievement is required is that of "overtraining" for police work. The college graduate, usually with high aspirations for a career, must begin police work at the bottom. In a typical department only a few among any recruit class will eventually be promoted to positions of real command responsibility and appropriate salary and status. The unpromoted college graduate may be bored, disgruntled, and can respond to the frustration of ambition and the non-use of college-acquired skills either by leaving the department—perhaps even leaving law enforcement forever—or if he stays in the department may become a low-morale grumbler, or, in some cases will stir up excitement by becoming a real trouble-maker.

The monotonous and routine nature of most lower level police assignments may not be suited to the highly intelligent recruit. Industrial studies have shown that bright people do poorly on monotonous jobs; the challenge they need isn't there. In police work the exceptional moment, the occasion of crisis which arises, does tax the judgment and intellect of the brightest; but these moments are few and far between. The long intervals of weeks or months or years may find the over-trained applicant mismatched to his job.

As long as the seniority system is operating and the only road to supervisory and administrative positions is up through the ranks, the recruitment standards must reflect a dilemma. If the standard is set high enough to assure the educational attainment of the administrator, as Vollmer implied in his demand that anyone in public service who enforces law and controls behavior have a college education and more recently as Germann has suggested, then the entering recruit is destined to face boredom, frustration and perhaps a growing sense of irritation or despair. If on the other hand the standard is set low, let us say at the high school diploma level, then those who do stay in the department and get promoted may find themselves with duties which they cannot handle. Here is the too-often observed tragedy of the present-day department; its administrators conscientious and dedicated, but untrained and unfit for the responsibilities which their position imposes upon them.

There are, of course, two alternatives to the dilemma. One is to provide lower level standards for recruitment, but to make eligibility for promotional examinations dependent upon further educational achievement. This system, practiced in some European nations, would for example allow a high school graduate to enter the department and to rise as high as sergeant, but in order to become an inspector or lieutenant he would have to complete junior college, and to become captain, director, or chief he would have to finish college. For such a system to work the department would have to encourage off-duty studies. Some departments do just this; Berkeley, for example, subsidizes an officer's education at the near-by School of Criminology at the University of California. Other departments are resistant; assignment policies are made more difficult by having to adjust assignments to class times and there can be a loss of working time as men take time off to study or attend special school events. These hazards can be too much for some departments. In addition some administrators, themselves lacking formal education, may feel uneasy about their subordinates becoming educated. The administrator feels threatened and, disguising his own lack of self-confidence, attacks schooling as "ivory tower" or a "frill."

The other alternative to the dilemma is lateral recruitment to command positions. This method, also used in Europe, allows non-police personnel to enter police service as lieutenants, captains and chiefs. It defies the seniority system and the democratic notion that every man has equal opportunity to rise from the ranks. Lateral entrance is based upon the achievement of special educational levels; ordinarily degrees in law, public administration, or criminology. It does provide highly trained and socially respected persons to fill the most responsible administrative posts. It does not rule out promotion from below, for the system can declare that anyone is eligible who has completed the educational and experience requirements. Nevertheless in a society such as ours where seniority concepts are basic to promotion and where at least the hope for equality of opportunity is fostered, the lateral system faces strong opposition.

It is apparent that the educational standard for police entrance cannot be considered apart from the broader issues of police respectability and police image, the preparation of a trained administrative cadre, the admission of monotony and frustration as conditions of work at the lower levels, the current ideas about seniority and opportunity, and finally, the extent to which the professionalization of police is desired and, if it is desired, whom among the police must be professionals. The one thing we should not do is to set our educational standards without regard for the great implications they have for recruitment, later training, and basic concepts about the future of the police.

PHYSICAL, EMOTIONAL AND MENTAL STANDARDS

The minimum standards for selection usually require certification of physical health, the presence of given levels of visual and auditory acuity, the ability to pass tests of agility, and conformance to standards of weight and height. They may also specify freedom from emotional or intellectual defect. The underlying assumption is that job performance requires particular physical and mental capacities. As far back as 1909, Fuld wrote: "The most important asset of the ideal policeman is unquestionably his physical constitution and condition."[5] Recent standards do not indicate much change in thinking.

Aside from the presumed relationship between bodily capacity and work, several other explanations have been offered for the importance attached to physical condition. One explanation holds that the police are exceptionally favored in the amounts of benefits awardable in the event of job-incurred injury, as compared with other work groups. The awarding of high injury compensations is believed by some to be linked to the contention of relative infrequency of injury among police. As a consequence high standards are said to be maintained so that disabilities, either acquired or congenital, will be infrequent in police service; thus assuring continued public and governmental support of present pension and benefit programs; programs which assure high compensation for those who do become disabled.

Another explanation for the importance of physical condition has been advanced by the English anthropologist Gorer who argues that the police are "culture heroes" and as such they must represent the ideal man in the culture in which they work. In our society physical prowess is admired. Our heroes are strong tall men, capable fighters with fists and gun, brave and resourceful, able to hold their liquor and to conquer women by the bedful. Without being aware of this ideal, both police and the public may strive for it in their law enforcement personnel; as a consequence it is held that police selection standards reflect a cultural demand more than any physical prerequisites for the work itself. Nevertheless if the public *do* demand such "Jack Armstrong" types, (and this has not been proved) it might very well be that the psychological demand of the public is every bit as important a consideration as the physical requirements of police work itself.

Other reasons advanced for the existence of physical and health standards include: (a) the necessity for the safe operation of potentially dangerous equipment; guns, and automobiles for the most part; (b) the necessity to protect fellow workers and the public from contagious illness, and (c) the need to detect existing defects so that these do not become the basis for later disability claims.

Whether or not we grant the role of the policeman as culture hero (and there are times when we must all feel he is more often thought to be the culture villain), it is evident that an ideal physical type is in mind when agencies set their physical standards. The stricter standards certainly do not fit the average or "normal" man. Consider for example one major metropolitan police force which rejects a large number of its applicants on the basis of physical standards. In 1961, this department had 7,092 applicants of which only 304 were finally selected; even though this meant that the department never reached its authorized strength. Obviously the potential recruitment pool is much restricted by insistence on ideal standards. It is well, at this point, to note the findings of Hanman[6] who compared worker physique and health with job requirements from various positions. He concluded that *"not more than 1 per cent of all workers is physically fit for all work."*

In considering selection standards based on physical and mental health and defects, it is necessary to ask to what extent the

assumption of permanent work incapacity is met, for it is clear
that men with deficiencies which are easily corrected through
training or are otherwise modifiable may not need to be excluded
at the time of selection. Some handicaps, whether induced by
disease or injury or inherited, are permanent. Others are temporary. Some are completely disabling; others are only partially disabling and still allow a man to function well in jobs which do not
put demands on his deficiencies. Some defects are permanent but
may be compensated for, either by nature herself in which case
the man overcomes his defects, or by physical devices and prosthe-
tics, in which case medical care and rehabilitation provide aid, as
in eyeglasses, hearing aids, arch supports, hernia belts, wheel
chairs, or false teeth.

What seems to be a simple matter of setting a physical standard
is shown to be complex. How *is* one to decide what natural or
artificial supports or compensations are unacceptable, what degree of disability is incapacitating? Observing operating agencies
one finds working officers who met the standards at the time of
employment but who, at some later time, suffered disability. One
sees men with glasses, men with arch supports, men with false
teeth, men with bad hearts, bad livers, ulcers, prostate trouble,
even men with limbs missing; and they are all at work. It is obviously not just physical incapacity which makes the difference;
it is also their interest, their skill, their "place on the team," and
the administrator's convenience which must be considered in
deciding whether or not a given physical condition is disabling.
Indeed, if we were to give careful physical examinations to *all*
of the members of any police force, it is a good bet that the majority would not meet the physical and health standards required of
the recruit at the time of entrance.

There are special situations in which the ideal physical type
is a liability in police service. Consider the undercover operation
to which a red-cheeked, clear-eyed young man of six feet weighing
a muscular 190 is assigned. Chances are that he will immediately
be pegged as "fuzz" and provided with about as much confidential
information as a newspaper reporter at a Cosa Nostra banquet.
But assign a wizened little fellow about 5 feet 2 with a gimpy leg

and a clever (if not somewhat larcenous) brain to the job and the chances are that he will bring in the evidence.

The illustration suggests the generalization. Standards should fit the job, not the preconceptions. For many functions; driving, shooting, using force on a person resisting arrest, walking a beat, minimal standards can be decided upon. Some departments sensibly require only such capacities that enable the officer, without corrective or compensatory physical devices (for it must be assumed that glasses or hearing aids may be broken or lost at one or another occasion), to perform his duties—protecting the public, his fellow officers and himself—for limited emergency periods. But if the principle of safety and protection is to be agreed upon, then departments must also do two other things; they must not assign incapacitated men to posts involving high risk of danger—whether it be driving, riding a motorcycle, or covering a beat; and they must do their best to maintain the physical prowess of their personnel through periodic reexaminations and through continuing training and fitness programs.

While mental and emotional defects may be excluded in the same statement which sets forth physical standards, the evaluation of the candidates for these defects is not done by the medical examiner but by psychologists and psychiatrists. Chapters V and VI of this book deal with their work in some detail. It is sufficient here to observe that job requirements can be set forth in terms of social and intellectual skills and that procedures for evaluating men on these characteristics can be developed. Chapter V shows that police performance is related to personality, vocational interest, social attitudes, and intelligence.

APPEARANCE

Appearance including manners, dress, expression and the personal qualities inferred from these is the traditional basis for judgments employed by an oral board. The operation of the oral board and techniques which can be employed to improve its work are described in Chapter VIII. Our discussion here will, therefore, be limited.

The appearance standard is hard to define, but comprises the impressions which the oral board have about a man's social skills, his maturity and alertness, his integrity and judgment, and other aspects of his personality. Behind these impressions and inferences there is likely to lurk in the minds of each interviewer the ideal which he has of how a police officer should look and act. There is implicit the question, is this the kind of man that I want to work with? It this the kind of man that I want the public to have in mind when they think of the police?

These are perfectly legitimate questions, but as every experienced interviewer knows, appearances can be deceiving. Just as there is scientific evidence—from studies by psychologists—to the effect that "expressive movement," that is how people talk and walk and gesture, can in fact provide valuable clues to personality and future behavior, there are also studies which show how easy it is for interviewers to err in the judgments they make. One excellent suggestion, offered in Chapter VIII, is to provide the interviewers with a wealth of supplementary material on each candidate so that interviewers have more to rely on than their own impressions. Another device, sometimes employed, is to have several sets of interviewing boards, each of which acts independently. Men who are consistently rejected are at least agreed upon as undesirable whereas those who are subject to disagreement among various interviewers are not summarily rejected, but are given more careful study by supplementary methods such as special psychological evaluation or further background checks.

In some European departments, interviewing officers are not required to justify their rejection of a man on the basis of his appearance. They report, "If we don't like his looks, if we don't feel comfortable with him, we reject him. That is all there is to it." This method is satisfactory as long as there are ample numbers of recruits, as long as rejected men do not protest their treatment and demand a show of cause, and as long as the department is pleased with the personnel they acquire over the years. On the other hand, in the absence of any of these conditions, it behooves a department to consider what its standards for appearance are and to justify them in terms of work requirements.

It is a commonplace finding among zoo keepers, animal psychologists, and students of human behavior that primates (men, monkeys, and lemurs) tend to distrust strangers; specifically that the human animal along with other primates reacts with fear and aggression when individuals very different from himself are brought into view. Humans have strong emotional reactions to those who look different, whereas they tend to be at ease with those whose appearances show they are members of the same tribe, social class, ethnic group or what-have-you. It has also been shown that these fears and extreme reactions—of which one may not even be aware—diminish over time as we remain in contact with the strangers and become used to them. Studies in race relations for example illustrate how "equal status" contact over periods of time—in military units, on shipboard, in schools, in housing projects, and on the job,—leads to the reduction in prejudice and negativism and to the reduction of concern about differences. Since there is no reason to believe that police commanders who are interviewing applicants are any different from other humans, nor that they should necessarily be aware of their own tendency to be suspicious of persons looking or acting "differently," it is very likely that some of the rejections of candidates arise from group differences rather than from any genuine defects in the applicants. Given the evidence for the effects of "equal status" contact, it is also likely that once such "different" men were hired and did perform effectively, they would become integrated into the police group's "self image" and would not continue to be a source of suspicion, fear, or doubt.

In addition to our instinctive animal response to strangers, judgments of appearance are also affected by our own personal idiosyncracies and problems. As a consequence our appraisal of others sometimes tells more about us than it does about the person being assessed. Our preconceptions, fears, and unresolved personal problems may distort the judgments we make. When those judgments are part of the selection process, the distortions weaken the excellence of the selection tool, that tool being the judge himself. The sources of distortion that lie within us are so great that they cannot be ennumerated here. What is important is to recognize the possibility that the standard employed in the interview situation may be an unconscious one inside our minds rather than the written one set forth as an operating policy of the interview board. While there is no sure way of detecting these self-imposed errors, one warning sign is a strong emotional reaction within ourselves to a candidate; a reaction which we cannot reasonably attribute to anything he has said or done.

In setting forth this psychological fact we have moved from external considerations of jobs, job analysis and derived standards to the beliefs and values of the men who set the standards. No concern with selection can overlook the role of the police administrators doing the selection; it will be their open-mindedness, curiosity, and hard work which will ultimately determine whether any standard is reasonable and useful or not.

WOMEN IN LAW ENFORCEMENT

Historically police work has been a man's job, but beginning with World War II women were pressed into employment where manpower shortages existed. The trend continues and in police work we find women employed not only as matrons in a jail, but as criminalists, meter maids, and policewomen charged with juvenile crime control, communications and identification work. In England they are also to be found on foot patrol.

The resistance of men to women in police work has been strong but not necessarily rational. The standard of the male police officer as the ideal officer may be difficult to justify as one considers the capabilities of women for many varieties of work. It is true that the woman lacks the physical strength to conduct a battle royal with rioting teenagers or to tackle a fleeing burglar. On the other hand her general health and longevity is superior to men and there are many situations in which her presence might be advantageous.

It is necessary to disentangle the cultural prejudice which finds us appalled at the idea of a gun-toting female shooting it out with bank robbers from the fact that a woman can be trained to use a gun quite as effectively as a man; Annie Oakley be our witness. While it is unquestionable that a female patrolman would, in certain situations, be placed in high risk of her own safety—or chastity—because of her sex; it is also likely that there are many situations in which violence would *not* occur just because of the presence of a female rather than a male officer. In some psychiatric hospitals for example, when male attendants serve on wards for the most disturbed male patients, there is a great deal of violence, swearing, and aberrant behavior. When female attendants or nurses are introduced in these wards—and the male attendants removed, these same violent patients behave themselves better and even begin to supervise one another to make sure that untoward conduct does not occur. In Holland, in the famous Van der Hoefen Clinic which houses some of the most dangerous and violent Dutch criminals, over half of the staff are women, the director is a woman, and no person carries a weapon. In this setting the inmates limit their misbehavior to verbal and procedural matters and do not attack the staff. Similarly, observations on resistance to arrest suggests that the conduct of the arresting officer is more likely to account for whether the offender resists than is the mood or personality of the latter. The firm, calm officer who does not expect violence, nor encourage it through his own ambivalence or hostility, is not likely to experience much resistance.

On the basis of these analogous situations it is possible to suggest, although not yet to prove, that female patrolmen might be in less risk—and be more effective—in dealing with offenders than would male patrolmen. If this were to be the case—and it very much needs a test—a whole new concept of fitness for law enforcement would be introduced.

ORDER OF SCREENING

Let us presume that the present minimal standards will be modified and rationalized, but that future selection will follow the same basic sequence as is presently in use: a series of different evaluation methods each designed to reject candidates who fail to meet predetermined standards. The question is, what shall the order of these steps be? Which screening is to come first?

At present the choice of selection steps is based upon cost and convenience. The easiest and cheapest steps come first so that fewer men will have to be evaluated by the more expensive and time-consuming procedures. This is reasonable from the standpoint of time and costs; it may not be reasonable in terms of selection efficiency. As an improvement Stone and Kendall[3] offer a technique called the "successive hurdles" method. Here all factors (standards) shown by research to be related to performance are set forth in the order of their importance. The standard which best predicts work success comes first, the second best comes second, and so on. The selection steps are arranged in the same order; the most efficient hurdle being the first evaluator and so on down the line. Only those who pass the first hurdle go on to the second.

The advantage of this method is that one does not carry along a host of candidates who have passed the first screener, but because that screener has a low order relationship to work, it is known that many of those who have passed will sooner or later be found unfit for employment. At the same time some of those who have been rejected will have been rejected in error.

Typical among the irrational cheap tools now in use as a first screener is the civil service written examination. It is easy to give, is costs practically nothing, and it eliminates a large number of applicants. The only thing wrong with it, as is shown in Chapter V, is that scores on the typical civil service written have but little to do with intelligence or with police service. It is a poor predictor and as such not only accepts men who will later be rejected (presuming the excellence of later selection tools) but rejects men who would have done well in police service. Under the approach suggested by Stone and Kendall, and heartily concurred in by ourselves, such inefficient screeners would be eliminated.

In order to construct a rational series of selection steps it will be necessary to know, in statistical terms derived from research, just how useful each selection tool is in predicting to job performance. What is implied here is that the administrator must be informed about the goodness of each standard and of the methods used to evaluate men according to it. To have information the administrator must make objective observations. These observations require that preconceptions be abandoned, that experiments be tried, and that trained observers be invited in to participate in the study of the methods in use. These are the requirements imposed on any science or any sensible policy maker. Their application to the study of standards and selection tools is heartily recommended.

REFERENCES

Part I: References Cited in the Text

1. Chruden, Herbert J., and Sherman, Arthur W., Jr.: *Personnel Management*. Cincinnati, Southwestern Publishing Co., 1959, 670 pages.
2. Germann, A.C.: *Police Personnel Management*. Springfield, Thomas, 1958, 251 pages.
3. Frost, Thomas M.: *A Forward Look in Police Education*. Springfield, Thomas, 1959, 290 pages.
4. Columbia Round Table: *What Makes an Executive*. New York, Columbia University Press, 1955, 179 pages.
5. Fuld, Leonhard Felix: *Police Administration*. New York, Putnam & Sons, 1909, 551 pages.
6. Hanman, Bert: *Physical Capabilities and Job Placement*. Stockholm, Nordisk, Rotogravyr, 1951, 167 pages.
7. Stone, C. Harold, Kendall, William E.: *Effective Personnel Selection Procedures*. 2nd., Englewood Cliffs, Prentice-Hall Inc., 1956, 433 pages.

Part II: Supplementary References

1. Adkins, Dorothy C., assisted by Brimoff, Ernest S., McAdoo, Harold L., Bridges, Claude F., and Forer, Bertram: *Construction and Analysis of Achievement Tests*. Washington, The United States Civil Service Commission, 1947.
2. Anastasi, Anne: *Psychological Testing*. New York, The Macmillan Company, 1954, 682 pp.
3. Bingham, Walter V.: *Aptitudes and Aptitude Testing*. New York, Harper and Bros., 1937.
4. Blum, Richard H., Goggin, William L., and Whitmore, Earl: A study of deputy sheriff selection procedures. *Police*, Nov.-Dec., 1961, Springfield, Thomas.
5. Blum, Richard H., Goggin, William L., Whitmore, Earl, and Pomeroy, Wesley: A further study of deputy sheriff selection procedures, *Police*, March-April, 1962, Springfield, Thomas.
6. Bohardt, Capt. Paul H.: Tucson Uses New Police Personnel Selection Methods. *FBI Law Enforcement Bulletin, 28*: No. 9, Sept. 1959, pages 8-12.
7. Frost, Thomas M.: Selection methods for police recruits. *The*

Journal of Criminal Law, Criminology and Police Science, Vol. *46:* May-June, 1955, pages 135-145.

8. Gourley, G. Douglas: State standards for local police recruitment and training. *Journal of Criminal Law, Criminology and Police Science,* Vol. *53:*Dec, 1962, pages 522-525.

9. Gourley, G. Douglas, and Bristow, Allan P.: *Patrol Administration.* Springfield, Thomas, 1961, 373 pages.

10. Jenkins, James J., and Paterson, Donald G., editors: *Studies in Individual Differences.* New York, Appleton-Century Crofts Inc., 1961, page 774.

11. Lawshe, C.H. Jr.: *Principles of Personnel Testing.* New York, McGraw Hill Book Co., 1948.

12. Los Angeles City Civil Service: Medical Standards for Police and Fire Service. Mimeographed material dated Nov. 1962.

13. Peacock, William G.: Police selection and training. *The Police Journal.* Brooklyn, Vol. *XLVI:* 4-14, No. 2, 1962.

14. Piffner, John M.: *The Supervision of Personnel.* Englewood Cliffs, Prentice-Hall Inc., 1958, 500 pages.

15. Pomeroy, Wesley A.: Supplementing Sworn Police Personnel as Seen by a Police Administrator. Presentation before the Administrative Institute for law enforcement officials, on Dec. 7, 1962, Peace Officers Assn., of Calif.

16. Santa Clara County: Medical Standards for Deputy Sheriff. Unpublished material, dated 1956.

17. Super, Donald E.: *Appraising Vocational Fitness by Means of Psychological Tests.* New York, Harper and Bros., 1949.

18. Wilson, O.W., *Police Planning.* Springfield, Thomas, 1952, 492 pages.

Chapter IV

RECRUITMENT

THE BEGINNINGS

PROBLEMS IN POLICE recruitment were relatively few during the formative years in America. Some community-conscious individuals volunteered their services; others were drafted to serve on a rotation basis. As time passed, those who were faced with assignment to police duties were able to escape their period of service by hiring someone else to take their place. Ultimately, however, the task of policing their neighbors became sufficiently unpopular to cause communities to hire paid, full-time police personnel.

The means of selecting new officers in those days were "informal," to say the least. Many were chosen on the theory that it "takes a crook to catch a crook." As a consequence, in some communities one needed a program to differentiate between the "good guys" and the "bad guys." Recruitment was primarily "word of mouth"—the mouth of the local alderman or councilman as he doled out patronage.

As populations expanded, essential governmental services, including police agencies, grew at a prodigious rate. Law enforcement was forced to act in a new role—an employer competing on the open labor market. This was complicated, of course, by the public image of the police. Consequently even those few departments that deliberately sought high quality applicants experienced difficulty in recruitment. This picture was further complicated by the fact that many police administrators preferred to devote all their time to the more glamorous (and newsworthy) task of "crime busting." The problem of recruitment was one they worried about on the day someone quit, was fired, or who upset the retirement board by dying.

EVOLUTION AND REVOLUTION IN RECRUITMENT

For many years police recruitment was likened by some to a refined form of seduction wherein great concessions were obtained with very little promised in return. Low salaries, poor working conditions, and little or no community appreciation were offered in exchange for a lifetime of hard work and hazard. In more recent times police have sought to change this picture to make the job more attractive. Slowly but surely many jurisdictions have been able to improve conditions of employment. Surprisingly enough, however, the overall results of recruiting have not materially improved.

Part of this has been due to police reform itself. Those agencies who did (willingly or otherwise) undergo moral and political purges to "cleanse themselves of sin" shifted into new and unfamiliar roles of respectability. Much like a reformed sinner, they now felt it imperative to follow the path of pious conservatism. As a result, much of their recruiting efforts were based on the theory of waiting for the applicant to come to the agency —the theory that "everyone will recognize how good we are and come knocking at our door." Their "soft sell" technique and unrealistic standards may have been successfully employed to recruit missionaries, but it did nothing towards recruiting good police material. The one really valuable product of this shift to high ethical standards was the break-away from "incestuous recruitment" (producing bodies from within the departmental family), and patronage appointment of political hacks.

In many areas the city's personnel agency began gradually assuming more and more of the initiative in recruiting policemen. This occurred because police administrators weren't overly concerned with devoting a great deal of time to recruiting, and secondly, because the police were unable to accurately define the type of person they were seeking. They could tell you what they felt a policeman *shouldn't* be, but not too much about what he *should* be. As a consequence, any guidelines for recruitment that were formulated by enforcement agencies tended to become nothing more than generalities.

STANDARD RECRUITING PROCEDURES

All departments are engaged in spirited competition with others in their area for recruits. Because of differences that usually exist, particularly in salaries, the smaller departments are hard put to recruit in the same labor market with big departments. As a result they are forced to accept something less insofar as ideal standards are concerned, or they must face the inevitable loss of at least part of their better personnel to higher paying or more attractive agencies. In some instances it has meant that the small department serves as a training ground where ambitious young men gain experience as they await openings in other area departments. One can philosophize that a department actually benefits by the employment of high quality personnel, even though for a short time. It would appear, however, that a high turnover rate can be disruptive both to departmental programming and personnel inter-relationships. Even worse, perhaps, it gives rise to anguished cries of "piracy" by frustrated department heads who steadily lose their better prospects to another agency.

(It might be profitable to analyze those departments where these losses occur consistently. It might well be that not only is their recruiting technique in need of major overhaul, but they simply aren't "delivering" the product they have so glowingly advertised.)

Many jurisdictions schedule tests only when a vacancy occurs. Usually there is a brief consultation between the department head and the personnel agency, and in essence the personnel agency is requested to scour the state for candidates and produce the best "by a week from Tuesday." Faced with this urgent ultimatum, civil service will hurriedly shuffle through their testing schedule and decide they can squeeze in the police exam between the more important tests for Parking Meter Collector and Hospital Attendant, providing they aren't holding first-aid classes in the high school gym on Saturday.

The "scope" book is dusted off and perused for an appropriate examination announcement. After these announcements are printed they are usually mailed to other departments and agencies in the area where they mysteriously wind up in the "circular file," or are tacked on the bulletin board among countless other job announcements.

When funds are available, the local and/or area newspapers are contacted and ads placed in the HELP WANTED columns. The usual ads tend to be helpful as screening devices, since their size serves to eliminate all except those with excellent eyesight. (Something else to ponder at this point is: Are we really looking for people who are unemployed?)

The third most commonly used method for recruiting is direct contact by members of the department. Probably one of the most effective methods, it also has the built-in danger of individuals presenting erroneous information concerning the position and the department.

ALTERNATE METHODS

Joint Recruitment and Testing

Many departments possess the highest sort of motivation to recruit the best possible candidates. Unfortunately they may not possess the funds and recruiting rescources that would enable them to accomplish this goal successfully. One answer to this predicament appears to lie in Joint Recruitment. In such a situation contiguous jurisdictions with comparable wage scales and working conditions would pool their resources towards one big effort, rather than two or more less effective ones. The ultimate in this direction would be where the county civil service department would serve as the recruiting and testing agency for all cities within the county. Thus professional staff would be available to those without it, the machinery essential to adequate personnel selection would not be duplicated in every city in the county, and better procedures could be utilized at lesser cost.

Continuous Recruitment and Testing

The young adult that police agencies seem most interested in is often attracted by announcements about job opportunities in the field of law enforcement. While this interest is high it is to the advantage of the police department and the personnel agency to lure him into the selection process. When there is a delay between filing and actual testing of several weeks or months, candidates often lose interest or find other jobs. It is essential therefore, when there is a predictable turnover sufficient to justify such a step, to seek candidates on a continuous basis and make it as convenient as possible for them to enter the testing process.

One means of doing this is through a referral (by civil service) to the departmental personnel officer when an applicant expresses interest by filing an application. This interview would serve to determine whether or not there is any reason why the applicant would seem unsuitable for police work. It would also serve as a vehicle for "selling the department" to the applicant. If nothing appears in the interview that would disqualify the applicant, he will then begin the testing procedure. The entire procedure may be completed within one day or it may take as long as several weeks, depending upon the ease with which all interested persons can adjust their time. (A modified form of this system could be "periodic testing," wherein the test cycle is begun every 90 days, on a year-round basis.)

The main advantage here of course is that the department (internally or through the personnel agency) is able to immediately test a prospective candidate while he has an interest in joining the department and before he makes other commitments.

Career Day Programs

Nearly every high school, junior college and college has some sort of "career day" each year at which recruiters from various professions are allowed to "hawk their wares." Although its potential has been virtually untapped by police agencies, it has proven a fertile field for corporations, government agencies and the armed services. Obviously the best time to recruit career personnel (or stimulate their choice of a career) is when these individuals are in the process of selecting their future vocation. When a police department assigns intelligent and neat-appearing young officers to make a "sales pitch" for law enforcement at these programs, the results can be highly productive. The student will be provided a palatable living "image" with which he can identify—an image that presents law enforcement in its most attractive form. These people may be hirable immediately as police cadets, radio dispatchers, identification clerks, etc., or their entry into the department may be delayed by age minimums and the desire for additional academic training. In any event, it means "getting the body while it's warm"—expanding the recruitment pool of the future.

Radio and Television

The cost of advertising today on radio or television is a relatively expensive proposition. Some police wags caustically point out that the cost would be nearly as high as items in the Chief's annual budget for meetings and conventions. In any event, the value of TV and radio commercials is a proven fact—a fact so important that nearly two-thirds of the top one hundred advertisers in the United States utilize these media in selling their product. If lack of funds does constitute a barrier to their commercial use, consideration should still be given to an approach to radio and TV stations based on requests for "Public Service Announcement" time.

Most stations feature "spot announcements" of ten, twenty, or sixty seconds duration. These announcements, usually made during station breaks, require written copy for live commercials, or pre-taped messages designed for radio broadcast. Television "spots" involve still-art and photography in the form of slides (usually 2" x 2" transparencies) or live announcements made in conjunction with station identification.

Considerable success can be achieved in utilizing these media through public service announcements. A personal visit with the managers of local stations will give one the necessary information regarding the type of announcement they can make and how it must be prepared.

Public Relations and the Police Image

Success in recruitment does not hinge on efforts commenced on the day the need for additional personnel becomes known. It begins and continues as a dynamic day-to-day program of attaining satisfactory public contacts. Because personal contact between individual officers and individual citizens occurs infrequently, this effort can be intensified through planned public appearances. Qualified speakers, using departmental approved material, can do much to build increased public respect throughout the community. By reaching a large proportion of the public during the course of these speaking engagements, the "image" of professional competency can serve as a magnet to attract good candidates. A sound, continuous Public Relations program provides one component for effective recruiting.

Profiting from the Press

American newspapers serve as a daily reminder that just about any product can be sold if it is presented in an appealing form. It is too often the case that a police or personnel agency will simply furnish the local press with its printed job announcement and expect the newspaper staff to develop some sort of interesting copy. The resulting material, if printed at all, is seldom the eye-catching and appealing type of article that will do a good recruiting job.

If police hope to get effective material in the daily editions and supplements, the copy must be well-planned and include some kind of "news peg" that will titillate the fancy of the editor who must approve its publication, as well as those who represent the potential market. (Many papers frown on running feature stories about job openings that are, in a sense, competing with paid advertisers. It might be wise then to submit articles and pictures at the same time one contracts for Classified Advertising in the Help Wanted Columns.)

The basis for creating successful copy is to avoid the routine approach. One should think about the particular recruitment problem differently than would others, and then try to say it differently.

It is important to consider when one should "time" the release of copy. Releasing it too far in advance, of course, lessens its effectiveness. People delay in filing and often put it off until it is too late. There is a natural reluctance too, on the part of the papers, to run material over a long period of time because it fails to hold reader interest. Thoughtful timing about what day you submit copy might also ensure that your material will appear in the weekly shopping news and throw-away editions, in addition to the daily issues.

Thought, imagination, originality, planning and timing—all these will serve to showcase your product in an appealing form that will reach a wide market of potential candidates.*

---

*See Appendix I for illustrations of imaginative copy.

OTHER RECRUITMENT MEDIA

In addition to radio, television and the press, police agencies should not hesitate to borrow freely from the other techniques of commercial advertising.

This would include the use of illustrated circulars (mailed to high schools, colleges and military installations, other departments, related agencies, etc.) as well as bill-boards and posters placed in strategic locations throughout the community. Still another outlet is found through the utilization of space in the printed programs used at athletic contests, cultural programs and major civic events. Lastly, we can consider placing advertisements in the so-called professional journals. (We use the term "so-called" in view of the existence of some publications alleging to be spokesmen for police professionals that are little more than fund-raising ventures for police groups or printed outlets for assorted experts whose experience in dealing with criminals is limited to the books and lectures from which they have pirated their material.)

The success of commercial advertising techniques is such that one can scarcely ignore it. It is so important that these techniques legitimately deserve consideration in any planning and research efforts by the department. These efforts can be sophisticated and complex, or as simple as doing basic research in the section of the local library dealing with Advertising. Either way it would do much to lift recruiting from the doldrums of prosaic, dull and unproductive methods.

THE RECRUITMENT BASE AND ITS IMPLICATIONS

Most administrators would like to feel that only "Don Strongheart, the All-American Boy" would venture in off the street to fill out an application. Somewhere in between this dreamworld and the cold, hard facts of everyday life is the unexciting truth that we can only hope to get what is available in our own particular community, or area. Instead of playing to the hilt the role of a spinster waiting for her Prince Charming, we should take off the rosy-colored glasses and accept the fact that some of our applicants won't have straight teeth, flat ears and a Doctorate in

Criminology. As a matter of fact, many of them will look and act just like the fellow next door.

If this premise be true, and we feel it is, a starting point might be in considering the recruiting standards and how they affect both the recruitment base and the recruitment pool towards which our efforts are directed. First we should understand that the terms "standards" and "limitations" are synonymous. Any arbitrary standard we establish will in itself set up a limitation on the number of eligibles we can reach. There is certainly nothing wrong with this procedure, since it tends to screen out those we don't wish to consider for employment. On the other hand, we must again stress the point that Utopian recruitment is fallacious recruitment. For example, seeking the tall Texan in short-statured Cincinnati will only lead to administrative ulcers.

Disregarding for the moment the complicated formulae expounded by various personnel "experts," one can utilize very simple and extremely available means of comparing existing standards with existing manpower in specific areas. This would involve reference to U.S. Census information, statistics from area Selective Service sources, the State Department of Employment, and other statistics selected from material furnished by various insurance company research surveys.

Probably the real bonanza is found in census information. This gold-mine will produce, for example, data concerning how many of the local labor force fall within your age limitations; whether or not your offered salary is a competitive one; how many can meet residence and citizenship requirements; what percentage meet educational requirements; what the unemployment rate is; what the predominant occupations of eligible employed males are; how many in the potential market are unavailable because they are enrolled in schools, are in the armed forces or are confined in institutions, etc. It provides, in other words, a fairly accurate picture with which we can compare our existing standards. If the available potential manpower pool is sufficiently large, then blame for difficulty in recruiting cannot logically be placed at this point in our system. However, if our standards have unrealistically narrowed the local field from which we can draw, then serious consideration must be given to modifying our demands. It could very well be that an intelligent candidate from another city, who is an inch shorter and a year older, is really better than no candidate at all.*

To see briefly how such an evaluation can be made, let's examine a medium sized city (San Mateo, California), population 69,870. It would appear that starting with such a substantial total would guarantee an ample market. It is disheartening to find this isn't true when we consider the primary screener—the number of males in the labor force. Census information provides the following:

	Age of Persons in Labor Force	
Males:	18 to 24 years old	1,513
	25 to 34 years old	3,982
	total	5,495

As can be seen, the fact that we're only hiring males within a certain age group would automatically screen out 92 per cent of the local population.

The second standard customarily employed is that of educational requirements. This particular city, as do all others in the same area, requires high school graduation. When we examine education status in the 1960 census we find that of all males twenty-five years old and over only 4,958 have completed four years of High School.

Working then with a potential market of approximately seven per cent of the total population, one begins to further decimate the recruitment pool by imposing additional qualifications related to:

1)	Residence.	4)	Physical agility.
2)	Height and weight.	5)	Citizenship.
3)	Vision and hearing.	6)	Mental normalcy.**

---

*It is something less than comforting to point out that the Government, in defining census statistics, lists policemen almost at the bottom of the list. Listed together with police in a general category of "service workers" are such glorious jobs as waiters, cooks, bartenders, theater ushers and chambermaids.

**In other areas of the United States, even race could be an important consideration.

All these factors inexorably chip away at the available re-cruitment pool. The result, often-times, is the formation of an "applicant's market" where a few applicants are sought by many. When this becomes evident, it signals the need for an agonizing re-appraisal of standards (refer to Chapter III). The basic issue then becomes one of finding where modifications can realistically be made without compromising our responsibility for quality.

SPECIAL RECRUITMENT POOLS

Cadet Programs

An earlier discussion noted the value of police participation in Career Day Programs at high schools. Related to these efforts is the establishment of Cadet positions in those police agencies large enough to provide a variety of functions in which they can be utilized.

Under such a system a cadet must meet all of the minimum qualifications required of a regular police officer, with the ex-ception of age. Normally a cadet would be assigned to non-critical functions in the department such as clerical work, switchboard and teletype operation, etc. When he becomes twenty-one the cadet can be promoted directly to the rank of policeman, with or without additional testing.

Some of the advantages of a Cadet Program are:

1. It gives the department head substantial time to take a long, hard look at the cadet's potential for a law enforcement career before the individual dons the protective armor of civil service.

2. The department can train the cadet in its own way while he is still in the habit of learning.

3. The cadet commits himself to a career in law enforcement as soon as he graduates from high school, although he is not yet old enough to qualify as a regular officer.

4. It may also provide more highly motivated individuals to fill non-enforcement positions, as opposed to run-of-the-mill, civil service employees.

Although Cadet Programs have certain drawbacks in terms of higher turnover and special training needs, they do create a needed additional resource from which to recruit.

Junior College and Four-Year Colleges

Police training programs in most junior colleges are unique in that they provide a special curriculum to many students who will never be able to use it. Little or no correllation exists between minimum standards for police and minimum standards for police science students. Until this hurdle is overcome, recruiting efforts at the junior college level are rather limited.

In order to strengthen this recruitment source, local departments must work with the colleges in setting up standards wherein students are accepted in police science courses only if their physical and mental capabilities qualify them to apply for police employment.

Here then is created a realistic recruitment potential. It can be further enhanced if the director of the college police program eliminates additional students who, during the progress of the course, demonstrate that they are obviously unsuited for police employment.

Four year colleges and the universities constitute a somewhat better manpower pool in that they provide an older and, hopefully, more mature prospect. Such individuals are also demonstrating that their career goals are more firmly fixed than at other levels.

Recruiting emphasis here, however, should not be limited just to those persons involved in police administration or criminology programs. Special "pitches" should be made to those in the Social Sciences, pointing out how their special and unique knowledge of human development and behavior are most sorely needed in the field of law enforcement. One could also point out that they could attain higher entrance level salaries in law enforcement than in many of the fields of employment for men with Bachelor Degrees. As for those students who plan to go on to graduate schools to obtain their Masters or Ph. D degrees, it will surprise them to learn that they can expect to make more money as a police administrator than they could ordinarily hope to make as college teachers or research workers.

The Military

Many departments seem to refute their claim of being a semi-military organization by ignoring altogether the military itself as a source for recruiting policemen. A great many cities have or are near military installations. By establishing communication with the personnel officers at these bases, local departments can familiarize themselves with the standards of the military, the number of qualified men who are slated for separation in the near future, and how one can arrange to contact them to discuss law enforcement as a post-service career. (One would also enjoy the advantage of dealing with persons who have fulfilled their military obligations and wouldn't later be lost through the "draft.")

Another potential recruitment pool to be found in the military is those who have reached retirement age, after twenty to twenty-five years of service, and are interested in law enforcement as a second career. Many in this category are still relatively young persons with a background of qualifications unmatched by any other potential applicant. Departments should seriously consider this source of manpower in their area as one of the possible solutions to recruiting problems.

SUMMARY

Police recruitment, admittedly off to a poor start in the beginning, has improved its position very little in recent years. Many of the so-called "standard recruiting practices" in use today are still characterized by a striking lack of imagination and willingness to experiment with change.

Primary emphasis has been on the development of personnel *after* their entry into law enforcement. Nearly all the efforts and resources of a department are channeled towards this goal, failing to keep in mind that a satisfactory finished product is possible only when you have sufficient raw material from which to begin.

The time is past when police agencies can realistically blame others for their inability to recruit personnel. It is time, therefore, to discard recruiting procedures that prove to be unproductive. It is time to divert the resources of the organization from certain of their traditional paths. Planning and research programs must be established that will continuously seek to identify the techniques and methods that will best aid the department in procuring manpower within its own particular community. In addition, there must be developed throughout the department a growing awareness of the important role recruitment plays in the future hopes and goals of the agency.

Procurement of manpower remains one of the biggest challenges in the police field today. By accepting and meeting this challenge, law enforcement will benefit both itself and the community at large. What more could a "professional" ask?

Chapter V

PSYCHOLOGICAL TESTING

T HIS CHAPTER discusses the use and future potential of psychological tests in the selection of police officers. It will attempt to provide the reader with information which will enable him to evaluate the current status of tests in police selection. It will also attempt to provide guidelines for the innovation of testing programs within departments. The chapter will present three kinds of information as follows:

a. Consideration of the purposes, limitations, and advantages of psychological tests in police personnel selection.
b. A discussion of tests which are likely to be useful in such programs.
c. Presentation of the results of research on the use of tests in police personnel selection.

On the basis of the information presented certain recommendations will be made in regard to the introduction and use of tests in police settings.

LIMITATIONS AND ADVANTAGES OF PSYCHOLOGICAL TESTS

The primary purpose for which one would employ any psychological test in selection work is to predict how the applicant will perform on the job if he is hired. A test is designed as a short-

Acknowledgements: The author wishes to acknowledge a grant from the Insititute of Social Science, Professor Herbert Blumer, Director, at the University of California in support of the preparation of this chapter and for the final stages of research work reported here. For their major contributions to the experimentation in selection procedures and to the studies themselves, thanks are due to the following: Undersheriff Wesley Pomeroy, Capt. Gene Stewart, Director Edward Comber, Lieut. William Osterloh, Capt. Earl Lewis, Capt. Jewell Ross and Capt. John Guidici.

For administrative support and guidance we are indebeted to Sheriff Earl Whitmore, Chief Thomas Cahill, Sheriff Frank Madigan, Chief Addison H. Fording, Sheriff John Gibbons, Capt. John Meehan, Capt. William Beall, Mr. James Newman, Mr. Donald Macrae, Mr. F. V. Routt, Mr. Phillip Berger, Mr. Herbert White, Mr. William Goggin, Dr. Harold Chope and Dr. J. J. Downing.

For statistical consultation and assistance Dr. William Meredith deserves thanks, and for their unfailing work as research assistants Mrs. Mary Lou Funkhauser and Mrs. Kay Gilman must be given special praise.

cut, as Ghiselli and Brown[12] point out, a substitute for actually hiring and observing an applicant in the work situation. One expects of a test that it will save an agency time, money, and disruptions in operation by helping to select men fit for the job while eliminating those who are unfit. In police work it may also serve a secondary purpose of providing an acceptable device for cutting down the size of a large applicant list. Even when used in this latter fashion it is necessary that a test have the known characteristic of not eliminating potentially good men while selecting the unfit. The necessity to know at least this much about tests is often overlooked when administrators choose screening hurdles which are meant to cut a list of applicants down to a manageable number.

The decision to use any test, or a battery of tests, rests upon having knowledge about whether or not the test can in fact predict success or failure on the job. In order to decide to use tests we should also know that the test can predict either more efficiently or more economically than traditional screening methods already in use. There would be no point to adopting a test if it could predict no better than methods already in use unless, of course, it could be shown that testing has some advantage over the traditional methods, as for example in being cheaper or easier to employ.

Any psychological test is a miniature life situation from which one seeks to gain information about a person which can be generalized to other aspects of the person's behavior. The assumption which is made in constructing a test is that what the person does or says under the test conditions will be related in some regular way to what the person will say or do when he is outside the test situation. We expect certain consistencies in human behavior. We anticipate that conduct in a test situation will resemble conduct in later life situations; we expect that characteristics or qualities of the person which are associated with his behavior in one setting will also be related to his behavior in other settings. Generally one expects the consistency of human conduct to be greater from one situation to the next the more alike those situations are, the more the person is asked to do the same thing in each situation, and the less the individual has himself changed over time in regard to his abilities, his motives, and his understanding. We can see from the foregoing some of the reasons for the inevitable inaccuracy in prediction.

In a testing program one requires that those abilities or personality factors which influence work performance be assessed during test performance. Insofar as the work itself will be complex or variable, calling on different sets of skills, motives or personal qualities, then the process of building or using tests also becomes more complicated and more subject to error. Insofar as the settings in which varied tasks are to be performed also changes, either over time or from place to place, there is added difficulty in finding a test which can predict conduct in a variety of life situations. To these difficulties is added our recognition that as human beings we change over the years or even from moment to moment. Psychologists and other scientists have not yet identified many of the internal or external factors which account for these at present inexplicable vagaries in human behavior. Until we identify and measure the effects of the many unknown factors which determine human behavior there can be no tests which identify and measure them for the purposes of prediction.

Generally speaking tests are most successfully employed when they measure some simple stable element of performance in order to predict that performance on the job. The closer the test requirement and the job requirement the easier the task. A test of typing proficiency among men who have learned to type does not have too much trouble predicting typing proficiency once a man is hired. But even here one is confounded by the unexpected; typing proficiency may decrease because of poor morale or irritation; it may increase with high interest or raised morale. Even simple tasks such as typing are subject to error in predicting dependent upon change in social settings, in work conditions, or the health, personality or motives of the individual.

Among men who have not yet been exposed to instruction on how to type, the prediction of who is potentially a better typist becomes immediately more difficult. Instead of measuring a skill achieved, we are trying to measure an aptitude or a potential for the acquisition of that skill plus the capacity to execute that work skill on the job. Here one tries to identify factors associated with the ability to learn to type. Vision, finger dexterity, fine movement coordination, the simple ability to read and write, interest in clerical work, intelligence, personality, immediate memory can all enter in.[12] So it is that the prediction of aptitudes rather than achievements or abilities is a more difficult undertaking.

We find even more difficulty when we move away from relatively well-defined tasks such as typing or radio operation to attempt to predict to performance of presently inexperienced persons in an occupation which requires various skills applied in changing circumstances as is the case in police work. To begin, we need to know what a policeman really does. Only when we know his job can we identify the skills he must possess and make inferences about personal characteristics which are likely to contribute to his success in one or another work situation. Once a number of skills or attributes are identified as likely to be associated with work performance, one can begin to think in terms of a battery of different tests, each one of which measures one ability or aptitude component of the job. It may be that carefully constructed tests will already exist to measure some of these components; if so one can experiment with these tests to see if their use can be immediately extended so as to predict police performance.

It appears that many of the concrete skills required of policemen are of the kind which have been studied in other areas of occupational test development. There exist a variety of tests to measure aptitude for or proficiency in clerical work, for abilities in handling or repairing mechanical or electronic equipment, for auto driving, and the like. Insofar as the policeman's work assignment requires of him only that he perform such well-defined tasks it is possible to make reasonably successful predictions about his response to training and his later performance on the job. Yet it is a rare department in which police personnel are hired on a specialty basis and are required to perform on other than specific technical or clerical duties. Even if a department were to select some of its officers on the basis of specialty skills which would lead to permanent specialty assignments* there would still be a ma-

---

*Current trends suggest that the specialist is less and less likely to be a *police* recruitment problem. The growth of civilian staff positions to serve as typists, criminalists, meter maids, file clerks, communication personnel, electronic data processing technicians etc. will no doubt be acompanied by increasing use of aptitude tests for the hiring of civilians. The problem of choosing line officers for general police work remains undiminished by the growth of civilian specialty staff positions.

jority of the force whose work would not be limited to such tasks and for whom line work assignments would be more varied, social and complex. For the majority of policemen job performance would *appear to* depend upon broader and less easily measured characteristics such as judgment, intelligence, flexibility, emotional stability, honesty, freedom from race bias, capacity to accept discipline, sociability and the like.

In this regard it is worth noting what police administrators believe to be the necessary qualities in a recruit. A review[4] of qualities listed by exceptionally able administrators produced the following desired features: good appearance, ability to speak up, forceful, able to fit into discipline, capable of being trained, sincere, flexible, uses good English, energetic, mature, sustained interest in personal advancement, genuine interest in becoming a peace officer, stability, wholesomeness, conscientious, well-adjusted.

Undesirable qualities listed included selfishness, oversensitivity, extreme introversion, opinionated, lack of objectivity, immaturity, psychopathic personality, inability to perform under pressure, uncertainty about life goals, lack of understanding of law enforcement principles, vacillation, lack of drive, egotistical, failure to understand what are key issues, poor voice, too security conscious, poor health, inability to handle finances, unstable employment history, poor driving record, too emotional, passivity, uncertainty, lack of enthusiasm or energy, lack of experience with or awareness of social conflicts, daydreaming, appearance not conducive to respect, poor thinking ability, failure to understand human nature, delinquent trends, inability to exercise authority, nervousness, lack of temper control, overaggressive, impulsive, anxious, rigid personality, unsophisticated, homosexuality, effeminate, tries too hard to please others, autocratic, or softness (lacking courage, determination.)

Accepting at face value the (at present unproven) relationship of these qualities to successful police work, we find but few of them which are easily identified, agreed upon, measured, and predictable by ordinary means. Furthermore, there is good reason to believe[2,3,6,7,26] that police selection is made more hazardous by the attraction of the profession to a number of persons whose background and qualities one assumes to be undesirable in policemen. We see evidence of this in a study[4] in one jurisdiction which reviewed the quality of a small group of applicants and found that 25 per cent had significant criminal records, 30 per cent had poor driving records, 30 per cent had moderate or severe personality problems, 20 per cent had defective judgement or intelligence, 33 per cent had questionable motives for entering law enforcement and background investigation revealed important negative information on 56 per cent of the applicants. A repeat study on applicants to the same department for the following year[5] found 22 per cent with emotional disturbance, 44 per cent with test evidence of character defect, and 54 per cent with important negative information revealed by a background investigation.

On the basis of these applicant characteristics it appears that a considerable number of the men who apply for police jobs are "risky" characters. Until more research is done we cannot say if the proportion of police applicants with criminal records, personality problems, or poor driving histories is higher than the proportion of such men among applicants to business houses, fire departments or industrial concerns. In the meantime, on the basis of the information we do have, we can recommend the need for care and caution in evaluating applicants for police work.

The qualities of applicants which are of interest to police administrators are also of great interest to psychologists, for many of these same attributes play an important role in other social situations. As a result psychologists and others have been working for many years to develop tests which can measure these characteristics and have been doing research on the relationship between test results and actual behavior in various circumstances. The tests that have been developed fall into four major categories: intelligence, interests and values, attitudes, and personality. The four categories are by no means unrelated.

Police administrators and psychological research workers who share an interest in the identification of human characteristics which enable one to predict what people will do will also share an understanding of some of the specific difficulties entailed in that prediction. They will recognize the difficulty in sampling from a small portion of behavior such as an oral interview or a test in order to generalize to much broader settings. They realize that appearance can be deceiving and that it is necessary to tap something other than superficial best-foot-forward behavior. They realize that it is difficult to know in advance which among a variety of characteristics or behavior potentials possessed by a man will become paramount in time and which will be elicited by any given situation. Both the police administrator and the psychologist further realize that situational factors strongly influence human behavior and that it is often not possible to anticipate the kinds of situations to which persons will be exposed. Furthermore, two persons with relatively similar characteristics will, if exposed to consistently different life situations, organizational requirements, or institutional atmosphere, be very likely to grow and learn in different directions, developing new habits, outlooks, vices or virtues which will in turn further shape their conduct.

Because the police administrator already knows how difficult it is to predict human behavior, it is hoped that he will keep this knowledge in mind when appraising the potential usefulness of psychologists and tests in his own department. He must be realistic in his expectations; neither discounting their work as unrelated to his own interests or of no potential value to him, nor, at the other extreme, of expecting their tests to make perfect predictions or their judgments to be without error. There is no magic in any of the social or behavioral sciences or in their applications. The special tools that the psychologist can offer to the police administrator are only those of a developing science which is hard at work trying to make careful observations which must be continuously checked for their stability and accuracy.

These tools have demonstrated their value elsewhere and it is very likely that they can demonstrate their usefulness to police selection as well. There is ample evidence from industry, the armed forces, universities, and other organizations that tests can improve selection programs. However, before tests are put to work in police screening it is necessary that both the administrator and the psychologist have evidence that the proposed tests do work in their new environment by adding accuracy and economy to prediction.

Too often the administrator can be "sold a bill of goods" by test enthusiasts who by virtue of their optimism, their lack of research training, or their commitment to unexamined clinical methods persuade an agency to adopt tests which have not demonstrated their utility in the police field. One must guard against naiveté just as much as one must guard against the opposite extreme of opinionated rejection of any testing program because there is general distrust of methods which are unfamiliar or "academic" or which threaten established practices.

EMPLOYING AN EXPERT

It is unfair for the police administrator to demand too much of himself. He cannot be expected to be an expert in everything. Consequently when it comes to the business of adopting tests for his own department he should not take it upon himself to chose the tests or to design the research program which evaluates the tests to see if they work. What he should know is that competent psychologists can assist him in evaluating his selection program and making suggestions for innovations and research. He should recognize that these professionals, like any other, come in all sizes of competence, and that he must exercise due care in *their* selection. Ordinarily one can rely on the recommendations of a reputable university psychology department, or local mental health or government agencies which employ Ph.D. psychologists skilled in research and knowledgeable about test methods or the fields of industrial, social and clinical psychology. Local industries with Ph.D. personnel administrators or consultants may also be useful sources for recommendations.

TESTS WITH POTENTIALS FOR USE IN POLICE SELECTION

The first group of tests which have application to police performance are those which have been considered as measures of potentiality or proficiency for *specific* work techniques. Here are included a number of tests usually well known to personnel people; tests which predict among those not now possessing a skill the aptitude to respond to training or which assess already present requisite skills or knowledge for tasks such as typing, clerical work, operation of communications equipment, equipment maintenance and repair, proficiency in knowledge or handling of firearms, automobile driving, and so forth.

Such tests are already employed in departments seeking to evaluate persons for specialized job assignments. Since these types of measures have demonstrated their ability to predict specific skill trainability or performance over many years, there is little need to dwell upon them here. They have shown their value for the specific purposes for which they are employed; consequently current personnel selection sees them in wide use. Since this is the case, and since few of these specific skills constitute the demon problems which plague contemporary police administrators, we shall not dwell further upon them here.

SCHOOL ACHIEVEMENT TESTS

We have indicated that aptitude and proficiency tests can be used quite successfully, but that they do not ordinarily contribute to the prediction of performance beyond specific skills. A second set of standard tests is sometimes used in personnel selection under the assumption that their general nature will make them better able to be effective screening devices. We refer here to a variety of tests of knowledge or school achievement. Tests of this sort are usually verbal tests designed to tap an applicant's knowledge about a subject area, as for example civics, arithmetic, law, or the broader content of high school curriculum. These tests are employed under one or several assumptions; either that a certain minimum level of knowledge, as measured by the test, is related to the ability to be trained or to perform as an effective policeman, that some means must be used for pruning from among a large number of applicants and knowledge is as defensible as any measure to employ when one lacks a more rational means, or finally, that regardless of any demonstrated relationship between knowledge and aptitude, the department does not want to consider applicants who fail to possess a level of knowledge about certain subjects. In the latter instances there is almost a moral sentiment, or one based on a notion of reputation, that one *ought* not to hire a man who knows no civics even if there is no evidence that he will not perform well as a policeman.

Closely related to the school achievement test in its emphasis on knowledge of one sort or another is the general information test so commonly employed by personnel or civil service bureaus. These tests are, typically, constructed by asking educators, police administrators, or personnel men to submit questions which they *believe* tap information an applicant ought to possess. Questions may range from asking about who has won the World Series to who was Amerigo Vespucci, from naming the ranks in an ordinary police department to citing statistics on crime to stating the second law of thermodynamics. These typical civil service test scores ordinarily correlate with amount of education and, to some varying extent, with intelligence. Ordinarily their content must change each year because they are open to public inspection after an examination. Given this latter requirement—and the usual unavailability of trained personnel or absence of funds for careful work in testing their validity—these widely used tests are not supported by any body of data showing that they do, in fact, work as good predictors of police performance. For the most part civil service tests are unstandardized rather than standardized.*

GENERAL PSYCHOLOGICAL TESTS

There are many instruments which strive to measure more general human characteristics such as interests, personality, intelligence and so forth. There exist among the tests of this sort a number which have been employed in police selection or which have potentials for such employment. Too often they have been more widely used than scrutinized so that there is more information on their use than on their usefulness. Among those tests that have been subject to careful development, the following hold special promise for police selection—

Interest Tests

Strong Vocational Interest Blank: A questionnaire (inventory) of interests which the applicant completes. Careful and continuing research has shown that scores and patterns of scores dif-

---

*A standardized test is one which has a set form, has careful directions for conditions of use and specific instructions for administration and scoring, has norms established showing range of performance on the test for various groups, and ideally has been validated, i.e., has been shown to measure what it purports to measure.

fer for persons in various occupations. Results of the test show whether or not the interests of the person taking the test correspond to or are different from those of persons working in each of a number of vocations. Norms* for policemen allow one to say whether the applicant's own interests are expressed so as to be relatively similar or dissimilar to those of working policemen. The limitation is that norms are based on a relatively small group of peace officers and cannot be said to represent the variety of range of personnel found in this country. Further research is needed.

The Kuder Preference Record-Personal: measures preference for personal and social activities in the following categories: working with ideas, being active in groups, avoiding conflicts, directing others, and being in familiar and stable situations. Combined with the Kuder Vocational Preference Record it should provide information on vocations compatible with the interests of the applicant. Research on its use in police settings is recommended.

Value Tests

The Allport-Vernon Scale of Values has long been used to measure the direction of broad interests and personal values of a religious, economic, social, political, aesthetic, and theoretical nature. Scores on this test are related to occupational choice and to personality factors such as dogmatism. The test has potentials which should be explored by selection research.

Attitude Tests

While specific tests are fairly easy to construct to measure particular attitudes toward such matters as drug use, capital-punishment, civil liberties, minority rights, there is no evidence that attitude scales of this sort have been tried out in research on policemen. There exist several attitude tests which have been widely used and shown to be closely related to more general personality and opinion factors. These are as follows:

The "F" Scale measures fascist-tending extremist views and is

---

*Norms are statistics which report the performance of other individuals who have taken the same test. They show the distribution of scores, usually among various designated groups, and are used in comparing a given person's score ordinarily obtained on the test.

related to ethnocentrism (the belief one's own group is superior and others are inferior). This short test is derived from extensive research on authoritarian personality and political and racial extremism.[1]

The Dogmatism Scale more recently constructed by Rokeach[25] measures open versus close-mindedness. Scores on it are associated with authoritarian personality and with traits such as openness to new ideas, willingness to examine issues for oneself, general fear of the world and anxiety over threat from other persons, over conformity, difficulty in synthesizing new ideas and the like.

Not unrelated to dogmatism and the attitudes which underly the authoritarian personality is rigidity or flexibility in the approach to specific problems. A test for this is the Gough-Sanford rigidity scale which is one part of the broader California Psychological Inventory to be discussed below.

Personality Tests

The Minnesota Multiphasic Personality Inventory (MMPI) is widely used for the diagnosis of neurotic or psychotic tendencies. It includes important scales for the detection of homosexual or psychopathic personality trends. (The latter persons being amoral and asocial ones likely to engage in certain criminal activities. Scores on this scale differentiate groups of delinquents from non-delinquents) This test can be given in a paper-and-pencil* form to groups of applicants but it must be interpreted by a professional clinical psychologist, or psychiatrist, who has had experience with it.

The California Psychological Inventory is a newer paper-and-pencil test which measures some of the same features as does the MMPI, but is more directed to general non-pathological functioning. It includes the Gough-Sanford rigidity scale and has many other scales including ones designed to measure self-assurance, maturity, responsibility, and intellectual efficiency. There are norms based on 13,000 cases.

The Rorschach Ink Blot Test is one of the best known projec-

---

*By a "paper-and-pencil" test is meant one which needs no professional person to administer it. Like ordinary school tests or questionnaires the person is given a booklet with questions and records his replies with a pencil.

tive* tests. It is best given individually but for screening purposes it can be given in a group form. In the hands of a skilled clinical psychologist it can be useful in describing complex personality organization including such things as emotional stability, self-control, the presence of neurotic or psychotic features, sensitivity, anxiety, maturity, etc.

The Cornell Index is a paper-and-pencil test which proved useful in screening psychiatric cases for the military. It has been shown to be effective with civilian populations and has been modified for use in large scale mental health surveys. It is quickly given and scored and may easily be used in conjunction with the routine medical examination for, in its full form, it contains many questions about physical health which are of interest to the examining physician as well as to the clinical psychologist.

The Machover DAP is another project test which in the hands of a skilled clinician has been shown effective in the detection of persons with overly aggressive or disturbed delinquent or psychotic tendencies.

Judgment Tests

The Cardall Test of Practical Judgment is not widely used but purports to measure the ability of a person to draw logical conclusions from practical everyday situations. It is reported to be relatively independent of the person's intelligence or academic and social background. Preliminary work with it in police research suggests it to be deserving of further study.

The Social Intelligence Test (Moss, Hunt, Omwake) purports to measure social judgment, observation of human behavior, sense of humor, recognition of mental state of speaker, and memory for names and faces.

Intelligence Tests

For the most accurate assessment of intelligence it is best to administer individual tests such as the Wechsler Bellevue. For the purposes of mass screening it is standard practice to employ

---

*A projective test is one in which the subject is presented with an ambiguous stimuli which he must organize in his own way. The assumption is that whatever organization is imposed is a projection of the subject's own personality on to the ambiguous material. Ink blots, vague photographs, incomplete sentences, drawings to be made, all constitute ambiguous stimuli employed in such tests.

group tests of the paper-and-pencil variety. These have the advantage of economy of administration. The disadvantage is that some persons suffer language or cultural background handicaps which, if not recognized in advance and responded to with special tests, lead to their getting low scores on the group test; scores which reflect their handicap rather than any necessarily low intelligence level. This problem should be considered and corrective steps taken if the applicant group includes members of disadvantaged minority groups (Negro, Spanish-American) who may not do as well on tests with essentially unfamiliar materials.

Among the group tests of intelligence which are commonly employed and which have trustworthy reliability and validity are the following:

Otis Quick Scoring Mental Ability Tests of which the Gamma test series is for use with persons of high school and college backgrounds. There are several forms of this test which can be machine scored.

Army General Classification Test, civilian edition, measures general learning ability and has been used to predict school and occupational success. Among applicants with higher educational backgrounds there is a tendency toward high scores which may not produce refined discrimination among persons in such groups.

Thurstone Test of Mental Alertness measures linguistic, quantitative, and general learning abilities. It is claimed that it is especially useful in measuring the ability to understand relationships, think flexibly, etc.

Ohio State University Psychological Test has no time limit and is useful for populations who are slower in their thought processes.

Revised Army Alpha Examination is derived from adult tests first developed during World War I. In a revised form by Wells it is quick to give and to score.

Miller Analogies Test is for use in the selection of candidates for high level positions from among persons already known for their advanced education and high intellectual abilities.

For a detailed survey of available tests see Buros, *Fifth Mental Measurements Yearbook.*

POLICE USE OF PSYCHOLOGICAL TESTS

As with so many other advances in police work, it was Vollmer in Berkeley who first introduced psychological testing. Holmes[15] and Dudycha[8], in reviewing the history of screening programs, point out how a number of departments followed Vollmer in the 1920's by testing their personnel with the Army Alpha intelligence test. Average scores varied widely among departments ranging from high (A ratings) in Berkeley where the average score was 149 to a low (C rating) in Detroit where sergeants averaged scores of only fifty-five. What was apparent then remains apparent now; that departments differ widely in the characteristics of their personnel and that departmental needs must be considered in setting standards for performance.

The use of aptitude tests other than intelligence in selection was begun in the 1930's and has gradually expanded since then. This growth, which has been proportionately greater in California, in the West, and in East North Central Regions, has not usually been accompanied by research programs to test the tests. Oglesby,[24] in a 1958 survey of selection practices in the one hundred and eleven largest American cities, learned that fourteen employ psychiatric and/or psychological screening devices to weed out men with emotional and personality problems. However, the interview was the primary device employed with only six cities out of one hundred and eleven reporting the use of paper-and-pencil or projective personality tests.

O'Connor[23] suggests that the use of psychological tests and psychiatric screening is positively correlated with the administrative progress or efficiency of a department; a development which is in turn associated with a trend to be more selective about hiring. In 1956, among cities of population of 25,000 and over, an average of seventy out of 100 applicants was rejected; by 1961 an average of seventy-eight out of 100 were rejected. O'Connor finds that Berkeley's average success rate of only 14 per cent hired is one of the most selective in the nation. In reviewing these figures O'Connor wisely notes that today's most common selection approach is based on the rejection of men assumed likely to fail rather than being based on the choice of men with characteristics known to be associated with varying kinds of successful performance.

In this regard it is well to take note of a recent article by Kahneman and Ghiselli.[17] These authors examined the statistical relationship between test scores and the criteria for job success and job failure and found that the factors which account for success on a job may be quite different from those which account for failure. Thus, while a high degree of success on one job may require intelligence it cannot be assumed automatically that lack of intelligence will be responsible for actual failure. One must bear in mind that personal qualities or aptitudes associated with *average* job performance may be quite different from those associated with superior performance and, also, traits which are required in moderate amounts for statisfactory job performance certainly do not necessarily lead to superior performance when the necessary trait is present in greater amounts.

To illustrate each of the foregoing points, it can be seen that the intelligent man may make a superior police administrator, but it does not follow that the man of low intelligence can't squeak by in some police administrative duties; it may well be that actual failure as a police administrator would be related to the absence of political savvy or personnel handling skills but not simply to the absence of high intelligence. To illustrate the second point above, one can imagine a department in which average performance in police work would be found among solid unambitious fellows who move along routinely from day to day while in that same department the outstanding performance would be by quite different sorts of people; ones who are highly ambitious and who, enjoying change and challenge, chaff under monotony and routine. As an illustration of the third point, one can easily imagine a department in which satisfactory performance required the policeman to have a moderate flexibility, a willingness to change his mind or his operating methods in the face of new situations, information, or demands. On the other hand, there would be no necessary reason to believe that the man who was very accommodating, changing his ideas, methods, and decisions every time he was challenged or some new suggestion came up, would be a superior worker.

As a result of their studies, Kahneman and Ghiselli warn that a psychological trait showing some relationship to job performance need not lead to better performance as the presence of that trait increases (as measured by a test) nor is it necessary that the reduced presence of that trait will correspond in any one-to-one fashion with chance of job failure. The emphasize the lack of one-to-one correspondence between increasing trait or ability magnitude and increasing job success, pointing out that the maximum validity of tests which rests upon such one-to-one measures (referred to in terms of a symmetrical or linear homoscedastic relationship) is of the order of correlation coefficient/ (r) *=.50. The authors also point out that is is possible to achieve correlations equivalent to .70 or .80 by using more refined statistical techniques for prediction, ones that take into account the possibility of non-linear, asymmetrical or perhaps better said "qualitative" differences among workers failing, those doing average work, and those doing superior work.

RESEARCH ON POLICE SELECTION

If we restrict the scope of our survey of research to studies which have been made by trained social scientists using acceptable

---

*A correlation is a statistic which expresses a relationship between two sets of scores or other ordered sets of data. It describes for example how well one can predict the position of a person on one test by knowing his score on another test. (Ordinarily expressed as "r=--", a perfect correlation would be r=1.00 (either + or—) whereas a moderate correlation would be r=.45 or r=.55. When there is no relationship at all between scores on one test and scores on another test, r will be close to zero. A correlation of .50 accounts for 25% of the observed variation. (To find the variance take the square of the correlation) that is, the square of the correlation coefficient tells us the proportion of the observed variation which can be predicted from the variable with which we are concerned. Thus if there is a correlation of r=.60 between intelligence and job success as a police administrator we would square. .60 to get .36 per cent which we would interpret as the proportion of police administration success due to intelligence and we would know that the remainder, .64 per cent, was due to factors other than intelligence. To use another example, suppose that there is a correlation of r=.40 between interest in police work as measured by the Strong test and success as a patrolman (measured by supervisor's ratings.) Squaring .40 we find .16 per cent which means by knowing the Strong police interest scores we can predict only a little (16%) as to how a patrolman will be rated by his supervisors on the job. In this case 84 per cent of the components which account for those ratings will be found in factors other than police interest as measured by the Strong test.

scientific methods for observation and treatment of data, we find that there has been very little such work directed to the evaluation of the usefulness of psychological tests for the selection of policemen. Those studies that have been done provide very important information. In the following paragraphs the major studies and their findings will be set forth.

Ghiselli and Brown[12] reviewed aptitude tests conducted between 1920 and 1952 and noted how little work had been done in finding how best to select persons for public safety and protective occupations. On the basis of the studies available to them they concluded that tests of intelligence and of spatial factors (speed of perception, location, etc.) had "substantial validity"-on the order of correlations from .30 to .46-with trainability, that is in selecting men who responded well to training programs in protective work. As far as predicting performance on the job was concerned, as opposed to simple trainability, the highest correlations obtained were between tests of intellectual factors with $r = .26$ for general intelligence and personality, $r = .24$. These are very low correlations and are not satisfactory in themselves for establishing screening program. The reviewers were aware of this; for example in another article Ghiselli (11) noted that most validity coefficients were moderate or low, and that it appeared that "no single type of test will give satisfactory predictions of success for any occupational group. Clearly the indication is that batteries of tests will almost be a requirement if a reasonable level of accuracy in selection is to be achieved." Ghiselli observed that the variation in coefficients for a given trait or attribute among men in the same occupation working in different organizations was considerable, suggesting that the requirements for actual performance were quite different from one organization to the next. For this reason he suggests that research on tests for screening must concern themselves with work demands by agency or organization so that aptitude for performance in particular circumstances may be specified.

Within an organization or occupation there is a wide range of ability which can exist in regard to a trait or attribute without any apparent prejudicing of job success. For example Ghiselli and Brown reporting a survey by Stewart[29] of intelligence test scores for various occupations find that the average I.Q. for policemen was 109, with 50 per cent falling between an I.Q. of 96 and 118. This means that one fourth of the police tested had I.Q. scores over 118 and one fourth under 96.* We can see from this that it was possible for a small proportion of men from some departments to function even though they had only dull normal intelligence.

An important study by Thorndike and Hagen[30] followed up on 17,000 air force cadets tested on intelligence and on numerical, perceptual-spatial, mechanical and psychomotor aptitudes during the war. On these tests those one hundred and nineteen men who had become policemen in a number of different departments by 1955 did not demonstrate any very specialized aptitudes as measured by the original tests. Neither policemen nor detectives scored particularly high on any of the limited aptitudes measures; there was considerable variability within each occupational group. Except for an eye-hand coordination test (rotary pursuit) police group scores were below the average but within the normal range.

A comparison of the test score profiles (patterns of scores on the battery) shows policemen and firemen to be similar on the aptitudes tests. Biographical information was examined and showed the police group to be characterized by limited education both for the men and their parents, and by few books in the home. The policemen had not done well in school subjects such as algebra, physics and trigonometry. They were high only in physical training; most had indicated a liking for adventure and a desire to prove that they could "make good" as reasons why they had originally volunteered for Aviation Cadet training. Compared with the other cadets the policemen were less likely to have gone to college and their parents were less likely to have been high school graduates.

Concerning their study as a whole Thorndike and Hagen caution that "we should view the long-range prediction of occupational success by (these) aptitude tests with a good deal of skepticism and take a very restrained view of how much be accomplished in this direction." It appears that those differences among occupational groups in personal background and aptitudes were what

---

*A score of 100 is average and "normal" intelligence range between 90 and 110. High average is from 110 to 120, while dull normal is from 80 to 90.

would have been expected by a sensible analysis of the occupations.

Another rather negative finding in regard to particular tests and police performance is reported by Germann,[10] citing an unpublished study by Hammond and David, who reported that memory and observation tests were unrelated to job success of (Colorado) state patrolmen. Unremarkable results were also obtained by Martin[21] in 1923 who used eleven ability tests to test a group of policemen whose work was well known to and rated by their superiors. The highest correlation between performance and any one test was r = .39 for a test of number copying.

On the positive side of the ledger a study by Mullineau[22] in Baltimore found a correlation between AGCT scores and trainability, as defined by standing in the police academy, of r = .75. What relationship exists between academy standing and later on-the-job performance is not indicated.

Studies on personal preferences based on the Kuder Preference Record, Personal, suggest that men in protective services do have preferences which distinguish them from other occupations. Two scales on the Preference Record stand out. It is reported in a study cited by Sterne[28] that policemen prefer, more than other groups, to direct others,[19] and tend not to prefer to avoid conflict. Putting the latter a little more sensibly, one can make the inference that policemen perfer conflict more than some other occupational groups. In a more recent study by Sterne[28] no significant correlations were found between general efficiency in police work and any scale score on the Kuder Preference Record, Personal. This means that the scores of the men rated as the best policemen were no different on the Kuder than were those rated as poor policemen. Nevertheless Sterne did find that as a group the policemen in his sample once again showed preferences for directing others and for conflict (or in the language of the test, for preferring not to *avoid* conflict).

Sterne asked two sophisticated raters to describe the personal characteristics of those policemen who received the most extreme scores in the conflict preference scale. The raters said they were complainers, inconsiderate, eager, easily offended and capable of intense hatred. Given these attributes we can see why low scores on this scale are not associated with ratings of superior police work performance. Men with high scores on Scale E, the one which purports to measure preference for directing others were described by raters as capable, neat, etc., while low scorers on that scale, men with preferences in a direction unlike most policemen, were said to be polite, respectful, willing etc. One can see that Kuder E scale scores show no necessary validity if one takes behavior ratings as the criterion for validity.

A study by Kole[18] compared civil service applicants (including forty applying for police positions) with eighty medical students of the same age on tests of intelligence, anxiety, psychosomatic and physical complaints, motivation and vocational interest. He found an average I.Q. of 126 for medical students and 113 for police applicants. The police applicants and medical students appeared to have superior emotional adjustment and to have fewer symptoms of anxiety and psychosomatic illness than ordinary groups.

In examining his data Kole found that civil service applicants, both for fire and police service, describe themselves — on the Edwards Personal Preference Scale—as being more willing to take orders, to accept routine and to do things in a conventional way in contrast to college students and others taking the scale. The civil service applicants report little need for independence, little aggressiveness and little feeling of personal inadequacy. As for the Strong Vocational Interest Blank, Kole reviews the literature and finds a relationship between Strong interest scores and *job satisfaction* but little correlation between Strong scores and actual *work ability*. Among his sample, the police candidates scored higher than any other group on the Strong policeman (interest) scale. Their interests were close to those of others in social service occupations. There were significant differences between the police and fire applicant sample on sixteen out of the forty-eight Strong interest scales; these marked differences in interest are in contrast to his finding of no difference between police and fire candidates on intelligence, emotional adjustment or personality needs.

Zaice[31] has also studied the characteristics of men doing superior police work; in this case those on the Portland (Oregon) force. Using the AGCT he found evidence of greater intelligence among detectives than among patrolmen, and greater intelligence among command personnel than among detectives. Examining personality needs as measured by the Edwards Personal Preference Scale, Zaice reports that the Portland men had strong desire for achievement. Using the Strong tests he found that patrolmen had higher police vocational interest scale scores than did command personnel, but that the command personnel had interests much the same as public administrators outside of police work. In conclusion Zaice drew attention to the fact that these superior performing policemen were well above average in intelligence and, by inference from the Edwards tests, were ambitious and without psychological characteristics which would interfere with their effective work.

A study by Humm and Humm[16] in Los Angeles reports on the use of the Humm-Wadsworth Temperament Scale. In giving this test the authors predicted probable success as a police officer on the basis of the scores on the Scale. The Scale was given to beginning officers appointed to probationary status. Studying a group of policemen hired during World War II—among whom 20 per cent were fired for cause—the authors indicate their predictions corresponded with on-the-job failure (as measured by terminations) in 91 per cent of the cases. Studying a group of men hired under (presumably more rigorous) civil service procedures, the authors state the Humm-Wadsworth predictions agreed with final (termination) action in 80 per cent of the cases. Among a few command staff tested, the test-based predictions were said to agree with work success in 68 per cent of the case.

This study, while an interesting one, requires reevaluation of the data to provide a broader and more conservative view of the capacity of the Humm-Wadsworth Scale to predict performance. While the data in the article are not presented in such a fashion as to make their reworking an easy matter, it appears that among a total of 669 men tested seventy-nine resigned, 233 were fired, and 357 remained with the department. The ratio of men fired to men resigned is most unusual and suggests a very special situation in the department in which the Humms did their study.

At the time of testing the Humms predicted that 359 out of the total 669 would do poorly in police work and that 310 would do fair or good work. Among those 359 predicted to do badly, an actual 168 or 47 per cent were fired. Among 310 perdicted to do fair or good work, 245 (79%) did so. Conversely 53 per cent of those predicted to do badly did in fact get along well (were not fired) while 21 per cent of those predicted to do well or fairly well did badly. Our criteria for these statements consider a resignation as "doing well" since there is no evidence that quitting the department was associated with problem behavior or was a sign of job "failure" as the Humms assume. Viewed in this fashion one finds the rate of false positives (men who are predicted to do well but who in fact get fired) is 21 per cent while the rate of false negatives (men predicted to do badly but who do well) is 53 per cent. Viewed another way one could say the Humms expected 54 per cent (359/669) to do badly whereas only 34 per cent (233/669) really were fired. Among these 34 per cent fired, the Humms had correctly identified 72 per cent by their testing program.

Using the Humms' own criterion of quitting as a criterion for job failure (along with being fired) one calculates and finds that of 359 predicted to do badly, 58 per cent did badly and 42 per cent did well. Among 310 predicted to do good or fair work, 66 per cent did well and 34 per cent did badly. Among the 312 doing badly the Humm-Wadsworth Scale had correctly identified 73 per cent.

Concluding this review of the Humm-Wadsworth Scale one may say that it appears to work well as a selection instrument, that it deserves further research, but that our reevaluation of the claims made for it suggest its success may not be as dramatic as is implied. For the police administrator one may draw the moral that a claim for dramatic success of any selection instrument needs to be very carefully reviewed and the data upon which such a claim is based should be subjected to cautious, even skeptical, scrutiny. This is suggested as a wise rule for the police administrator not just in evaluating the Humm-Wadsworth Scale, but in evaluating the claims or conclusions of any professional "experts" in the field, the present author included.

As a final reference in a related work specialty, that of correctional officers, Gough[13] found that the California Psychological Inventory could be used to predict correctional officer performance with a correlation coefficient of $r = .35$. A single scale on this test, called the So scale, which was designed to measure honesty, conscientiousness and dependability did better in predicting work performance than did any pattern or profile using several different tests or scales. Gough went on to develop a special inventory to measure a person's interests in and attitudes toward correctional work. His conclusion is suggestive for research in the police field. He wrote, "Special testing devices constructed so as to focus directly on the job prediction problem seem to be much superior to standard tests for which psychometric calibration only is attempted." With Gough's suggestion in mind one might well wish to develop special methods for predicting police performance for possible use in conjunction with or even as replacements for standard psychological tests with demonstrated predictive value to police performance.

Within the last seven years the author of this chapter has been engaged in research on selection methods in police work. While progress notes have been published from time to time[4,5] there has been no full report of findings. In this chapter the most recent results from the several on-going studies will be presented.

PERSONNEL EXPERIENCE OF DEPARTMENTS NOT USING PSYCHOLOGICAL TESTS

Several brief surveys have been made of the personnel experience of police and sheriff's departments which do not use psychological tests or psychiatric interviews in their screening. The departments studied were all well-administered ones using ordinary civil service selection devices coupled with routine physical and oral board screening procedures. Data from these departments gives us an idea about the differences from one department to the next in personnel problems, and in a crude way, can provide a basis for comparison with the experience of departments which have used psychological tests as additional screeners. These departments of course differ in size, policy, supervisory practices, quality of recruits, and kind of police tasks involved.

Department A: A city in the 100,000-200,000 population range. Department A is well-reputed and recruits many of its men from college graduates with degrees in police science. Beginning with all men hired in 1956 and following through to the year 1962 we find that Department A has hired only 22.4 per cent of all men appearing for examination. We see that Department A is average for percent of men selected according to O'Connor's national survey.

In following the progress of each year's recruits we find that the rate of personnel loss through voluntary termination or being fired is quite regular from one year to the next. At least within the relatively short time span under observation there is no increase in turnover as men stay in the department longer, that is, later years are not found to have higher proportions of men lost than earlier years.

A total of 150 men have been hired from 1956 through 1962. By the end of 1962, nineteen had quit or been fired. The average rate of loss has been 4 per cent, that is, each year 4 per cent of the original group hired are lost to the department. Of those terminated, for every man fired, two quit without any evidence of misconduct or other disciplinary or efficiency action.

Department B: In a city under 50,000, Department B has hired only three men since 1956. None of these three has been fired, has quit, or is reported to have been a disciplinary problem. Department B's proportion of men selected out of those applying has been 6.5 per cent. This is a highly selective screening.

Department C: This department serves about 65,000 persons. In the period 1955 through 1962, it has hired twenty-six men of whom four have quit and two others have been fired. In this department all those terminating had done so within four years of time of hiring (out of a span of seven years of observation). If we calculate an annual rate of loss we find it is nearly 4 per cent per year.

Department D: This department serves a city of nearly one million persons. We have information only on rate of loss for men hired during 1956 and 1957. Out of ninety-three men hired in those two years, nine have quit by 1963, one was fired, one retired on medical disability and one died. Considering turnover exclusive of the two medical problems (retirement and death), one finds over seven years an 11 per cent loss from the original group which is occurring at a rate of less than 2 per

cent per year. Examining for periods of loss, one finds peak turnover during one year from the time of hiring, and again after
five-six years on the job.

Department E: Located in a major metropolitan area, this
Sheriff's Department serves about one million people in the incorporated and unincorporated areas of its county. From 1956
through 1962 it has hired 179 men from among 2745 applicants
taking the examination. This selected proportion of 6.6 per cent
is very discriminating in comparison with the national average
reported by O'Connor (of which 22% of those applying are
hired). An opportunity to study the excellent department personnel records allows us to describe some detailed aspects of its
personnel problem. First as to disciplinary problems, among the
179 men one finds that over the seven year period there were
sixty charges and complaints of sufficient severity to require
official action and records notation. Thirty-six men were involved in these sixty incidents while 143 men were free from
serious charge or complaint.

During the seven-year period, thirteen men were fired for
cause; eight of these men were among the thirty-six involved
in one or more serious complaints or changes. During this same
seven-year period, forty men (22% of those hired) quit the department; twenty-five to take jobs in other law enforcement
agencies. Of the forty quitting only four had been involved in
serious disciplinary problems. If one combines the number
being fired with those additional men cited on serious charge or
complaints, one finds a total of forty-one men whose conduct
represented a serious source of trouble and disappointment to
the department; this constitutes 23 per cent of all men hired
during the seven-year period. If one examines the time served
on duty prior to getting into trouble, one finds that the majority
are disciplined within the first three years after appointment
(keep in mind the restricted time span for observation of these
relatively recently-hired men). Limiting our analysis to those
hired in 1956 through 1959 (105 men hired of whom 23 got in
serious trouble) we find that twenty-one out of the twenty-three
who got in serious trouble did so within the first three years on
the force.

Looking at the thirteen men who were fired we find that
eleven were terminated by their third year on the force, and

among the forty quitting by early 1963, thirty-five had quit before the end of three years service.

The conclusion from the study of Department E is that the rigorous use of traditional police screening methods (in this case the routine medical and agility tests, the civil service written, and the oral examination) is no guarantee that the men hired will not present a department with very serious personnel problems. We have heen that Department E has 22 per cent of its men quit within a short time after being hired and that another 23 per cent get into serious trouble. It is reasonable to conclude that this department has selected a high number of "bad apples" even though its screening measures drastically pruned from among a large number of available applicants. Given the high turnover rate among the men who did not get in trouble, one may also surmise that this department has suffered from administrative difficulties which may have served to magnify rather than to control performance and morale problems.

NEW STUDIES IN THE USE OF PSYCHOLOGICAL TESTS FOR POLICE SELECTION

We now turn to a review of the results of a series of studies conducted by the author and his colleagues on the use of psychological tests in police selection programs. We shall report in this section on the findings in four different departments where tests results can be compared with on-the-job police performance.

I. A Follow-up Study in a Suburban County Sheriff's Department

One of our studies focused on a sheriff's department in a suburban county of about 500,000 population. One aspect of the research there was to study a group of applicants for Deputy Sheriff who had passed a routine civil service screening test and a physical agility test. There were twenty-eight men in the group studied. Each of these men was given a battery of psychological tests, was given a careful background check where an investigator called on neighbors, employers, schools and agencies which had knowledge of the applicant, and for whom record checks were made with the FBI, the State Bureau of Criminal Identification, and the State Department of Motor Vehicles. Ten with adverse psychological test results were referred for psychiatric examination. Results were compared with judgments independently made by an expert oral board of police administrators. Findings were as follows:

> Using the Minnesota Multiphasic Personality Inventory as a means for diagnosing potential character defects, measured by the scores for psychopathic deviate, lying, and homosexual trends, it was found that eight out of twenty-seven men taking the MMPI were rated as having some character defect. Using the information from the background investigation and the criminal and driving records, psychiatric examination, one finds that seven out of these same eight men had shown evidence of past bad behavior. Nevertheless, the man who had the highest psychopathic deviate score on the MMPI had no derogatory information in the supplemental material. Looking at the supplemental material for evidence of dishonesty, it was found that nine men had past misconduct. Among these, five had high psychopathic deviate scores on the MMPI, one scored high on homosexual tendencies, the remaining three had no MMPI signs of character defect.

> In this group of limited size the MMPI performed relatively well; producing 12 per cent false positives* and thirty-three false negatives.*

> Scores on the O'Rourke test showed some relationship to oral board decisions. Among the nine men scoring the highest on the O'Rourke eight (89%) were judged suitable for police work by a "blue ribbon" oral board. Among the middle scorers six were judged suitable by the oral board, and among low scorers five were judged fit. Combining the middle and low scoring group one finds 61 per cent passed the oral examination.

> A slight relationship between motives for or interest in police work and actions by the oral board was shown. Using scores on the Strong Vocational Interest Blank plus an evaluation of an essay written by the candidates on why he wished to enter police work, one finds that among 18 men with high interest and expressed motives judged adequate, 14 or 78 per cent

---

*A false positive is a man identified by a test as having a defect but who is found on the basis of other information to have no defect. A false negative is a case found on the test to be free of defect but found to have defect on other measures.

were judged suitable for police work by the blue ribbon oral board. Among the nine men with low interest or questionable motives only 56 per cent were judged fit by the oral board.

Extreme scorers on the "F" scale, a test for authoritarian personality trends, were compared. There were seven with relatively high intolerance scores (144 or above) of whom six were judged to have emotional disturbance on the basis of psychological test data, five had strongly adverse background reports. Among the seven men with relatively low authoritarian scores, (109 or below) only one had emotional disturbance inferred from psychological tests and two had strongly adverse background information reported.

One test which was employed was to ask candidates to describe their experiences during examination the day before including a description of the examiner's clothes. They were also asked to organize their life history summary information. Among the six who received "excellent" ratings on report writing and organization, five either had previous police experience or fell in the high scoring groups on the civil service test or on the AGCT. Only one of the four persons receiving poor ratings on report writing had received high AGCT or civil service scores. None of the four had had police experience. It was concluded that report writing as a test was too closely linked with past work experience or intelligence to justify further use.

Limited psychiatric time was available. Ten men with psychological test data suggesting mental disturbance were referred to the psychiatrist. The psychiatrist's ratings showed that he agreed with the psychological test findings in only 66 per cent of the cases.

The actions of the oral board, which did not have any of the test or background data before them when they made their decisions, were compared with psychological test findings.

Among eight men characterized by a psychologist to have moderate or severe disturbance on the basis of test performance (Group Rorschach, DAP, MMPI) six, 75 per cent were passed by the oral board. Among nineteen men characterized as having *no* emotional or mental disturbance, the board passed only 69 per cent.

Among eight men characterized by a psychologist as showing character defects, based on MMPI scores, the oral board passed four men, or 50 per cent. Among nineteen men not said to have character defect on the basis of MMPI scores, the oral board passed fifteen, or 79 per cent.

A second study was made in the same sheriff's department with a second group of candidates the following year. The procedures were changed for this selection process so that the civil service test was given but scores on it were not used to pass or fail candidates. Secondly the oral board was given the results from all tests, psychiatric interviews, criminal and motor vehicle records, and background investigation prior to the meeting of the board. None of these records were themselves used to pass or fail. All passes and fails, except for the medical screening, were made by the oral board on the basis of the information before it plus their direct evaluation of the candidate.

Findings from this study were as follows:

The traditional civil service written test eliminates men who would otherwise be passed by an expert oral board; men on whom there is no other adverse information judged by the board to be significant. Among forty-one men examined eleven were passed by the board. Four of these eleven had received scores of below sixty which ordinarily would have been the basis for their being dropped from further consideration.

The written examination used, one prepared by a State personnel agency, correlates .70 with Otis intelligence. This correlation shows that intelligence is an important factor contributing to performance on the civil service written examination. Nevertheless, if it is intelligence one wishes to select for, then it is instructive to learn that had the civil service test cutting point been set at seventy out of 100, as recommended by the agency, 90 per cent of all applicants whose intelligence was in the normal group range, as measured by the Otis intelligence test, would have been excluded from further consideration. Had the civil service test score of sixty been used as the cutting point, 57 per cent of all candidates of normal intelligence would have been dropped. It seems apparent that men of normal intelligence are lost to potential police service through the uncritical use of civil service tests as screening devices. The majority of such civil service tests are not standardized and not validated. It seems foolish to employ them as screening devices when standardized and validated intelligence tests can be used in their place.

There are three kinds of psychological observation which, when adverse, correspond perfectly—in this limited sample—to the decision of the oral board to fail a candidate. Because the board had this information before them at the time of decision it cannot be said whether they relied heavily on the psychological observations, or whether these observations corresponded with those made by the Board. All four canditates with an I.Q. below 90, i.e., falling below the normal range of intelligence, were failed by the board. All eight candidates who were observed by the psychologist during the two-day testing period to be nervous or to cheat were failed by the board. The ten men who were rejected most often (22 times or more) by fellow candidates on a sociometric choice test were all failed by the board.

The potential utility of sociometric testing as a means for identifying men likely to be failed by a police board must be considered. Further research on this device is to be encouraged. The sociometric procedure used in this study is found in the Appendix of this volume.

Among men adversely rated by a psychologist using the MMPI, The F Test, the Rorschach, and the DAP, the oral board passed about one third and failed about two thirds.

In comparison to the findings on the previous study, the MMPI did not sustain its predictive abilities. Twelve out of eighteen applicants with character defect inferred from the MMPI were found to have misconduct histories based on records and background investigation. Among twenty-two men with unfavorable background reports, only eleven had MMPI character defect ratings. The rate of false positives for the MMPI, using the background check as criterion, is 33 per cent. The rate of false negative is 50 per cent. The change in relative usefulness of the MMPI from one study to the next stands as a warning about the danger in generalizing from small sample studies, as these are.

A review of the results of both this and the previous study supports the conclusion that careful evaluation work which includes background investigation, psychological examinations, and psychiatric interviews which are then made available to a high caliber oral board which is sophisticated in test and inter-

view interpretation is of considerable potential use as a selection method. Whether this method is superior to strict adher-
ence to test cutting points upon which rigid pass or fail recommendations are made should be tested by means of comparison
through long term follow-up research.

The third step in the sequence of studies in this department
is now under way. It is the follow-up of men tested to see whether
success or failure on the job relates to the test performance of
those carefully selected men who were passed by the oral board.
One approach has been to compare the experience with men carefully selected—as was done for 1961 and 1962 with men less carefully selected, as was done for years prior to 1960. The 1960 group
are a special problem; for although a variety of selection methods
were applied to this group, no results were made available to the
expert oral board. The purpose in that year was to see how an
expert oral board independent judgment and action compared
with the findings from a variety of selection techniques. On the
other hand, test and background investigation results were made
available to the sheriff's department itself before actual hiring;
as a result screening was done using the findings in making selec-
tions from the eligible list. Of nineteen eligibles, only six were
hired. Because of this the most conservative course is to consider
the 1960 group as having been selected with the help of special
information.

Among the twenty men hired in 1960, 1961, and 1962 by 1963
one had been fired, one was in trouble over finances, and—at the
opposite extreme—two had been promoted or were eligible for
promotion. Among the thirty-five men hired in 1957, 1958, 1959,
by 1960 one had quit, four had become disciplinary problems,
and one was in financial trouble over debts. None had become
eligible for or been promoted by early 1960. Looking at the two
groups each over the same time period, no striking differences
occur.

Proceeding to examine the experience of the 1957, 1958 and
1959 recruits through the period of 1960-1963 we find a considerable change. Within these last three years three more men have
been fired, four have quit, two are in trouble over finances and

six have become disciplinary problems. By 1963, three of the original thirty-five have been promoted or are on an eligible list. On first glance it would appear as though conduct problems in this department emerge only after a few years on the force. If this is the case, not enough time has passed to enable us to compare the carefully selected men of years 1960 through 1962 with the less carefully selected men of years 1957 through 1959.

On the other hand we find that 1960 was a crucial year for personnel administration in this department. During that year a major revision in personnel practices was instituted; it was reflected in the appointment of a captain's rank personnel director whose task it was to supervise and discipline men. This administrative change is reflected in the decision to begin an experimental program in personnel selection which, as we saw, led to the use and evaluation of psychological tests and background investigations. It is the opinion of the administrators in the department that personnel supervision became much stricter beginning in 1960 and that men whose records show no work problems for 1957-1959 may have been problem cases not identified as such during more lax years of primary supervision by sergeants and lieutenants. If this is the case, as departmental officials believe it to be, then one may make a partial argument for the comparison of the 1957 through 1959 recruits for the entire period 1957 through 1963 with the 1960-62 recruits for the shorter 1960-1963 observation period. Admittedly any such comparison puts the earlier recruit group at a disadvantage for they have had more opportunity to leave or to get in trouble.

If we do such a comparison, being aware of its tenuous assumptions, we find that the recruits selected without full records or background check and without psychological tests or psychiatric referrals produce the following personnel experience: Out of thirty-five men hired, three have been fired, five have quit, three have had financial troubles and eight disciplinary problems have arisen (among men not being fired). A total personnel or case "Trouble Count" is nineteen out of thirty-five or 54 per cent. On the positive side of the ledger a total of three men have been promoted, or 9 per cent.

For their part, the more recent recruits, twenty in number, show a trouble count of only two (one fired and one in financial trouble) or only 10 per cent. As for promotion, two have been promoted or again 10 per cent.

Using the foregoing method of comparison whereby the experience of the more recently hired men is compared to the men hired earlier, a comparison which admittedly loads the dice in favor of the more recently hired group, there is a dramatic difference which shows that fewer personnel troubles arise among the men who have been more carefully selected. The trouble count for the latter is 10 per cent; the trouble count for the former is 54 per cent.

In the opinion of the personnel captain in this department, the men hired under the careful selection program are as a group, "head and shoulders above those hired in earlier years . . . they have a greater potential, a better attitude toward the work." He commented that the rigours of the screening process were in themselves a screening device; only those with genuine interest and perseverance stuck it out through the three days of arduous testing and observation.

II. Test Results Compared with Personnel Ratings in a Rural-urban Sheriff's Department

A second study took advantage of the availability of psychological tests and personnel records on sheriff's deputies and command personnel in a department serving a large rural county which had an urban center as county seat. About 1956 this department instituted a testing program among men who were being hired and among selected staff members. Testing was hit or miss and we were not able to learn what its aims had been or what criteria had guided the selection of men to be tested.

One hundred and twenty-four men had been given the Minnesota Multiphasic Personality Inventory (MMPI), eighty-one were given the MMPI, the Cardell Test of Practical Judgment and the Army General Classification Test (AGCT) and three men were given the MMPI and the AGCT. Scores on these tests were compared with average personnel ratings which were obtained by summarizing all personnel ratings as found on the standard forms in a man's folder. Separate averages were made of personnel evaluations in each of five categories of work assignment; patrol, detective, operations, detention, and "other." These evaluations were on a scaled point system with high evaluations receiving more points than low evaluations on a scale of one to five. Separate averages were obtained for evaluations of personal characteristics and for performance per se. Extremely good or bad ratings, commendations and disciplinary actions were also noted.

Because of the inadequacies of the personnel rating system and the records, because of our lack of knowledge of the selection criteria for testing, and because of the relatively few men falling in groups of *special* interest, i.e., men rated high on personnel evaluations or men being fired, our data are lacking in those safeguards necessary for us to view the results with confidence. Inspection of the data shows the following non-significant patterns:

1. Using clinical judgments of the MMPI profiles presented by two clinically-trained psychologists who placed men (without knowing anything of their personnel records) in one of four categories ranging from predictions of probable good job adjustment (category one) through prediction of great likelihood of job difficulty (category four), it was observed that there was no significant difference in MMPI ratings between men who quit the department versus those who remained in police service. Men being fired and receiving the poorest personnel ratings (N-13) had average MMPI clinical ratings of 1.54, men receiving moderate personnel ratings (N-97) average MMPI ratings of 1.62, and men receiving high personnel ratings (N-14) received average MMPI ratings of 2.00. The direction here is opposite from that expected; the greater the personality problems shown by the MMPI, the higher the average personnel rating.

2. Examining AGCT scores—which correlate highly with intelligence as measured by other tests—we find no significant difference among the poor, medium and highly rated (personnel evaluation sheets) men. There is a tendency for the men who quit the department to get higher average AGCT scores (91.7%-ile) than those who did not voluntarily terminate (average AGCT percentile 89.2).

3. On the Cardell test groups of men rated high or low on

personnel evaluations were particularly small and no consistent trends were observed in the data. We do find a non-significant higher Cardell score for men getting in trouble than for those not getting in trouble; again a finding contrary to expectations.

The results of this study tell us very little about the relationship of psychological test scores to police performance beyond cautioning us about the use of available data when records are inadequate and where testing programs are without rational design. The findings here show that psychological test scores for police work groups can be found which are contrary to common sense expectations. While the results here may reflect errors due to sampling or records error, they nevertheless warn us there is by no means any perfect, consistent or inevitable relationship between intelligence or personality and measures of performance or records of disciplinary problems, firing and quitting, within a particular police agency.

III. A Long-Term Follow-up of Test Scores and Job Performance in a City Police Department

Our third opportunity for study arose in a city with a population between 100,000 and 200,000 which has had a testing program in effect for many years. The tests which it has relied upon for use in personnel selection are primarily intelligence tests. In this department we have been able to relate scores on several different tests (different tests were used in different years) to the major work performance measures of: (a) being fired during the probationary period; (b) voluntary terminations; (c) being fired for cause after the probationary period; (d) promoted to the rank of inspector or less, and (e) promoted above the rank of inspector.

The tests employed at one time or another by this department have been among those commonly used by police and civil service agencies for measuring variants of intelligence: the Army Alpha, the Otis, the Moss Mental Alertness and the Moss Social Intelligence. In addition trial periods of use included the O'Rourke Policeman's Adaptability Test. The variety of tests given over the years has reduced the chances for statistically significant results to emerge from our data analysis; this is the case because greater differences must be observed to obtain statistically significance when the sizes of groups being compared are small.

Test scores were available on 145 men hired over the last thirty-five or so years. No men in our follow-up group were tested more recently than fifteen years ago. Most had been tested in the 1920's and 1930's. Table I below summarizes their scores on each test and on each performance measure.

TABLE 1

AVERAGE RAW TEST SCORES OF POLICEMEN ON SIX MEASURES OF WORK PERFORMANCE
(Number of men with test scores on each performance measure appear
in parentheses)

Name of Test	No. Taking Test	Dropped During Prob. Period	Fired	Quit	Stayed on without Prom.	Promoted up to Inspector (or Less)	Promoted beyond Inspector
O'Rourke Policeman's Aptitude	44	89.6 (5)	96.5 (2)	95.3 (23)	92.9 (14)	----	----
Moss Mental Alertness	78	160.3 (10)	147.5 (2)	155 (36)	151.1 (9)	152.9 (14)	152.6 (7)
Moss Social Intelligence	102	120 (11)	129.3 (3)	118.1 (48)	117.3 (13)	115.9 (20)	116.7 (7)
Terman-Merrill (Int. Test)	62	190.9 (8)	195 (1)	185.6 (28)	184.5 (25)	185.6 (12)	190.2 (6)
Army Alpha (Int. Test)	77	167.3 (11)	181 (1)	166.3 (38)	168.7 (9)	170.2 (13)	168.4 (5)
Army Alpha form SB	34	188.7 (6)	196.5 (2)	189.8 (14)	183 (1)	201.9 (7)	196 (4)
Otis	61	177.2 (9)	188.6 (3)	185.8 (27)	176.2 (12)	191 (11)	200.5 (4)

Inspection of the scores in Table I shows no fully consistent trends among the several different tests used for measuring intelligence. Furthermore, statistical treatment of the data reveals no significant differences* between any of the performance groups

*It is a practice or convention when dealing with data which is analyzed by statistical tests to term "significant" those differences which, on the basis of the statistical tests, are unlikely to have occurred by chance more than five times out of a hundred. Thus when one says of a difference between two groups, let us say in intelligence, that it is statistically "significant" it means that the observed differences are not likely to be due to change factors.

for any one test. One finds, for instance, that on the Moss Social Intelligence Test the men who are dropped during the probationary year or who are fired have an average 5.5 points higher (intelligence) than those who stay in police work. This difference is significant to the .10 level but not to the .05 level conventionally accepted as a standard for statistical significance.

Looking at those who quit the department versus those who stayed in it, we find that on three tests (Moss Mental Alertness, Moss Social Intelligence, and Terman) those who quit average higher scores than those who stay. In contrast on three other tests (Army Alpha, Alpha SB and Otis) those who stay get higher scores than those who quit. None of the differences are statistically significant.

Comparing those promoted with those not promoted, one finds the promoted personnel averaging higher scores on the Moss Mental Alertness, on the Terman-Merrill, on the Army Alpha, on the Alpha SB and on the Otis. Only on the Moss Social Intelligence Test among the intelligence measures (neither the O'Rourke nor the Telford are intelligence tests) is there a contrasting direction. While one must be reluctant to combine scores on different tests, one can cautiously point out that on five out of six intelligence tests the promoted men average higher scores than non-promoted men.

The results of this comparison of intelligence test scores (plus the O'Rourke Test which is not known to measure any relevant traits or abilities) with police career terminations and promotions, used as measures of performance, shows no statistically significant relationships between intelligence and police career records. Other than a trend for promoted men to score higher on intelligence tests than men not promoted, there are not even trends worthy of note.

One may attribute the lack of results to several possible factors. For one, the tests were used in selection and at the time of hiring; as a result only those men with high intelligence were hired. The observations over the thirty plus years are limited to a highly selected and intelligent sample. Within that select group there is not much possibility of wide variations in scores and, in consequence, differences among sub-groups of men in the department could not be very large. Further, if one assumes that once minimal intelligence levels are met, career records in police work are then dependent on qualities *other than* intelligence, one would not then expect to find gradations in already high intelligence levels as important factors in determining police performance.

Another likely factor is, of course, the demand which statistical tests make upon data. So long as the groups compared are small in size and the differences among them are moderate, statistical significance is hard to achieve. In this study that problem has been compounded by the use of several different kinds of intelligence tests. This has meant that the sub-groups taking any one test are relatively small, especially when these sub-groups are in turn divided into several categories of career and performance.

These qualifications which are imposed upon the findings should not divert us from a necessary conclusion: in this department which selects men of high intelligence for police service we have no evidence that intelligence is associated with the chances for a man's being fired, quitting, or being promoted, nor do we have any evidence that men of higher command rank are any more intelligent than are men of lower command rank. These findings do not disprove a general relationship between intelligence and police career records, but it can be inferred that if one hires only men of high intelligence when their later police careers are compared, their progress will be determined by qualities and events unrelated to their intelligence.

IV. A Seven Year Follow-up of Systematically Tested Police Recruits

In 1956-57, each recruit hired by a major metropolitan police force was tested. The tests played no role in the selection process itself; the latter depended upon medical and agility examination, an unstandardized civil service written test, and an oral interview: the traditional selection devices employed by most cities. Once the tests were given the results were filed and not made known to any of the supervisors of the men tested. Seven years later, in 1963, each recruit's file was carefully reviewed and, with the assistance of departmental personnel officers, some judgments and recordings of performance on a variety of measures were made.

The following tests were given to each of eighty-seven recruits:* the Minnesota Multiphasic Personality Inventory, the group form of the Rorschach Ink Blot Test, the Strong Vocational Interest Blank, the Machover Draw-a-person test, the "F" Scale for the measure of authoritarian personality trends, and the Otis intelligence test. The projective tests (Rorschach and Machover DAP) which do not yield scores were judged by clinical standards and recruits were rated on a scale of from one to four, with one representing optimal personality integration and a score of four representing serious personality disorder. On the basis of all the test data—but no personal knowledge of the recruits or their background—the author predicted performance as a police officer on a scale of from one to three; one being the prediction of satisfactory performance, two being for questionable cases, and three saying that the officer would become a disciplinary or efficiency problem because of some personality difficulty, lack of intelligence, or insufficient interest in police work. All tests were scored, interpreted and summarized into a prognosis score in 1956-57.

In 1963, data was gathered from personnel folders to describe for each of the eighty-seven his conduct history on the following work performance variables:

(a) Department commendations officially recorded.

(b) Public commendations, including letters of praise from citizens.

(c) Serious charges of misconduct leading to formal hearings before the Police Commission.

(c_1) Evidence of exceptionally serious misconduct. (This criterion is based on analysis and actions taken from criterion "c" above).

(d) Minor charges of misconduct handled by supervisors or bureau heads and made a matter of record.

(e) Number of vehicles accidents while driving own or departmental vehicles.

(f) Number of incidents leading to his own reported injury.

(g) Number of different periods when time off was taken for illness.

(h) Total number of days lost due to illness.

---

*An eighty-eighth recruit was tested but died early in police service. His case has been excluded.

(i) Record of terminations: voluntary or for cause, from the department.

(j) Assignment progression: record of transfers from bureaus and precincts (from which inferences were made by two senior police administrators as to the on-the-job efficiency and desirability of each man) .*

Data were analyzed statistically: computations resulted in a correlation coefficient describing the extent of relationship between each test, or between each scale on tests with several scales, and each of the eleven performance criteria cited above. This technique allows us to say how much of a relationship exists between each of the tests, or test sub-scales and each of the performance criteria. In addition the overall predictions were correlated with each of the criteria, enabling us to describe the extent of the relationship between prognosis in 1956-57 and performance during the intervening years until 1963.

It is not feasible or necessary to present all of the nearly three hundred correlations which emerged from the data analysis. The procedure for presenting the findings is to list each work performance criteria (a) through (j), above, and to tabulate all of the correlations of .20** or better between a work criterion and the tests or test sub-scale predictors. These correlations are presented in decreasing orders of relationships, from high to low. There are two regular exceptions to the rule of presentation of correlations of only .20 or better. One exception occurs when no predictor (test or test sub-scale) correlates as high as .20 in which case the highest correlations that do emerge are presented. The second exception is when a predictor does not correlate .20 with a criterion but where the correlation is nearly that and where there

---

*The personnel folder contains a record of each new assignment given a man. These were recorded and submitted to two senior police officials for evaluation. The administrators evaluated the record and placed the man on a one to five scale; one being evidence of his being highly thought of as inferred from his progress to more and more desirable assignments. A placement in category five meant that his assignments demonstrated his inefficiency or undesirablity. Promotions could not be recorded because none had been made. In this department promotions are generally not made until a minimum of eight years service as a patrolman.

**All correlations reported are rounded off to the nearest hundredth.

is an interesting practical or theoretical link between the predictor and the work criterion; one which will be worthy of noting.

There follow a set of tables, Table II through XII, each of which presents one work criterion and the test predictors correlated with it. In reading the tables be sure to note the negative correlations which are indicated by a minus (−) sign and an "n" in parentheses. All correlations are positive unless so marked. A negative or inverse correlation means that as the value or magnitude on one variable (measure or criterion) rises the value or magnitude of the other is reduced. Thus one finds in Table V a negative correlation between interests (on the Strong Vocational Interest Blank) corresponding to those of working psychologists and the frequency of evidence of serious misconduct on the part of policemen. This means that as a policeman shows more interests that are like those of psychologists his record will show less evidence of serious misconduct and, conversely, as a policeman's interests are less like those of psychologists the greater the chance (within the modest limits of a low correlation) for his record showing evidence of serious misconduct. As another illustration, in Table VII one sees that a high score on the "F" Scale correlates negatively with public commendations. This is interpreted to mean that the more authoritarian, dogmatic, fascistic a man's attitudes are (and presumably his personality which those attitudes express) the less likely he is to receive praise and commendation from the public.

In reviewing Tables II through XII one may come to these major conclusions:

1. Some relationships exist between psychological characteristics measured by tests at the time of hiring and later work performance on each of eleven major work measures. On all but one work variable, assignment progression, correlations between predictors and performance criteria of over .20 were obtained.

2. The magnitude of the relationship between any one psychological characteristic and any one work measure tends to be low. Among 324 correlations run, only thirty-six reached $r = .20$ or higher. Among the latter only three were .40 or above; the highest of these being .47. (Recollect that an r of .47 accounts for only 22 per cent of the observed variation.)

TABLE II
RELATIONSHIP BETWEEN FREQUENCY OF VEHICLE ACCIDENTS AND TEST RESULTS
AMONG POLICEMEN ON A METROPOLITAN FORCE*

Predictor Variable	Test	Correlation
Intelligence (I.Q.)	Otis	.30
Interests corresponding to those of physicians	Strong VIB	.30
Interests corresponding to those of psychologists	Strong VIB	.28
Interests corresponding to those those of physicists	Strong VIB	.26

TABLE III
RELATIONSHIP BETWEEN MINOR CHARGES MADE A MATTER OF RECORD AND TEST
RESULTS

Variable	Test	Correlation
Schizophrenic personality trends	MMPI	.29
Obsessive-compulsive personality traits	MMPI	.27
Attitudes indicative of authoritarian dogmatic personality	"F" Scale	.26
Bizarre and unusual responses to questions	MMPI	.23
Impulsive, selfish, insensitive behavior	MMPI	.23
Prognosis of poor job performance	clinical interpretation	.21

TABLE IV
RELATIONSHIP BETWEEN FREQUENCY OF SERIOUS (FORMAL) CHARGES AND TEST RESULTS

Variable	Test	Correlation
Schizophrenic personality trends	MMPI	.29
Interests corresponding to those of author-journalists	Strong VIB	.23

---

*For readers who are not familiar with how to read a table such as this, we shall explain. The main point to keep in mind is that Table II gives information about the extent of the relationship between the number of vehicle accidents which police officers experiencd after being hired, and their scores on psychological tests given at the time of hiring. Tables in this series present only those test scores which were found to bear a relationship of r=.20 or higher. (See the footnote on page 101 for a discussion of the meaning of the correlation coefficient. Thus in Table II one finds a low positive relationship between intelligence and several interest sub-test scores and the frequency of vehicle accidents. In view of the low positive correlations of about .30 one can say there is a tendency for the brighter men and the ones with scientific interests to have more accidents. Why there should be such a relationship we cannot be sure. One can speculate that, on the basis of industrial research which has found that brighter men more easily become dissatisfied on monotonous jobs, the bright and "experimentally-minded" men make things more interesting by driving more dangerously.

Reading Table III one sees that men whose psychological tests showed several kinds of personality disorders of character problems are more likely to be brought up on minor charges within the department. This relationship between personality problems and getting into trouble is easy to understand.

TABLE V

RELATIONSHIP BETWEEN EVIDENCE OF EXCEPTIONALLY SERIOUS MISCONDUCT AND TEST RESULTS

Variable	Test	Correlation
Schizophrenic personality trends	MMPI	.47
Bizarre and unusual responses to questions	MMPI	.42
Obsessive-compulsive personality traits	MMPI	.40
Prognosis for poor job performance	Clinical Interpretation	.38
Paranoid personality trends	MMPI	.34
Impulsive, selfish insensitive behavior	MMPI	.32
Interests corresponding to those of physicians (n)	Strong VIB	−.28
Personality disorder	Rorschach	.20

TABLE VI

RELATIONSHIP BETWEEN FREQUENCY OF DEPARTMENTAL COMMENDATIONS AND TEST RESULTS

Variable	Test	Correlation
Interests corresponding to those of carpenters (n)	Strong VIB	−.24
Intelligence	Otis	.22

TABLE VII

RELATIONSHIP BETWEEN FREQUENCY OF PUBLIC COMMENDATIONS AND TEST RESULTS

Variable	Test	Correlation
Attitudes indicative of authoritarian, dogmatic personality (n)	"F" Scale	−.28
Interests corresponding to those of carpenters (n)	Strong VIB	−.24
Lying in response to questions	MMPI	.18
Interests corresponding to those of physicists (n)	Strong VIB	−.19
Self-centered, amoral, thrill-seeking, dishonest behavior	MMPI	.16

TABLE VIII

RELATIONSHIP BETWEEN NUMBER OF DIFFERENT PERIODS WHEN TIME WAS TAKEN OFF FOR ILLNESS AND TEST RESULTS

Variable	Test	Correlation
Interests corresponding to those of carpenters (n)	Strong VIB	−.24
Artistic, Intellectual, sensitive or effeminate traits	MMPI	.23
Intelligence	Otis	.20
Lying in response to questions (n)	MMPI	−.20
Self-centered, amoral, thrill-seeking, dishonest behavior	MMPI	.20
Vocational interests correspond to those at higher more complex occupational levels	Strong VIB	.20
Bland, overly-dramatic, mercurial behavior	MMPI	.19

TABLE IX
RELATIONSHIP BETWEEN TOTAL DAYS LOST DUE TO ILLNESS AND TEST RESULTS

Variable	Test	Correlation
Interests corresponding to those of policemen	Strong VIB	.22
Atttiudes indicative of authoritarian, dogmatic personality	"F" Scale	.22
Bizarre or unusual responses to questions	MMPI	.20

TABLE X
RELATIONSHIP BETWEEN NUMBER OF INCIDENTS LEADING TO INJURY AND TEST SCORES

Variable	Test	Correlation
Intelligence	Otis	.27
Interests corresponding to those of physicists	Strong VIB	.22
Interests corresponding to those of carpenters (n)	Strong VIB	−.18

TABLE XI
RELATIONSHIP BETWEEN ASSIGNMENT PROGRESSION IMPLYING MERIT AND TEST RESULTS
Note: No correlations reaching .20 with this criterion

Variable	Test	Correlation
Prognosis of job performance	Clinical Interpretation	.14
Personality disorder (n)	Machover DAP	−.13
Lying in response to questions (n)	MMPI	−.13
Intellectual, artistic, sensitive or effeminate traits	MMPI	.12

TABLE XII
RELATIONSHIP BETWEEN POLICE CAREER TERMINATIONS BY TYPE OF TERMINATION AND TEST RESULTS

(For purposes of this analysis men staying in the Department were put in category No. 1, those quitting voluntarily were put in category No. 2, and those being fired for cause were put in No. 3.)

Variable	Test	Correlation
Anxiety, depression as emotional disorders (n)	MMPI	−.22
Personality disorder	Rorschach	.15
Artistic, intellectual, sensitive or effeminate traits	MMPI	.15

3. The largest number of correlations above .20 and the highest correlations observed were found to describe the relationship between evidence of exceptionally serious misconduct among policemen and test variables indicative of personality disorder.

Here there were eight correlations reaching .20 or more, three of which were at .40 or more.

4. The tests which most often were found to show a relationship with work performance variables were the MMPI and the Strong VIB. MMPI sub-scales correlated .20 or better on six work criteria; all in all fifteen MMPI sub-scale correlations of .20 or better were obtained with work criteria measures. Among two MMPI sub-scales, one the measure of schizophrenic tendencies (the Sc Scale) and the other a measure of unusual and bizarre response to questions (the F scale) each correlated .20 or above with three performance measures. The Strong VIB correlated with eight work criteria; a total of eleven sub-scale correlations of .20 or greater being obtained. Rather oddly the carpenter interest scale most often correlates, always negatively, with performance. At the other extreme the Machover DAP showed no relationship (at .20 or better) with any work measure and the Rorschach correlated with only one of these measures.

5. Reviewing the contents of Tables II through XII and combining performance criteria into the major sectors of work behavior and relating these in turn to major psychological characteristics measured by tests one can see the general kinds of relationships which emerge between personal qualities and later police performance. In setting up this summarizing scheme we have arbitrarily classified psychological characteristics as: (1) vocational interests (all Strong scales) ; (2) personality problems and pathology (all MMPI scales except the Mf scale measuring intellectual, sensitive or effeminate trends, and the Rorschach) ; (3) attitudes and orientation ("F" Scale and Mf scale on MMPI), and (4) intelligence (Otis). We have excluded the clinical prognosis predictor since it rests entirely on test result interpretation. We have also excluded all correlations less than .20.

    A. Getting in trouble and getting fired is related in order of frequency of correlations obtained to personality, vocational interests and attitudes and orientation. It is not shown to be related to intelligence.*

---

*Inspection of obtained correlation coefficients between Otis test scores and the three work criteria for trouble reveal no correlation whatsoever; no r is greater than .02.

B. Receiving commendations and praise is related to vocational interests, attitudes and orientation and intelligence. It is not related to personality measures.

C. Being subject to accidents, injury or time off for illness is related to vocational interests, intelligence, personality, and attitudes and orientation.

D. Restating A, B and C, one may conclude that personality problems loom largest in determining the chances for later misconduct as a policeman; they also play a role in risk for accidents and illness. They seem to play no role in whether or not a man is commended. Vocational interests play a larger role in determining the chances of accident and illness time lost and a lesser role in the risk of getting in trouble and in getting commendations. Attitudes and orientation are found to play a role in accident and illness risk, in the chance for getting commendations, and in the risk of misconduct. Intelligence plays a role in accident and illness risk and in getting commendations, but not in the risk of getting in trouble.

Turning now from the data of Tables II through XII with their conclusive evidence for the existence of relationships between characteristics present in policemen at the time of hiring and later work success and problems, we may now ask the practical question, "What would have happened if we had known in 1956-57 what we know now about the relationships between predictors and work criteria in this department and had used tests to screen out men with high risks for one or another undesirable forms of behavior?" The answer is that their use would have resulted in fewer men involved in undesirable or costly work problems, but one would not have been able to eliminate all men showing misconduct, high rates of illness or accident-proneness.

Take as an example the small group of four men who probably posed the greatest problems for the police administrator and for the city's citizens; the four who got involved in troubles resulting in formal charges and in the production of evidence of very serious misconduct. Using the test score that correlates most highly with getting in trouble, the Sc (Schizophrenia) subscale on the MMPI, one finds the four men scored as follows: 24, 32, 33, and 43. What if one decided to use 24 as a cutting point;* not hiring any men who scored 24 or above? Looking at all the scores, one finds that thirty-six men scored under 24; and (excluding the four men in trouble) another forty-five scored between 24 and 31. Only two scored 32 or above. By establishing a cutting point at 24 during the 1956-57 recruitment and using this scale alone, one would have rejected a total of fifty-two more men but would have eliminated all who got in serious trouble later on. By putting the cutting point at 32 one would have rejected a total of five men, three of whom would have been the ones getting in serious trouble later on. By such a simple expedient one would have lost only two good men through weeding out and would have rejected three out of four bad ones.

By adding another test sub-scale, say the Pt scale of the MMPI (obsessive compulsive) and learning that the one man in serious trouble above with an Sc score of 24 also had a quite high Pt score of 28, and then establishing 28 as a supplemental cutting point on the Pt scale one would weed out some good men (who scored 24 and above on the Pt scale) but by doing that one would have eliminated all four serious misconduct cases.

If one had an administrative goal of weeding out all four potentially serious misconduct cases while reducing the number of good men lost to recruitment, one might try to refine one's selection instruments by setting up a group or pattern of cutting points on various tests. For example inspection of the test scores reveals that the one man of the four in serious trouble who got the relatively low Sc score of 24 received a quite high Pt (obsessive-compulsive) score on the MMPI of 28. If a Pt score of 28 were used as a cutting point in addition to the Sc score of 32,

---

*A cutting point is any score (or point) on a graduated scale at which the decision is made to reject those falling on one side of a score and accept those receiving grades on the other side of a score. Thus a civil service test may arbitrarily establish a cutting point at 70; accepting all who score 70 and above; rejecting all those below. In the case of tests where higher scores mean the likelihood of more undesirable features, as above where higher Sc or Pt scores mean more psychopathology, than one rejects those scoring *above* a certain point. Where one sets a cutting point depends upon the correlation between the test and performance, the labor market and selection ratio, what are the adequate performance levels for the job, and so forth.

inspection reveals that only ten good men would have been screened out (of the 87 hired) while all four "bad" men would have been screened out. And looking at the ten "good" men so lost one finds that five subsequently were in trouble on either formal charges or recorded disciplinary actions by supervisors.

The above example suggests a number of refinements which can be undertaken by a department which is intent upon developing a maximally efficient selection system. Once standards of conduct are agreed upon by administrators as ones which they want their personnel to meet (clear definitions of undesirable conduct as well as standards for meritorious performance), once research has shown what tests or other psychological measures are related to conduct which conforms to the desired standards, it will be sensible to employ statistical devices (multiple correlations or factor analysis for example) which, in the hands of capable researchers, will provide a wealth of useful information. One could find out for example to what extent in the general population of applicants the men who have one desired characteristic for police work also have other desired characteristics; that is: can one isolate a general factor which predisposes men to do well in police work or if it the case that performance is very specific to particular traits and situations; implying that it would be better to select men for specialty assignments according to their special talents rather than to seek generally fit men who can work at a wide variety of assignments. Such research could answer the vexing question as to how general or specific police performance abilities are for a given department. Another practical step would be to analyze the *pattern* of test results so as to increase the efficiency of test use through statistical techniques (for example multiple discriminant analysis) which would enable one to set cutting points on a number of tests and sub-tests so as to screen out the highest number of undesirable men while, at the same time, reducing the number of potentially good men weeded out. It is reasonable to expect that the use of such batteries of tests with carefully-worked out patterns of scores as cutting points would raise the efficiency of selection considerably. For example, with the use of test batteries as opposed to single tests it is already possible to raise the correlation between test scores and work performance on some jobs to $r = .75$ (12) (17).

Regardless of the help which can be rendered by research and statistical procedures, the ultimate decisions rest with the responsible administrators themselves. The establishment of performance criteria—standards of performance to be sought—rests with them. Likewise it will be their decision as to how many good men can afford to be lost as one seeks to weed out the bad. Almost inevitably the greater the percentage of undesirable men screened out, the greater the number of good men also not hired. The ratios here will depend upon the correlations between predictors (tests) and criteria (standards); the absolute numbers in each category (good and bad) will depend upon where the administrator decides to set the cutting points. Where the cutting points will be established will depend upon the major factors: (1) the availability of applicants for the job; (2) their quality, and (3) upon the cost and distress which result from inefficiency, misconduct and terminations. These considerations must be weighed in the balance by the administrator not only at the beginning of a selection program based on research findings, but continually thereafter; for the selection standards must be under continual revision based on the conditions in the job market, departmental requirements, and—hopefully—from new information obtained by careful study of the department's own selection practices.

SUMMARY AND CONCLUSIONS

There is good evidence that psychological tests can measure human characteristics which are associated with various kinds of success and failure in work situations—including the performance of police duties. Studies to date indicate that no one test will be a sufficient predictive device nor will any single job standard be a sufficient measure of performance. The results are clear but moderate so far in showing relationships existing between traits or aptitudes measured by tests at the time of hiring and later police performance; correlations between single measures and single standards will rarely be greater than .50; in our own studies .47 was the highest correlation achieved. On the other hand refinements in research design, in testing, and in statistics offer genuine hope for increasing the capacity of test batteries to predict to, and thereby to select for, well-defined performance standards.

A review of the experience in departments which do not use psychological tests in their screening shows a wide range of difference in later job performance of the men hired. Some jurisdictions report so few problems with discipline, turnover, or efficiency that the cost of doing preliminary studies and setting up research-based testing programs seems unwarranted. On the other hand there are departments where as many as one fourth of the men hired by traditional civil service procedures get in trouble and another one fourth raise personnel costs through quitting soon after being hired. In such departments there is an apparent need for improved selection methods; a need that rational testing programs should be able to meet.

Based on these wide departmental differences it would appear that the first step in considering potentially new selection devices is to assess a department's present needs and problems to learn whether the men hired are performing without undue cost, incompetence, or disruption to the department and community. If things are going well psychological testing programs may not be worth the trouble; if things are going badly—or even with moderate inefficiency—research and innovation in selection methods should be considered.

Reviewing our own findings on the relationship between psychological tests and performance in four departments, one is impressed with the wide range of differences in the relationships between test results and job performance. Some of these observed differences are no doubt due to inadequacies in the original selection of men for testing and in the measures of performance employed. But even giving due weight to these important sources of biased information, one is left with the impression that the administrative standards employed in a department—and the working atmosphere in that department—influence the kinds of relationships which emerge between psychological characteristics and job success and failure. There is also evidence that if a department has selected carefully for one well-definined characteristic, in this case high intelligence, later performance in that department will then depend on other (unknown) qualities and will not be related to the relatively minor difference in the already high intelligence among the working force.

The suggestion which emerges from the foregoing considerations is that differences among departments are so great—in the quality of their recruitment pool, in the implicit selection standards and assumptions, in the quality of administration, and in the actual standards by which men are judged, that no constant relationship between any psychological characteristic and general police performance—regardless of department—will be found. Rather it is reasonable to expect that—given some probable minimum requirements for the capacity to work and get along with others—various types of departments will show characteristic relationships* between work success or failure and the personal qualities shown to be related to work standards. This of course implies the need—at this stage of the game—for individualized selection programs based on research within a department (or within departments of a similar type) to show what psychological qualities will be related to success and failure within that department.

In reviewing the two studies (I and IV) conducted by the author and his colleagues under a more systematic research design, one is led to conclude that typical unstandardized civil service tests might well be replaced by more carefully constructed devices; also that psychological tests may well be considered part of a larger selection process which emphasizes excellence of all phases of recruitment and screening (for other procedures the reader is referred to the accompanying chapters in this volume). The role of tests as an integral part of screening can be best established by continuing thinking and research directed to all phases of the selection process.

The results of studies I and IV indicate that a variety of personal qualities are related to police performance; among the qualities, we have evidence for the role of intelligence, personality (in terms of problems and pathology), vocational interests, and

---

*For an interesting study of several widespread types of organizations-as well as for excellent management advice-the reader is advised to refer to Likert, R.: *New Patterns of Management*. New York, McGraw Hill, 1960.

attitudes and orientation. Among the tests which correlate with performance one finds the Strong Vocational Interest Blank, the Minnesota Multiphasic Personality Inventory, the "F" Scale, the Otis (and other tests of intelligence), and the Rorschach Ink Blot Test. Sociometric ratings procedures also hold promise.

In addition other investigators report relationships between scores and work performance of policemen on tests of perceptual arithmetic and motor skills (spatial factors abilities) and—by generalization from other industrial studies—between specific tests for skills (typing, clerical, mechanical etc.) and success in work requiring the application of these special skills. There is also in the literature some evidence for the usefulness in police research—if not yet selection—of the Army General Classification Test, the Kuder Preference Record, Personal, the Edwards Personal Preference Scale, the Humm-Wadsworth Temperament Scale and the California Psychological Inventory.

While each of the foregoing tests—and probably many others as yet untried—have potential utility in police selection, one must recommend against the adoption of any one of them by police departments until after the department has given careful consideration to the nature of its tasks, to the standards which it wishes to have its personnel abide by, and the extent and kind of personnel problems which it faces in the present and is likely to face in the future. Once the administration has taken stock of its goals and problems—and has looked itself squarely in the face to be sure that it is not the administration itself which needs improvement before any kind of benefit from improved selection will ever be realized, then it is time to consider innovations in selection.

The decision to try to improve selection methods will require a commitment to support a new program, to deal with the problems of change as they arise, to enlist staff understanding and support for the new effort, and to deal effectively with other public agencies concerned. Once such policy commitments have been made, the department can turn to the relatively simple technical problems involved in finding a competent research or industrial psychologist—or perhaps a clinical or social psychologist with a statistician consultant—and working with him (or them) on the research and follow-up work necessary to find which tests work best under what conditions to select the finest possible policemen for the department.

BIBLIOGRAPHY

1. Adorno, T. W., Frenkel-Brunswik, E., Levinson, D.J., and Sanford, R. N.: *The Authoritarian Personality*. New York, Harper & Brothers, 1950.

2. Blum, R. H.: Police selection in Europe. *Police,* 1961, Part I 5, No. 4, pp. 39-43, Part II 5, No. 5, pp. 32-35, Part III 5, No. 6, pp. 72-74.

3. Blum, R. H.: Problems of being a police officer. *Police,* 1960, Part I, 5, No. 2, pp. 10-13, Part II, 5, No. 3, pp. 31-32.

4. Blum, R. H. with Goggin, W. L.: A Study of deputy sheriff selection procedures: Preliminary report. Unpublished. See *Police, 6:*No. 2, pp. 59-63, 1961.

5. Blum, R. H. with Goggin W. L., Whitmore, E. B., and Pomeroy, W. A.: A further study of deputy sheriff selection procedures. Unpublished study. See *Police, 6:*No. 4, pp. 77-79, 1962.

6. Brannon, W. T.: *The Crooked Cops*. Evanston, Regency Books, 1962.

7. Deutsch, Albert: *The Trouble with Cops*. New York, Crown Publishers, 1954.

8. Dudycha, G. J.: *Psychology for Law Enforcement Officers*. Springfield, Thomas, 1955.

9. Gallati, R. J.: Police personnel testing experience at the New York City Police Department. *Police, 4:* (May—June, 76-77), 1960.

10. Germann, A. C.: *Police Personnel Management*. Springfield, Thomas, 1958.

11. Ghiselli, E. E.: The validity of commonly employed occupational tests *University of California Publications in Psychology. 5:* pp. 253-269, 1949.

12. Ghiselli, E. E., and Brown, C.W.: *Personnel and Industrial Psychology*. New York, McGraw Hill, 1955.

13. Gough, H. G.: Predicting job effectiveness among correctional officers: Report of the 8th annual Training Institute for Probation, Parole and Institutional Staff, University of California School of Social Welfare, Berkeley, 1956.

14. Holcomb, Richard: *Selection of Police Officers*. Iowa City, University of Iowa, 1946.

15. Holmes, B.: Selection of patrolmen. *J. Crim. Law, Criminology, Pol. Sci., 32:*pp. 575-592, 1942.

16. Humm, D., and Humm: Humm-Wadsworth Temperament Scale appraisals compared with criteria of job success in the Los Angeles Police Department. *J. of Psychology, 30:*pp. 63-75, 1950.

17. Kahneman, D., and Ghiselli, E. E.: Validity and nonlinear heteroscedastic models. *Personnel Psychology,* Vol. *15:* No. 1, pp. 1-11, 1962.

18. Kole, D. M.: A Study of Intellectual and Personality Charatcteristics of Medical Students. Unpublished Master's thesis, University of Oregon (Dep. of Medical Psychology) 1962.

19. Kuder, G. F.: Manual for the Kuder Preference Record, Personal. Available from Science Research Associates, Chicago, Illinois.

20. Land, T. H.: The role of central personnel agency in police personnel problems, *J. Crim. Law, Criminology & Pol. Sci., 51:*pp. 471-475, 1960.

21. Martin, E. M.: An Aptitude test for policemen. *J. Amer. Inst. Criminal Law and Criminology, 14:*pp. 376-404, 1923.

22. Mullineaux, J. E.: An evaluation of the predictors used to select patrolmen. *Pub. Personnel Rev., 16:*pp. 84-86, 1955.

23. O'Connor, G. W.: An Analysis of Methods Used in Selection of Municipal Patrolmen in Cities over 25,000 Population. Berkeley, University of California, unpublished Master's thesis, 1962.

24. Oglesby, T. W.: Use of Emotional Screening in the selection of police applicants. *Police, 2:* (May-June, p. 49), 1958.

25. Rokeach, M.: *The Open and Closed Mind.* New York, Basic Books, 1960.

26. Rolph, C.H.: *The Police and the Public.* London, Heinemann, 1962.

27. Stern, M.: What makes a policeman go wrong? *J. Crim. Law, Criminology and Pol. Sci.,* 53, pp. 97-101, 1962.

28. Sterne, D. M.: Use of the Kuder Preference Record-Personal-with police officers. *J. Appl. Psychol., 44:*pp. 323-324, 1960.

29. Stewart, N.: AGCT scores of Army personnel grouped by occupation. *Occupations, 26:* 1947.

30. Thorndike, R. L., and Hagen, Elizabeth: *Ten Thousand Careers.* New York, John Wiley, 1959.

31. Zaice, J. E.: Measured Interests, Personality and Intelligence of Professional Policemen. Unpublished Master's thesis, Washington State University (Pullman) 1962.

Chapter VI

PSYCHIATRIC EVALUATION IN THE SELECTION PROCESS

T HERE ARE TWO major issues to be considered in this chapter. One is how to use the special skills of the psychiatrist efficiently. The second is to understand the limitations of the psychiatrist's skills and effectiveness. It will be found that the psychiatrist is a potentially useful tool for police selection. It will be found that this tool, like any other, is far from perfect and must be employed wisely.

The use of psychologic principles in the selection and screening of applicants is not an original concept. For almost any position other than the most menial service or one in which the personality qualifications are irrelevant, the employer will attempt to gain some impression of the prospective employee's suitability for the position in question. Hopefully, this impression should correlate with the employer's past experience with other individuals in similar positions. Thus, the selection is made on some basis more rational than pure chance. This evaluation may be done by the employer personally or by some representative, usually the prospective supervisor of the individual. In larger organizations, evaluation is sometimes done by a specially designated personnel director, a series of personnel workers or an entire department. In these cases the individual is relying either on past experience or training in personnel management rather than the highly specialized skills and techniques of the trained psychiatrist. This situation is gradually changing. A sub-specialty, industrial psychiatry, has emerged in which interest is directed toward the psychiatrically-oriented aspects of screening and selection.

Only a few large corporations are utilizing this method at present, however, and only a tiny minority of law enforcement agencies have added this procedure to their selection programs. Consequently there is very little precedent or experience to rely on and practically no definitive, statistically valid data upon which to base an evaluation of the results. The following chapter, therefore, will be devoted primarily to a discussion of the psychiatric examination in general, its application to police selection, and the limitations and potential usefulness of the examination. There will be reference to data in the meager literature available as well as observations from the author's personal experience.

Before proceeding further, it should be helpful to describe the nature of the psychiatric evaluation in general and the modifications necessary in a police selection situation.

THE PSYCHIATRIC EXAMINATION

The psychiatric examination may vary greatly but it contains certain essential elements which cannot be modified, at least at the present stage of development. We will consider these general characteristics.

The General Psychiatric Interview

Although psychiatric evaluations can take many forms (for example, a psychiatric evaluation of records alone), the evaluation is usually conducted in an *interview* situation. Although psychiatric interviewing is sometimes done in groups (group therapy) psychiatry's unique approach for personnel investigation involves an individual interview with the subject. To make full use of the psychiatrist's skills, the interview must take place in privacy. Some organizations, as in some types of military screening, have utilized an "assembly line" procedure with psychiatrists, i.e., short few minute sessions in a semi-public setting. The drawbacks of such a method are so great as to question even the value of the proceeding at all. The advantages, if any, of the psychiatric interview over other screening methods can be achieved only under circumstances allowing the application of the usual psychiatric techniques.

Conduct of the Interview

The interview is merely a special method of obtaining raw data upon which the psychiatrist will base his ultimate opinion and conclusions. This data is obtained from both the verbal and non-verbal communications of the subject. The observations of the psychiatrist, i.e., his personal subjective reactions to the individual, are recorded separately from the subject's own reactions to things. At times the psychiatrist's very subjectiveness is an equally important factor in reaching a conclusion. The interviewing technique then is an extremely flexible one. The subject is encouraged to discuss relevant material. The discussion is initiated either by the psychiatrist's suggestions, such as leading statements designed to draw out the individual, or by direct questions concerning the subject matter.

There are three general areas which should be covered. It is not necessary and is at times undesirable to take these up in a stereotyped orderly progression.

PRESENT PROBLEM. In the ordinary psychiatric interview, the subject is a patient or a potential one who is troubled with some emotional or behavioral problem or has been referred for the purpose of evaluation. This interview then naturally must deal with all or a good part of the material relevant to the patient's problem. In order to help the patient, the psychiatrist hopes to reach an ultimate conclusion from the elaboration, confirmation or verification of the initial impression he received from the patient's history. The direction and extent of the investigation will be influenced primarily by the nature and complexity of the patient's problem.

PAST HISTORY. This is material involving the individual's past behavior and experience up to the present time. It emphasizes those features related to the present problem or those that might be expected to have some bearing on it. This may include investigation of his family both in terms of personal contact and hereditary factors. Technically these factors are considered a separate subject.

SPECIFIC TESTS. At some point in the interview, specific test questions are asked to elicit information that would not be brought out by the investigation alone—tests giving a rough evaluation of intelligence, thinking ability, intellectual mechanisms, mental content, and subjective feelings. Sometimes testing brings forth certain emotional responses from the subject, for example, the psychiatrist applies pressure or irritation to him in the attempt to elicit anger or unhappiness.

GENERAL OBSERVATIONS. During the entire interview the subject's general behavior is observed and thus his present emotional state. The examiner notes his own subjective feelings re. the subject and records them in proper context.

Modifications in Police Selection Interviews

The personnel selection interview is different from the above in that the subject does not come to the examiner with any special complaint. He comes to the examiner with the opposite inference, that he is a "normal individual" and that the interview is for the determination of "normality," rather than "abnormality." The "present problem" is the interest or the desire of the individual to become a police officer. The referring source, the police department, is interested in the confirmation of their lay opinion that the subject is suitable or unsuitable for appointment. It is the author's firm conviction that the psychiatrist should never override the appointing authority in situations where the department does *not* feel the candidate is suitable. It would be an abuse of discretion on the part of the psychiatrist except under most remarkable circumstances, to "sell" the employer on a prospective employee who is not wanted by the employer. The reasons are obvious. The psychiatrist is to determine not whether the candidate is "suitable" in the abstract but whether the employer will *consider* him to be so. The employer will be responsible for the ultimate decision. It would be unwise for the psychiatrist to foist upon the employer an individual whose personality characteristics the employer does not like. It is unlikely that the employer will change his opinion during the policeman's probationary period. Furthermore a lack of confidence by the employer very probably will affect the performance of the candidate with unsatisfactory results quite probable.

Past History

Our investigation of the candidate's past history will therefore be directed to those areas relating to his desire and suitability for appointment in the police department. The areas of discussion and testing selected will be those which have been found to show some correlation with future performance, either by past experience or based on general psychological principles.

Specific Tests

The specific tests should be designed and applied insofar as they are relevant to the functions of policemen. Since police officers are expected to function well under stress, it is reasonable to duplicate, at least to a minor extent, a stressful situation to test the candidate's reactions. Then we attempt to correlate this experimentally-induced reaction to possible behavior on the job. One can test by pressuring the candidate—questioning certain obvious statements—or by abruptly throwing emotionally-charged subject matter at him.

Attention should be given particularly to areas which psychiatric theory and experience show to be reasonably correlated with interest in law enforcement work, for example, latent aggression, sadism, homosexuality, etc. In addition there are tests of intellectual mechanisms such as abstraction ability and inductive reasoning which might be involved in familiar law enforcement situations. It should be borne in mind that the actual procedure is highly variable and dependent upon the training, experience and personality of the psychiatrist involved.

CHOICE OF PSYCHIATRIST

Psychiatry is a medical specialty in which the emphasis is placed upon the diagnosis, treatment and disposition of all aspects of human behavior. There are other well-trained individuals in this field who do not have the medical degree. Therefore, we shall briefly discuss the particular value of the psychiatrist in police selection. The other professional fields related to psychiatry are principally those of clinical psychology and psychiatric social work. The qualified clinical psychologist has a Ph.D. degree in clinical psychology. A qualified psychiatric social worker has at least a master's degree in psychiatric social work. All of this training involves working with emotionally and mentally disturbed individuals in a clinical setting. However, there are certain advantages in the employment of a psychiatrist which justify his use in police selection programs.

Unlike the other related specialties, the training and experience of the psychiatrist involves not only exposure to psychiatric problems but includes the entire management and responsibility for these cases. In the usual clinical setting, the psychologist and the social worker cooperate with the psychiatrist but are still *additional to* the psychiatrist. He is the one who handles the final disposition of the case. The emphasis and training involving authority and ultimate decision, which are prominent in his orientation, are of distinct value in screening and selection methods. The psychiatrist supplies an all-around approach to the problem rather than just supervising psychologic testing or giving social evaluation as in the other fields. Lastly, to become a "qualified" psychiatrist, one must have a minimal degree of competence in all aspects of the subject. In the related fields, even if the training is good, there may be large areas in which the psychologist or social worker is not properly qualified. If a psychiatrist is not available for the selection procedure, it would be advisable for the police department to consult a psychiatrist for recommendations of qualified substitutes from the related fields. These individuals could then handle the psychiatric portion of the evaluation procedure or its equivalent.

Minimum Qualifications of the Psychiatrist

There is an extreme variation in the quality and emphasis in the training of the psychiatrist. At the present time, any licensed M.D. may hold himself out as a specialist in any field including psychiatry. Therefore, it is necessary that the psychiatrist selected have at least some basic qualifications on which the department can rely.

Probably the best requirement is the psychiatrist's certification as a diplomate of the American Board of Psychiatry and Neurology. This certification requires three years full-time training following completion of internship, at least two additional years of experience in the field of psychiatry and an intensive examination by numerous experienced psychiatrists selected by the American Board, a subsidiary of the American Medical Association. This Board examination requires a basic knowledge in all phases of psychiatry in spite of the fact that there are different theoretical approaches to human behavior problems and despite the fact that training programs emphasize certain aspects of psychiatry.

An accredited training institution must prepare him in all these phases. If there are no certified specialists available, or if the department is located far from such facilities or if certified men are unwilling to cooperate, then there is this solution. Choose a psychiatrist and be sure he is eligible for Board certification, indicating that he has completed the basic training and experience requirements although not completing the examination. Although Board certification or eligibility does not mean excellence in the field, it does insure at least the basic minimal qualifications that a layman could not evaluate. Unfortunately, emphasis in psychiatric training and experience is often directed toward individual patients just as in any other medical specialty. Consequently, the competent psychiatrist may have no experience in the sort of situation involved in police selection.

It is highly desirable that the psychiatrist chosen have additional experience or training in the community aspects of psychiatry. By community aspects we mean rapid evaluation of large numbers of individuals for some specific purpose. There are not too many opportunities for this sort of experience however. It may be difficult to recruit such a psychiatrist for the selection program. The best background for this type of work may perhaps be military experience where the psychiatrist is often involved in numerous boards, hearings and evaluations, requiring him to perform in a semi-administrative capacity. Similar experience can be gained by work in conjunction with courts and mental hospitals where there is a rapid turnover of patients. However, these latter situations require evaluating presumably "sick" individuals whereas in police selection the evaluation is of more or less normal individuals. Ideally, the psychiatrist should have experience in the selection of police candidates, and preferably, experience working with a police department, but this is unusual and probably will not be available for the average department. Obviously the psychiatrist becomes of more value as he gains experience in the selection procedure.

The Psychiatrist as an Individual

The psychiatrist's general personality makeup is of equal and perhaps even greater importance than his training and experience.

It is difficult to describe his desirable and undesirable characteristics but they vary in psychiatry as in any other occupational
group. Those to be desired are maturity, confidence and the ability to understand and implement the needs of the department
during the selection procedure.

Characteristics to be avoided include immaturity, lack of confidence, or an obvious emotional bias which interferes with his
objectivity. The psychiatrist should also be flexible enough to
overcome any personal image he may have as to the "ideal policeman." Thus he will not eliminate qualified candidates who just
do not happen to fit into his preconceived mold. This characteristic is difficult to assess but in general the rigid, pedantic psychiatrist should be suspect.

Finally, it is desirable that the psychiatrist be interested, even
enthusiastic about working in the police setting (but beware the
over-enthusiastic one with a "mission"). A psychiatrist's interests
very often can be noted by his participation in other community
aspects of psychiatry as compared to a pure dedication to private
practice. Remember however that many psychiatrists are looking
for an opportunity to function in a community area without
having had a chance to do so previously.

PLACE IN SELECTION PROCEDURE

The use of the psychiatric interview in the selection program
is determined to a large extent by both practical and theoretical
limitations. There are budgetary considerations. The psychiatrist's
time is expensive. Therefore, the psychiatric interviews are usually the most expensive portion of the selection process.

There is the problem of availability. There are only a handful
of law enforcement agencies in this country large enough to
justify the employment of a full-time psychiatrist. It may therefore be difficult to obtain the services of a qualified psychiatrist
for more than a limited time. If there is a problem in this regard,
the local or regional Psychiatric Association or Medical Society
should be of assistance. In order to cut down the time and money
spent on the psychiatrist, it is advisable to do as much screening
and elimination of unsuitable or questionable candidates as possible prior to the psychiatric exam. This has led, in many agencies,

to the policy of leaving the psychiatric examination as the last step prior to acceptance on the appointment list.

There are theoretical considerations as well. The time allotted to the psychiatrist (see below under "Limitations") may not allow a complete evaluation. The psychiatrist can use his time best if there is available to him the information collected from other sources. This would include test scores and background investigation reports.

The highly subjective nature of the psychiatrist's evaluation is one factor of great importance, usually underestimated by the selection agency. Laymen tend to expect a definitive answer from those to whom they refer their problems. They are frequently disappointed by the psychiatrist's indefinite and noncommital response. The nature of human behavior necessitates this and does not indicate the psychiatrist's incompetence or insecurity. In certain areas the psychiatrist can be as exact and definitive as any other medical specialty or nearly any other field of scientific endeavor. This relative exactness is possible in certain diagnoses and, to a lesser extent, the prognosis (prediction) of certain clear-cut psychiatric disorders. However, as the individual to be evaluated approaches "normal" the predictions become more difficult.

There are numerous variables which must be taken into consideration in order to achieve the accurate prediction of future behavior. Most of them cannot be completely evaluated in a selection procedure. A consideration of even a few of these variables makes this clear. Most candidates being evaluated are still fairly young, still in a process of maturation and change in their psychologic development. Most of them have had no experience equivalent to police work. Therefore, there is no data upon which to predict future adjustment by comparison. The policeman will react not only to his job but to his life circumstances which will be variable in the future and are difficult to anticipate at the present. The law enforcement officer works as an essential part of a particular department. The personnel and morale of this department change from time to time and the individual's reactions will change accordingly. His behavior can be largely unconsciously determined so that he may not understand his own motivation to become a police officer. The psychiatrist can estimate that unconscious motivation only by inference even under the best of circumstances. Consequently when the individual is faced with the reality of police work, his behavior might be quite different from that anticipated by himself or the psychiatrist. The interview situation is always an artificial one in that the prospective employee is attempting to impress the examiner favorably. This introduces distortion. Finally the psychiatrist's own subjective feelings about the individual may play an extremely important part insofar as objective information is absent. Most psychiatrists hesitate to base an evaluation entirely on unsubstantiated subjective feelings.

Most psychiatrists would not feel comfortable in the role of absolute and final arbiter with reference to a candidate's acceptability. Many, including myself, feel that the psychiatrist recommendation should be but one factor in the final decision. There are, as a result, two ways to introduce psychiatric findings into the decision-making process about each applicant.

One method calls for the psychiatrist to see all candidates before they appear before the oral board, but after psychological and background investigation reports have been made. When the oral board meets, it is given all of the information about each applicant, one portion of which will be the psychiatric report. The oral board would then make the final decision on each man. This essentially is the procedure employed experimentally in the San Mateo County Sheriff's Department.[1,2]

A problem in this method is that the psychiatrist must see rather large numbers of applicants; an expensive and time-consuming business. To reduce costs several modifications can be made of the foregoing sequence. One modification is that the psychiatrist, before the oral board meets, sees only those individuals about whom questions have been raised during the background investigation and psychological testing. Thus he will see the most likely "bad apples." After the oral board meets the psychiatrist can then see all those candidates who have been recommended for hiring by the board but who have not yet been seen by him.

A second approach to decision-making, more in conformity with my own experience, makes the psychiatric examination part of the medical screening. Adverse recommendations by the psychiatrist, as by the examining physician on physical matters, absolutely disqualify candidates. For borderline cases the final decision is not made, but a provisional acceptance "with qualifications" is recorded. In this sequence the medical-psychiatric review follows the oral board evaluation and is limited to the examination of candidates passed by the board.

USE OF RELATED PROCEDURES

Ideally the psychiatrist should have all available information at the time of the interview. This would include all background information from collateral sources as well as results of psychologic testings. Sometimes it is not practical for the background check to be completed by this time. As a compromise, and as an aid to the interviewer, the prospective candidate fills out a history questionnaire which saves considerable time during the interview and often directs the line of questioning. It is also helpful to have the candidate write a short statement indicating his interest in law enforcement work and in the particular department involved. Certain clues can be obtained here, indicating personality characteristics as well as the individual's intellectual functioning.

Psychologic test results should also be available. The test battery should include both an intelligence test and personality tests. It should be understood that psychologic testing can function either as a screening device or as an adjunct to some other phase of the selection procedure. If the candidate is eliminated on the basis of a minimal score or rating, the psychiatric interview would be superfluous. If he passed, this test information could still be helpful in the subsequent psychiatric interview. Another approach would be to administer psychologic tests solely for the purpose of gaining additional information for the psychiatrist or the oral board in its final determination. The psychiatrist should know the function of psychologic testing in the department he assists.

THE SCIENTIFIC STATUS OF PSYCHIATRIC EVALUATION

In recent years there have been a number of scientific investigations of the reliability and validity of psychiatric examinations.

The findings, which have recently been reviewed by Blum[3] show how difficult it can be for psychiatrists to agree with one another —or with psychologists—about diagnosis, especially in regard to refinements as opposed to gross categories. Validity is also difficult to establish and while the test of daily medical usage bespeaks the contribution which psychiatry can make to understanding and testing mental disorders, there is much less evidence about its ability to predict performance among normal persons. Ideally one would set up a scientific test of psychiatry in the police field. To do this properly one would need to conduct a long-term study in which psychiatric predictions were contrasted with actual performance on the job. It is to be hoped that one of the readers of this book will be stimulated to undertake such an investigation in his own department.

THE PROPORTION OF APPLICANTS REJECTED

How many applicants a psychiatrist will reject will depend upon several factors. The quality of the candidates will be one; the modus operandi of the psychiatrist, two; the standards of the department, a third; the job market itself will be a fourth. In times of plenty, that is when recruits are plentiful, the psychiatrist can be told to be very demanding in his requirements, consequently eliminating large numbers of men. In times of applicant scarcity, the psychiatrist can be instructed to lower his standards to rather minimum basic qualifications.

As far as the statistics on the proportion rejected by psychiatrists are concerned, these will depend upon the place of the psychiatric examination in the order of screening procedures. If the candidates are carefully screened by a number of devices before any are seen by a psychiatrist, the proportion he will reject from this select group is going to be low. If, on the other hand, the psychiatrist sees the candidates early in the selection process, before many have been weeded out by other means, the chances are that he will have a very high rejection rate. In reviewing the rates of rejection reported by various departments who employ psychiatrists, it is necessary to keep the foregoing in mind.

My own experience in the Berkeley Police Department, which consists of about 150 policemen serving a town of about 100,000, is illustrative of these selection rates at each step of the way. The department is one which enjoys a good reputation, has good morale, attracts a good grade of applicants, experiences relatively small turnover, and has relatively high qualification standards and reasonably demanding screening procedures. Over the last ten years selection experience has been such as to provide the following general picture.

For every two hundred applicants, approximately one hundred qualify on the basis of their application forms. After the written examination (primarily psychologic testing including a standard intelligence test requirement of I.Q. = 112) only twenty-five men remain to go on to the next step in the selection procedure. Three more will fail on the physical agility test leaving twenty-two men out of the original 200. Of these about four will be failed by the oral board. This leaves eighteen. The psychiatric examination will eliminate two men while one will fail the medical examination. This leaves fifteen men. Of these, one third, five, are rejected on the basis of background investigation. Ten men out of the original group of 200 will actually be hired. About 20 per cent of these are lost during the two-year probationary period so that eight permanent employees remain.*

VALUE AND LIMITATIONS OF PSYCHIATRIC EXAMINATIONS

Practical Limitations

The duration of the selection psychiatric exam must usually be shorter than that ideally desired for a thorough evaluation. The total time of evaluation and preparation allowed for a report is rarely over one hour. In the author's personal experience the usual time runs from thirty to forty-five minutes for the evaluation itself with a few additional minutes for preparation of the report.[4]

The use to which reports are put varies with the department. There might be some advantage in a complete psychiatric evaluation but this is time-consuming and of limited purpose when most of the screening has already been accomplished. In the event the

---

*It is quite apparent the earlier the psychiatric exam occurs, the higher the percentage of candidates it will remove early in the procedure.

psychiatric evaluation takes place before the meeting of the oral board, a complete psychiatric report can be very helpful to the board. Some departments require no report whatever but only a "pass" or "fail." Sometimes a "pass-fail" or conditional acceptance can be given and the psychiatrist retains his notes in case of some future difficulties. The author is accustomed to a procedure wherein a short summary is written which includes any significant data in the case of those that are passed and a more detailed report of the rejected men. The latter is necessary in case they reapply at a later date.

The typical short examination is ordinarily desirable except in those questionable cases when the psychiatrist would feel more confident of his opinion with a longer time allotment. The lack of confirmation of background information rendered by the applicant presents definite difficulties to the psychiatrist. The prospective candidate for an appointment is therefore likely to bias the examiner in his favor.

The theoretical limitations which were discussed previously, involve the uncertainty in predicting a man's future behavior in an ever-changing environment, coupled with the unavoidable subjectivity of the psychiatrist. Nonetheless, distinctive advantages can be achieved which justify the procedure. The psychiatrist is trained to think of unconscious mechanisms in human behavior and therefore looks for the unconscious basis for events of the candidate's life. He is trained to know what "the little things" in human behavior may mean. Many clinical manifestations may be "normal" and "healthy" in one individual but are distinct signs of pathology in another. Conversely an apparently "normal" "well-adjusted" pattern and appearance might be a defense by the aspiring policeman to cover up abnormal unconscious mechanisms. These could be seen only by one trained to assess such behavior. Certain patterns of behavior are indicative of pathology even though each part of the behavior pattern may seem "normal." Likewise real abnormalities may be insignificant when considered in the total context of the person's behavior and resources.

Because the psychiatrist is trained to investigate certain highly personal and sensitive areas of behavior which people do not usually tell one another, he can obtain such information comfortably. Others who might undertake such inquiries often do so either with extreme difficulty or with strong emotionality. Some important areas of behavior are not even noticed by non-psychiatrically oriented evaluators.

The psychiatrist is also better able than others to assess the importance for various kinds of work performance of whatever psychiatric disorders may be present in a candidate. Let us say that both the senior command staff and the psychiatrist recognize that "something is wrong" with an applicant, but that he has many very desirable qualities. "What is wrong" may be a facial tic or remnant of a stutter or some rather unobtrusive sign, but the non-psychiatric evaluator will be concerned about it, not so much because it poses any apparent limitation to the candidate, but because he does not know whether or not it signifies a personality problem which might very well interfere with performance. In this situation the psychiatrist performs a helpful service by discussing the signs and symptoms in his report, telling what they signify in a man's personality, and indicating how this affects or does not affect the various tasks ordinarily involved in police work.

The presence of a psychiatrist to provide such expert knowledge often serves to make an oral board, or others responsible for selection, much more at ease in the decisions they make. The psychiatrist can answer their questions about a candidate who shows some signs of distress or disturbance.

It is also possible that a candidate who seems to be free of any kind of undesirable quality, in the eyes of other evaluators, may be found by a probing psychiatrist to have some potentially serious disorders. Conscious masking and unconscious defenses may make it possible for a candidate to mislead non-psychiatric interviewers and to pass early stages in selection. When the psychiatrist identifies a hazardous quality in a candidate he performs a unique service for the department, but such "finds" are the exception rather than the rule. For the most part one can expect the judgments of the psychiatrist and sensible police commanders to be much the same; there will be agreement on extremely undesirable candidates, uncertainty about borderline ones, cautious accept-

ance of the middle ground, and good agreement on the outstand-
ingly desirable men.

CONCLUSION

Psychiatric evaluation has a distinct place in police selection
as long as a department clearly understands what it can do and
what it should not do. Its most dramatic contribution comes in
the identification of mentally disturbed persons who otherwise
go undetected but who, if hired, would be likely to pose serious
problems of efficiency, interpersonal relations, or safety to the
department and the community. Less dramatic but nevertheless
worthwhile contributions come from the valuable supplemental
information that a psychiatrist can provide about candidates, and
the reassurance he can give to responsible officials about the
significance of various observed traits about which the officials
may be uncertain. Psychiatric screening will necessarily eliminate
a proportion of the potentially good men and will occasionally
fail to identify men who later become problems to the department. Improvements in the psychiatric selection tool can be
brought about through research in police settings. In the meantime the wise police department will consider the use of psychiatric examiners as an important supplement to the screening process, but will recognize the need to select those psychiatrists with
care, to train them to understand the department's goals and
problems, and will neither expect too much from the psychiatrist
nor discount his contribution.

BIBLIOGRAPHY

1. Blum, R. H., Goggin, W., and Whitmore, E. J.: A study in deputy
   sheriff selection procedure. *Police, 6:*59-63, 1961.
2. Blum, R. H., Goggin, W., Whitmore, E. J., and Pomeroy, W. J.:
   A further study of deputy sheriff selection procedures. *Police, 6:*
   77-79, 1962.
3. Blum, R. H.: Case identification in psychiatric epidemiology;
   methods and problems. *Milbank Mem. Fund Quart., 40:*254-
   288, 1962.
4. Wilson, D. H.: The function of psychiatry in a municipal law enforcement agency. *Amer. J. Psychiat., 116:*870-872, 1960.

Supplemental Bibliography

Frost, T. M.: Selection methods for police recruits. *J. Crim. Law Criminol. Police Sci., 46*:135-145, 1955.

Kelley, D. M.: Psychiatry in police recruitment. *Police Yearbook,* pp. 194-199, 1953.

Oglesby, T. W.: Use of emotional screening in the selection of police applicants. *Public Personnel Rev., 18*:228-231, 235, 1957.

Rankin, J.H.: Psychiatric screening of police recruits. *Public Personnel Rev. 20*:191-196, 1959.

Reiner, H.: Another view on psychiatric screening of police recruits. *Public Personnel Rev., 21*:41-55, 1960.

Chapter VII

THE BACKGROUND INVESTIGATION

T HE PERSONAL history of an applicant for the police service should be above reproach. The facts concerning his personal behavior in the past should form a basis that will permit a prediction to be made that he will function successfully as a police officer in the future.

O. W. Wilson has said, "A policeman's character and reputation should be of the highest order. A police chief cannot afford to appoint to his force an applicant whose reputation is questionable or one whose character is such as to cast doubt on his future actions."[4]

Some ex-chiefs of police have said, "If I had only known what kind of a character he was I would never have hired him in the first place. He was responsible for my being forced to resign."

An examination of the personal history of an applicant will assist a department in selecting the best men from those who are interested and appear to be qualified, and will prevent a department from making costly, damaging mistakes.

WHAT IS BACKGROUND INVESTIGATION

A background investigation is the systematic collection of facts and opinions from persons who have known a candidate, or from persons who have custody of the records of his past performance. The report of the background investigator is reviewed, with all accompanying documents, to determine if the candidate is acceptable for appointment to the position of police officer.

Other terms meaning essentially the same thing are: *personal history investigation, character investigation, reference check, applicant check* or *applicant investigation.*

The purpose of the background investigation is at least three-fold. The major objective is to learn how the candidate has behaved under a wide variety of circumstances and from this to base a prediction concerning future performance as a policeman. The second is to verify all of the statements the candidate has made in his efforts to become a police officer. The third, to prevent the department from hiring a man who will prove unqualified so that the man and his department suffer the damage that occurs when an individual must be separated from the service.

HISTORY

Law enforcement history books are not very explicit concerning the origin of the background investigation as a formal technique in personnel selection. The procedure could have begun when a board of town trustees decided that it would be a good idea to "check the record" of a man they were considering for appointment to the position of town marshal. It could have begun, too, when the opponents of a candidate for county sheriff discovered they could defeat him by "digging up the dirt" concerning a lack of integrity where he last held public office. In both situations, the origins of the background investigation as a tool to assist in the selection of qualified men may be observed.

WHERE DOES IT FIT INTO THE SELECTION PROCESS?

It would be ideal if a complete history of the candidate were available at the very beginning of the selection process. The initial interviewer could use it to screen out those who are obviously unsuited for police employment and thus save the expense of all subsequent testing for those persons. Oral board members, psychologists, medical examiners and psychiatrists could also make good use of a factual documentation of the life history of a candidate.

Economically, however, the background investigation is the most expensive part of the process because it requires extensive interviewing, travel and correspondence. Most departments investigate only those applicants who have qualified for the eligible list and who are being considered for immediate appointment. Other departments conduct it after all other procedures have been completed but before the eligible list is established. In still others, men are appointed from the eligible list and assigned to a recruit training school, and then investigated. There are advantages and disadvantages in any specific plan or time schedule. Local laws, such as "tight civil service" regulations, may compel a department to appoint all men who qualify for the eligible list. Local custom, such as political control and interference in the administration of a department, may similarly require a chief to appoint all men who qualify in ridiculously simple written examinations but who meet what are considered to be important political qualifications. Ideally, the background investigation should be conducted after all other requirements are met but before the candidate is appointed to the job.

A significant point to bear in mind is that usually all other screening activities do occur within short, limited and economical periods of time. None of the procedures such as written examination, oral interview, physical agility test or medical evaluation proves that the candidate will do an acceptable job as a policeman. That he has survived each of the *screening out* processes may in part be credited to the fact that he has supplied uncorroborated information which, because of the pressure of time, has been accepted at its face value as the truth. Since the police service requires truthful men, the background investigation will serve at least dual purposes in corroborating all of the statements made by the applicant in his efforts to become a policeman and will establish that he has practiced truthfulness in his normal life. Facts concerning both of these facets will be useful in predicting future performance.

MODUS OPERANDI AND BACKGROUND INVESTIGATION

"Study the past if you would divine the future," Confucius said. A premise in personnel selection is that there is a certain constancy in human behavior, that an individual will consistently repeat behavior patterns when they have been successful in meeting life situations in the past. Theoretically, therefore, if we can determine the past behavior of an individual in a variety of social situations it will be possible to predict his behavior when similar situations occur in the future. This is a generalization that is not wholly accepted and one that has some obvious defects that will be commented upon later. For the moment, however, let us examine a variation of the premise that is found in the police investigative technique termed *modus operandi*.

Modus Operandi is a term of Latin origin meaning "method of operation." In criminal investigation, it refers to a technique that is recognized as being potentially helpful but is a less than perfect instrument. In applying it, an investigator studies the evidence gathered at a crime scene to identify habits, characteristics, peculiarities and traits that are the trademarks of the violator. He then endeavors to identify the individual who is responsible. He works with records of known offenders and in arriving at his list of suspects will bring into play all of his specialized skills, his training and experience in handling human beings, and will add his subjective judgment to the process. This judgment will unconsciously call into play his personal attitudes, knowledge and concepts concerning the method by which the crime was committed and the personality of the individual who committed it. *Modus operandi* is essentially the same when it is applied to the evaluation of a candidate for the job of policeman as it is in selecting the most likely candidate for the commission of a crime. The basis for the system is the belief that the behavior patterns in human beings will be consistent over a period of time. —The applicant who has demonstrated consistent good judgment, leadership ability, reliability in the handling of his finances and personal affairs, pride in the performance of his job, independence, and an ability to work in harmony with others under ordinary and stress conditions can usually be relied upon to conduct himself similarly in the future. Conversely, the candidate who has been a liar, a cheat, a frequent violator of laws or conventions, a reckless, drunken unethical, profane, prejudiced, violent, immoral or irresponsible show-off, can fairly be assumed to be the kind of a man who will repeat the errors of his past. Perhaps the contrast has been exaggerated here, but it provides a basis for understanding that the personal history of an applicant for the police service contains highly significant indicators as to the probability of future performance in the man who aspires to serve humanity and his community in the police service.

Although we do study the past history of an applicant to predict his future performance, we should recognize the imperfection of the system. The premise that adult human behavior is constant, given the same surrounding conditions, is not conclusively proven, and any experienced manager can cite a score of examples to the contrary. We do not know exactly what characteristics in human personality are subject to change with proper leadership. We do not know exactly what delinquent characteristics are unchanging. This may indicate that police administrators can find substantial benefit in the use of outside specialists, such as psychologists and psychiatrists, in applying the technique of *modus operandi* in the selection of candidates for appointment to entrance level positions in his department.

SETTING THE STANDARD

Industrial personnel specialists know that a functional analysis of a job will dictate the qualifications that must be possessed by the technician who will be employed to carry out the project.

This process has been attempted in relation to the vocation of policeman (or *Deputy Sheriff*, or *Law Enforcement Officer*). Bruce Smith,[5] August Vollmer,[6] and practically every other man who is respected as a pioneer in the field of police personnel selection, have analyzed, listed, discussed, hypothecated and proposed the qualifications that ideal candidates for the service should possess. In addition to the fundamental problems of varying human nature, they have recognized that the culture of a community and the motivating power of a police management team, among other factors, complicates the development of a simple formula or criteria that can universally be used in the United States to select police manpower. But most authorities tend to agree on one point, and that is that the "character and reputation" of the candidate should be compatible with the requirements of a policeman's job. As a basis for what will follow, therefore, the following is offered as a basic assumption or statement of principle:

The character and reputation of a candidate for the police service should be excellent. His personal history should reflect a pat-

tern of behavior that is compatible with the requirements of the policeman's job. Any doubt concerning his possession of desirable personal qualities should be resolved in favor of the community rather than the candidate.

The background investigation will endeavor to obtain all necessary information in order that each factor in this definition can be considered factually in arriving at a decision concerning the employability of the candidate.

THE MECHANICS OF A BACKGROUND INVESTIGATION

The Investigator

The officer entrusted with the responsibility for the conduct of the background investigation should substantially possess the qualities of an ideal police officer. His ability as an investigator, interrogator, reporter and evaluator of evidence should have been proven in the crucible of experience. His loyalty to the organization, the code of ethics of law enforcement and his proven interest in the professionalization of the police service should be beyond dispute. He should enjoy the complete confidence of his chief.

You may wish to challenge the foregoing statement. The basis for the strong definition is simple to understand. One of the most prevalent human characteristics is that of rationalization. Untrained and inexperienced human beings decide most issues in their lives on the basis of personal experience, attitudes and emotional reactions. We communicate by interpreting the tone of voice of the other person and read into his statement all of the hidden meanings that personal prejudice, bias, like or dislike permits. If this is a general truth, even with educated and experienced persons, it will be to the positive advantage of an organization to capitalize upon this psychological phenomena. The selection of the ideal policeman who is trained, experienced and oriented to the best objectives of the service will more likely result in interpretations that are favorable to the organization than the assignment of a man who will be inclined to overlook background facts because they reflect his own misconduct or weakness of the past. So, use a proven professional if you would employ additional men of like high standards.

The background investigator will be assigned to make all necessary checks and interviews to determine the qualifications of the applicant. He will be the chief individual who considers all of the facts before making a recommendation concerning the employability of a candidate. He should clearly understand that the facts of past behavior will be the foundation for predicting future behavior. He should have the ability to discriminate between what is and what is not important, according to the published criteria and the unwritten standards of his agency. He should understand what events constitute a basis for disqualification. He should know that evidence is required to justify his recommendation. He should understand the nature of prejudice and its influence on the thoughts, speech and actions of men. And, although this topic is capable of further lengthy development, he should understand clearly that the results of his investigation are intended for the confidential use of the head of his agency, but may be subjected to the critical review of others.*

While this general description of the qualifications of the background investigator may be sufficient to establish an understanding of the need for careful selection for the task, his training is a matter of additional importance. It is assumed that he has a background of training and experience for his basic job of law enforcement investigator.

The investigator should receive additional training through reading, discussion and formal education if he does not have it when assigned to the task. Some administrators believe that a

---

*Editor's note: One technique which should be considered is an occasional review of background investigation reports and of the decisions based upon them. This review, which should be aimed toward improvements in the existing standards and operations, can be conducted by the command staff of the department, by police consultants from other departments, or by citizens. One might wish to consider inviting a committee from the city council, delegates from important minority group organizations, etc. One might wish to consider setting up a police advisory committee composed of interested and prominent citizens representing a variety of community forces. The function of such a group, carefully guided by the department, would be to become interested in police problems and to provide helpful criticism and grass-roots citizen backing for the department. While many administrators might be wary of non-police "intruders," the department which is doing a good job and shows its responsiveness to citizen concerns can expect such a committee to become an important asset.

background investigator should have sound fundamental knowledge concerning the nature of emotional maturity, social dynamics and the general field of cultural anthropology. Supervisory, management and personnel training are of value. Admittedly, this point of view leans heavily toward the ideal. Lacking men with this qualification, however, a department should not sacrifice the investigation. Policemen daily have to evaluate human beings in terms of the evidence presented by eye-witnesses to an event, and the distance between this kind of investigation and background investigation is short.

The investigator should know the explicit standards of past behavior that will result in the disqualification of an applicant. He should know, too, that the department endeavors to select only men of proven integrity and that this quality should be reflected in the facts that are gathered. It is the chief administrator's responsibility to provide him with a list of standards and qualifications that will permit him to operate with the greatest economy of time. It is assumed that the investigator has demonstrated in other aspects of his police performance that his knowledge, judgment and ability to appraise facts are reliable.

Before leaving the topic of *the investigator,* it is recommended that the police administrator consider the desirability of assigning the responsibility on a continuing basis to one man, or the rotation of this duty between many officers of his department. The fundamental question is whether homogeneity or variety in recruit manpower is desirable. Even though each individual applicant is unique, it may be found that an investigator unconsciously eliminates all applicants except those who reflect his own concept of the ideal or satisfactory officer. He will investigate more thoroughly some individuals who do not measure up to his standards until sufficient facts are available to disqualify. Or, unconsciously favoring some aspect of the candidate's qualification, he will investigate more thoroughly to counteract negative information should it be developed. This can and does happen. Since every police official must constantly look to the future and realize that new ideas will be needed to match our changing times, it is suggested that rotation of men through the background investigation assignment can be a tool to produce recruits of diverse characteristics. The "blood lines" of a thoroughbred group may thus be improved.

The first job of the investigator will be to get organized and for this he will need some basic documents.

The Application

Having completed the preliminary steps for qualification, the applicant should be informed that he is being given serious consideration for appointment to the force. He should now be required to submit a detailed, supplementary personal history statement that will provide the basis for his background investigation.

The supplementary personal history statement, or application, and documents should provide sources of information on every aspect of past behavior that is to be investigated. It should reflect the explicit standards used by the department to measure the worth of a candidate. One example of a supplementary application form is included in Appendix III at the end of this book.

It is not uncommon for some persons for political or other reasons to voice public objection to the fact that a supplementary personal history statement is a deliberate device to frustrate young men and to discourage them from further efforts to become police officers. Granted that there is an element of frustration in any job that requires work, concentration, accuracy and effort, one can editorially wonder if the critic's objection is valid. One observation made by an experienced police personnel officer when confronted with this accusation was, "When a man is so easily frustrated by this 'paper work' requirement, the department is well off without him. The investigation and report of a simple injury traffic accident might later prove to be an insurmountable and emotionally traumatic event."

The supplementary personal history document should contain clear instructions that:

a. All questions are to be answered either by providing the requested information or marking the space as "not applicable";

b. False statement, material error or significant omission may be sufficient grounds for removal of the candidate from further consideration for appointment;

c. A stated list of supporting documents are to be submitted with the form;

d. All statements in the form and the attached documents are subject to verification;

e. If the space provided is inadequate, other pages may be added and should be identified as to the item to which it applies;

f. The signature by the applicant constitutes a certification as to the accuracy and truth of all information provided.

The documents that are most often required, and copies of which are filed with the supplementary application, are:

    Birth certificate

    Diploma satisfying educational requirement

    Driver's license

    Military discharge, separation papers or draft card

    Marriage certificate and divorce decree, if applicable

The department should obtain:

    Fingerprints and photograph

    Authority for release of information, several copies

    Authority for release of military information

Suggested Procedure

It is assumed that the background investigator will be provided with the complete set of documents that have been submitted and a report indicating what steps have already been taken to secure information concerning the candidate.

The investigation should begin with the sending out of fingerprints for reports from the Federal Bureau of Investigation and the State identification bureau, if any. Since several days will be required for clearance and report, this step should be initiated at the earliest practicable time.

The personal history statement and supporting documents should be reviewed and the facts contained therein should be evaluated. This preliminary examination should reveal completeness, attention to detail, and sometimes obvious discrepancies.

When it reveals omissions of periods of time in the residence or work history, the omission should be noted and checked out during the subsequent investigation. A failure to set forth all of the facts requested may be a deliberate means of withholding critical information.

Discrepancies are best revealed by carefully considering each fact that is recorded in relation to all available information. For example, a candidate may have an expensive automobile that is entirely out of line with his income and financial status. A written note should be made concerning any point that cannot be interpreted to reconcile with other information provided.

After the preliminary evaluation the investigator should either call in the candidate for an explanation concerning possible disqualifying entries, or proceed with the investigation.

The objective at this point is to develop two separate lists. The first will be an organized set of notes concerning each individual who will be personally contacted. The second, a list of individuals and agencies to whom letters will be directed.

As a general policy, the background investigator should endeavor personally to contact every individual who has personal knowledge concerning the candidate's behavior. From a practical, economic, point of view, there should be a geographic limit established inside of which the investigator is free to travel in securing his information. Outside of the limits imposed, the investigator should know that he will have to rely upon either correspondence with the source of information or a contact by the local law enforcement representatives.

Form letters and guide letters should be developed to simplify the process of securing information through correspondence. Samples of some of these are presented in Appendix III.

Letters requesting information should be sent to the following:

1. Police departments and sheriffs offices in all jurisdictions where the candidate has even lived, worked or attended school.*

---

*Editor's note: The quality of investigation reports which one may expect to receive from other police departments varies immensely. For applicants who have only recently arrived and about whom there is little or no local information, the weight of the background report may rest upon departments in other towns where the applicant has formerly lived. Unless one is sure that these other departments conduct their investigations as carefully as one conducts one's own, one will have doubts about the adequacy of these other reports, especially when they are clearly
(Footnote continued on next page)

2. Departments of motor vehicles or drivers licensing agencies in every state where the candidate has lived, worked, attended school or been stationed as a member of the Armed Forces.

Letters may be sent to the following where the addressee is located outside the geographic limits imposed for personal contact:

1. Schools.
2. Past employers.
3. Personal references.
4. Landlords.
5. Credit references.
6. Relatives. A typewritten letter and printed or mimeographed questionnaire may be used. See a sample questionnaire (Appendix III).

After all correspondence has been initiated, the most important work of the background investigator begins. The personal interviews he will conduct are potentially the most valuable sources of information concerning the character and reputation of the candidate. It is impossible to provide an all-inclusive guide concerning the questions to be asked and facts to be obtained. In some departments a sample list of questions have been developed for the purpose of providing guidelines for the investigator. See Appendix III for an example. During this phase of the investiga-

---

superficial. The more mobile Americans become and the more competitive does recruiting become, the more police agencies will have to rely upon one another for careful background investigations.

At present the variations in the quality of investigations points up the remarkably different standards of performance and administration from one department to another. At the present time there may be no solution for these inequalities, but we must over the long run make sure that interdependent agencies provide each other with the best in work and cooperation. If less effective departments do not improve and if national voluntary coordination is not enhanced, there will inevitably be many who will demand that national standards be developed and enforced through federal law. There will also be many who will view a national or federal police as the best answer to present local inadequacies. Indeed, since these latter suggestions have already been forthcoming, it is incumbent upon us to consider the advantages and disadvantages which federal standards or a national police would pose.

(On the basis of his appraisal of the impact of such steps, the author of this chapter has come to be strongly opposed to state or federal police systems replacing present municipal and county law enforcement.)

tion, the skill of the interview and interrogation will be applied in every contact. An appraisal should be made of each person interviewed to assist the investigator in assessing the reliability of the information that has been provided. Each person contacted is potentially able to provide information and additional sources that may be checked out. And, gradually and graphically the picture of the candidate's character, personality and abilities will be developed. Some specific suggestions are:

1. Have the facts concerning the candidate and the person to be interviewed immediately at hand. Know the applicant's full name, nicknames and aliases. Know the relationship between the candidate and the person being interviewed.

2. Conduct the investigation according to a geographic plan and time schedule. Organize the working notes to permit sorting and filing. Telephone and make appointments whenever possible.

3. Schools. In verifying educational data, the investigator should personally visit the school if possible. The counselor, teachers and other personnel who have known the candidate should be interviewed. The names of close associates during schooling should be determined for later interviews. Some of the kinds of information that may be obtained are:

a. Academic accomplishment or failure, and mental ability test results.

b. Activity in clubs, groups and social organizations; his ability to work in harmony with others.

c. Demonstrations of leadership, laziness, erratic behavior or constructive interests.

d. Absences due to illness or injury.

e. Reputation for honesty, integrity and other personal qualities, positive or negative.

f. Ability to accept responsibility and produce results.

g. Verification of statements in the personal history statement concerning any or all of the preceding items.

h. The nature of any disciplinary action, including the misconduct, involvement with others, and disposition made by the school.

4. Employers. Interviews with employers should develop information concerning the candidate's ability to work in harmony

with others, his reliability, dependability, reputation for honesty, need for close supervision, and other points. Some topics that should be covered would be:

a. Were the candidate's services routinely satisfactory? If not, why?

b. Why did the candidate leave that place of employment? Would the employer rehire if a vacancy existed and the candidate was interested in re-employment?

c. What was the candidate's attitude toward his employer and his job?

d. Were there any untruthful statements or misrepresentations in the personal history statement? or in the employer's personnel record when compared to the police application?

e. How many days of paid sick leave were taken? Why? Was there a pattern, such as immediately preceding or following regular days off?

f. Were there any industrial compensation type injuries received? What are the details? Any disability?

g. Is there any information available concerning the candidate's incompetence, unreliability, laziness, carelessness, drunkenness, "rabble rousing" or chronic griping? Or the reverse?

h. Did he take company property for personal use without permission? Tools? Did he ever set up his own business as a sideline activity in competition with his employer?

i. Would the employer welcome the candidate back as a policeman should an incident occur, requiring attention granting that the man would be trained in the proper handling of police responsibilities?

j. As a taxpayer, would the employer feel that he would routinely get his money's worth in public service from the candidate?

5. Credit references. The manner in which an applicant has handled his credit will often reveal whether he exercised foresight and mature judgment. Some suggested questions to be asked of all creditors are:

a. Did he pay his bills as agreed in the contract? Better than agreed?

b. If not paid on time, did he inform the creditor concerning the reason for the delay?

c. Was it ever necessary to sue the applicant, or turn unpaid bills over to a collection agency?

d. Would credit be extended to the applicant again if requested?

Does the entire credit picture of the applicant indicate the exercise of good common sense and an ability to live within his income?

6. Landlords. The candidate's reputation as a tenant would logically lead to an inquiry concerning his reliability in paying his rent. Other points might be:

a. The dates of residence, as a cross check on the accuracy of statements in the personal history statement.

b. Names and reputation of the candidate's friends, associates, co-tenants, enemies or other sources of information.

c. Reputation for sobriety, integrity, morality and other traits, desirable and undesirable.

d. Financial responsibility; management contacts by collection agencies.

e. Reputation as a motor vehicle operator, and respect for others when driving or parking.

7. Neighborhood checks. The objective is to determine the neighborhood reputation of the candidate concerning his personality, personal conduct, and any activities that would reflect positively or adversely upon the desirability of appointing the man as a policeman. Some suggestions are:

a. Check with the neighbors who lived in the house on each side and over the back fence from the candidate.

b. In an apartment house, try to check with at least four persons who knew the candidate while he resided there.

8. References, or Character Vouchers. Frequently the candidate will list persons of high standing in a community who may be barely acquainted with him. Often, too, they are friends who can be relied upon to give only favorable reports. In checking with them, therefore, one should determine just how close the acquaintanceship was and from them obtain the names of other

persons who may be more impersonal in their evaluation of the candidate. Genuinely close friends may be good sources, when approached properly, concerning the standards of morality, temperance, tolerance, prejudices, strengths and weaknesses of a man.

The preceding suggestions are to be considered only as a guide to some of the points that should be covered in the conduct of the personal interviews during the background investigation. Little or nothing has been said concerning many important facets of character that are significant to the police chief. Some of these are: membership in subversive organizations; association with homosexuals, prostitutes, racketeers or others whose influence would be detrimental to the best interests of the department; or, on the positive side, the achievement of special recognition for outstanding contribution in any phase of organization, community or civic life. The key point is that facts are obtainable from people, and the investigator should be sensitive to what people say and expand any interview when the opportunity presents itself. Facts will be the basis for his report. Facts will justify the appointment as an officer, and facts must justify the removal of a candidate from an eligible list.

The Moment of Decision for the Background Investigator

Sometimes the facts necessary to justify a recommendation are quickly obtained, and usually this occurs when the past behavior of a candidate has been such as to justify his disqualification. When this occurs, the investigator should stop investigating and confer with the official to whom he is accountable. The investigator should know that every fact upon which this decision is based should be verified. He should recognize the possibility of an appeal to a legally constituted agency. For this and other reasons, he should review the disqualifying information to determine if there will be any violation of a confidence should the information be revealed. When this situation prevails, he should investigate further, including additional interviews with the candidate if necessary, and secure corroborating evidence that can be revealed without violating a promise.

On the other side, the investigation may be completed successfully and it will be the pleasure of the investigator to reduce his information to a form for review by the appointing or recommending authority. Different methods are available to him, depending upon the choice of his agency.

The Written Report

Most departments require that the background investigation report be submitted in writing. It is helpful if there is a standardized format or outline that can be adhered to for the sake of uniformity. One example of an outline will be found in Appendix III.

The part of a background investigation report that is usually of the greatest value to a department head is that part wherein the personality, character and reputation of the candidate is described in brief summary form. It is recommended that this summary be placed at either the beginning or the end of the written document.

The summary should include the most important positive and negative characteristics that have been learned by the investigator. The report should end with the investigator's recommendation concerning employment and should be positive, negative, or indicate the need for additional processing before a decision can be reached.

WHO SHOULD MAKE THE FINAL DECISION?

The future of a human being will be decided each time a final decision is made as to the employability of a man in the police service. In the dynamic atmosphere of our times it is also possible that an individual decision may affect the standing of the agency in its relationship to the entire community it serves. Each decision is important, therefore, and consideration should be given to the possibility that it is sufficiently important to justify a review by more than one individual.

The review of the investigator's report and recommendation is most easily assigned to the Chief or another high-ranking official. It is simply assigned also to a departmental Personnel Officer, a Division Commander, or to a Joint Staff Review Board.

Some departments believe that the decision is so important

that it deserves an assist from several persons representing each echelon of the organization. Concurrences and non-concurrences are reduced to writing for top staff review.

The question as to who should make the final decision can be debated in many ways. The position taken by most competent police administrators is that the decision should be made by the Chief, or department head, with advice from at least one reviewer between the investigator and himself. This view is based upon the assumption that the department head may suffer the loss of his job if the hiring of inferior personnel results in improper, dishonest or inefficient police performance in the community. It is a valid position supported by many examples in fact. Another point of view is that every new member of a law enforcement organization should recognize from the moment of his appointment that he owes his tenure to the office of the Chief and that continuance in his job will be dependent upon his performance satisfying the head of the agency.

This debate can raise controversial issues also. An objection to the power of decision being placed in the office of the department head is that it will permit politics and favoritism to be practiced. In some communities, some groups state that bias, prejudice and unfair employment practices are fostered by this placement of power.

In the author's view, the power of decision should lie with the Chief or department head, subject to review in any contested case by the chief administrative officer of the local government.

PROBLEMS IN RELATION TO BACKGROUND INVESTIGATION REPORTS

The most common problem in using the fund of information that can be developed by background investigation is that of applying it to known standards or criteria.

Little or no difficulty arises so far as the basic standards for public employment are concerned. Where a candidate has been convicted of a felony crime as an adult, for example, most reasonable people will agree that he should not be appointed as a police officer. It is in the refined standards that problems begin to develop. Should a man be employed who has been convicted of disorderly conduct? Should the son of a person convicted of a notoriously vicious crime be hired? What should the limit be for the number of times one has been convicted of moving traffic violations? Should the fact that a candidate has been arrested by warrant on four different occasions for failing to post bail on parking citations be considered a disqualifying factor?

In the field of moral standards the criteria becomes increasingly more difficult to define. Whose moral standards should apply? When does "social drinking" become "alcoholism"? Does the fact that a candidate successfully defended himself in a paternity suit while suffering a loss in reputation render him unsuited for the service? Does the fact that he is known to often participate in "high stake" poker games with friends in private homes make him any more or less employable than the individual who appears to be addicted to "low stake" games of chance in legally established public parlors? How many divorces is the limit? The classic answer to most of these questions will vary according to the culture of the community in which it is asked. And it will vary in the same community depending upon the time that it is asked. This is no answer, but it emphasizes one of the hazards in attempting to establish standards that will be acceptable to the informed and interested leadership in any community at any given time.

A third problem is found in the mobile nature of the American population. This has been commented upon as being part of the great American tradition of independence, with fledgling citizens flying from their homes at the earliest possible time and often from one end of the country to the other. This movement about the country makes practically impossible the gathering of reliable information by personal interview. It also increases considerably the number of persons and agencies that must be contacted through correspondence. It removes the possibility of the background investigator having the benefit of "accidentally" getting information that occurs frequently during the course of personal contact. It provides an opportunity for the concealment of facts and the fraudulent misrepresentation of incidents in the life of an applicant. Although local residence as a qualification for police employment is being widely eliminated throughout the United States, there are some who point to its value in simplifying the problem of background investigation.*

A fourth problem grows out of that discussed in the preceding paragraph. A mobile population results in many cultural transplantations. Subtle and unconscious influences may be at work when investigators are developing information on candidates who speak with different accents, have a noticebly different physical appearance, or dress in clothing that is common in another part of the country but significantly different from that worn by local young men. A newcomer's customs, attitudes and social values may differ sharply from those of local residents. Although qualified in appearance, intelligence, education and experience, a candidate may be disqualified on the basis of too great a number of variations from accepted local norms. A reverse influence may also be true. One field of human error lies in the tendency to over-rate those who come from a distant place in preference to those persons raised in the familiar environment around us.

The major problem is evaluating the results of the background investigation lies in relating it to the standards of the agency. Despite the considerable amount of attention that has been given to the field of personnel selection for the police service, it is the exception rather than the rule to find a precise statement listing the criteria that will be used to disqualify men for further consideration for appointment. Many departments have such lists but the ones the author has examined have been primarily limited to the most obvious disqualifications, such as:

1. Conviction of a felony;
2. Conviction of a specific number of moving traffic violations within a recent one, two or three year period;
3. Dishonorable discharge from the Armed Forces;

---

*Editor's note: In this instance the desire to broaden the recruitment base comes into conflict with the desire to recruit from a population whose background can easily be learned. While the trend in the United States is to increase recruitment from non-local sources, other nations are much more restrictive. Some of the Swiss cantons not only require local residence from the applicant but demand that his family have resided in the region for two or three generations. This reflects the emphasis on continuing good citizenship by all members of a family over the generations as a condition for being selected. It also implies a belief in hereditary as well as environmental influences in determining conduct.

4. Conviction of a crime involving moral turpitude.

It should be obvious that there is considerable opportunity for research into this question of standards.

CONCLUSION

The background investigation is a necessary and important tool in the field of police personnel selection. As a process it has some imperfections, the most obvious of which are those that are dependent upon the exercise of subjective judgments by investigators, supervisors and the decision makers of the employing agency. If it will be accepted that all judgments are to be made in favor of the department, the community and the people who will be served by the police, the process will be a valuable tool in providing men of good character for the police service. Finally, there is much room for research in this field. One of the most important developments will be the production of a set of written standards that can be applied in evaluating the background and personal history of those interested in police employment. When developed, it should assist the police to even further refine their dedicated interest in the exercise of fair employment practices in this professional field.

BIBLIOGRAPHY

1. Coppock, Robert W., and Barbara Brattin: *How to recruit and Select Policemen and Firemen.* Chicago, Public Personnel Association, Personnel Report No. 581, 1958.
2. Germann, A. C.: *Police Personnel Management.* Springfield, Thomas, 1958.*
3. Holcomb, Richard L.: *Selection of Police Officers.* Iowa City, Bureau of Public Affairs, State University of Iowa, 1946.
4. International City Managers' Association: *Municipal Police Administration.* Fifth Edition, Chicago, International City Manager's Association, 1961.
5. Smith, Bruce: *Police Systems in the United States.* New York, Harper, 1949.
6. Vollmer, August: *The Police and Modern Society.* Berkeley, University of California Press, 1936 (out of print).

---

*Professor Germann presents an exceptionally well organized bibliography in this book, pages 236-245.

Chapter VIII

THE ORAL BOARD

P ROGRESSIVE POLICE OFFICIALS are attempting to solve their recruitment problems realistically. Their task is difficult because there is no real unanimity of opinion among the administrators as to the personal qualities essential to the adequate performance of police duty. The various qualities most often identified as necessary are, at best, opinions developed without the benefit of scientific measurement. There has been little basic research undertaken in the field of police personnel selection. Hence, as important as the police function is to the maintenance of society the procedures employed in the recruitment and selection of law enforcement personnel are still, in large measure, left to uncertain techniques.

The first standards adopted related to physical attributes and the successful completion of a medical examination. As the nature of police service has become more complex attention has been given to the need to consider other qualities of the candidate. Police administrators have become aware of the fact that some assessment must be made of each candidate's mental development, emotional maturity and stability, personal morality and occupational interest. There is considerable evidence to support the thesis that these less tangible qualities are perhaps more significant that the physical attributes. Standards of performance within the service are subject to continuous upgrading. With the advance of performance standards and the extension of specialization attention has been re-directed toward the up-grading of recruitment and selection processes.

The basic obstacle to more effective hiring of police personnel is the present limitation of testing devices and procedures used to screen candidates. Certain qualifications can be measured without difficulty, for example, "height" and "weight." However, other qualities such as "enthusiasm," "judgment," "adaptability," etc., present a real challenge. In addition to measurement testing devices must satisfy the requirements of "validity" and "reliability." The police administrator wants to select candidates who as policemen will exercise competent judgment in the many stressful situations that are common to police work. The problem has been to find a testing device that will prove discrete and will measure adequately the existence and extent of the desired quality. Some police officials question the value of some of the more sophisticated tests being used as psychological measurements. They tend to favor the personal interview approach and base the selection on personal reaction to the candidate. They admit the technique is not "scientific" yet the results are more direct and have been reasonably acceptable.* This expression of trust in the interview process gives support to the use of an "oral board" in personnel selection.

Many police and personnel administrators consider the oral interview particularly suitable to the selection of law enforcement officers. There are a number of reasons for this belief. Historically, the employment interview is undoubtedly the oldest selection device known to man. It is not difficult to imagine interrogation of job seekers by employers long before there are any formalized evaluation of applicants and their capacities. In a number of personnel selection systems the practice of questioning applicants and observing them in an interview situation is the most important phase of the screening process. In many other systems the oral interview is considered a valuable addition to a series of more formal testing devices.

Before considering the oral interview in detail and its relation to other screening devices it is important to review the objectives of an employment examination. An examination conducted to select police recruits should accomplish three basic goals:

1. The examination should test the qualifications of each candidate with respect to predetermined standards that have been established,
2. The examination should provide some measure of the potential capacity for growth and effectiveness in the service for each successful candidate, and
3. The examination should provide a means of ranking the various candidates as to their qualifications.

---

*This argument is only valid in a small department.

Obviously there are many candidates who, by every available standard or requirement, as imprecise as the standard may be, will possess acceptable qualities justifying their hire. The question remains, "Will they perform well during their long career as law enforcement officers?" It is not enough that applicants possess the requisite physical, mental, emotional and moral capacities for the job. The good candidate must also be motivated by a desire to perform adequately that will extend over his career even when confronted with frustrations that tend to over shadow job satisfactions.

Whereas the first two goals mentioned above related to the candidate and the job the third goal is a mechanical factor that is introduced solely to provide an orderly means of presenting candidates to the department administrator for appointment. This consideration arises due to the competitive aspect of the examination process within the philosophic framework of American civil service. It is reasonable to assume that some difference in potential will exist between the several candidates in a group. Ranking the successful candidates on the basis of test scores is a crude attempt to indicate relative capacities. Under the many limitations of personnel testing the ranking device is a more adequate measure of present capacity than it is of future potential for police service. The reduction of test scores to one numerical value for the purpose of ranking candidates tends to reduce the significance of the individual test measurements. Attempts have been made to counter this defect by weighting various test measurements in order of importance in job performance.

Intelligent personnel administrators are well aware of the problems associated with the assessment of men in relation to specific jobs. The direction of our efforts and the course of action we must pursue is clear. This fact is well documented in the several chapters of this book as well as in many of the references identified in the bibliography.

All authorities are in agreement that the examination and associated procedures used in the selection of men for law enforcement should be:

1. Valid,
2. Reliable,

3. Politically and socially acceptable,
4. Free from arbitrary manipulation,
5. Relatively simple to administer,
6. Inexpensive to conduct and evaluate, and
7. Possessed of a host of other "practical" virtues.

This is not to say that the field of law enforcement is totally lacking in requirements, standards, or testing devices which will measure applicants with reference to those standards. Many of these requirements and standards have been determined subjectively yet experience indicates that they have considerable demonstrated merit. For example, there is the general awareness that physical condition is an important factor in police performance. Most police executives and the public generally are of the belief that physical standards must be high. Thus, more attention is now given to the relationship of weight to height, superior motor coordination, freedom from potentially disabling defects and similar physical qualities. Devices to test these qualities are readily available everywhere. For another example consider the matter of police intelligence. We find broad acceptance of the proposition that law enforcement officers should be of above average intelligence if they are to function adequately. True the question of "how much" above is still being debated professionally but instruments are available which will tell us how intelligent a given applicant may be. However, a definite sense of uncertainty is felt when we move onward into the less well developed areas of personality and its testing.

It is certain that most police administrators will agree that a suitable police officer candidate will be characterized by such qualities as alertness, enthusiasm, loyalty; that he will possess a agree that no completely valid written tests have been found to measure the quality and quantity of each of these characteristics present in a given applicant. Of course research in these matters continues briskly. There has been some notable work done in high degree of initiative, resourcefulness, self confidence and that he will have some understanding of what he will be undertaking in order to avoid future discouragement and disappointment. Almost universally, observers of the field of personnel management isolating such personality characteristics as aggressiveness, dominance and recessiveness. The implications of this and similar research are still not clearly understood by police officials although this material might be useful in police personnel selection.

It is because of the "uncertain" elements in the above described testing methods that persons hiring police officers have turned to the oral interview. There is a substantial feeling that "experienced men" will be able to distinguish between those applicants who may or may not have the qualities which will make them successful policemen. The feeling persists that we are dealing with a situation in which the criteria for successful police performance are not clearly defined and where testing methods are not perfect.

Some justification for this point of view may be found in the fact that many men of good qualities have been selected for employment without formal testing procedures. Frequently these men have been hired solely on the basis of an oral interview. Yet serious doubts exist about the values of the interviewing technique. Ordway and O'Brien[1] comment;

> "The oral process has been open to criticism because of the nature of the personality factors, if any, utilized; the kind of evidence, if any, adduced; and the subjectivity of the standards, if any, employed in rating."

And Stahl[2] notes in his text:

> "The oral test has long served as a basic selection tool in private employment but has been more slowly accepted in the public field. This conservatism arises out of three considerations: (1) the difficulty of developing valid and reliable oral tests; (2) the difficulty of securing a reviewable record on an oral test, and (3) public suspicion of the oral as a channel for the exertion of political influence through the destruction of anonymity."

This observation by Stahl opens two topics for discussion. The first is the distinction between "private" and "public" employment. The second topic concerns the safeguards that seem necessary and which create such concern in the personnel selection practices for public employment. In differentiating between private and public employment we recognize that all employment involves a contractual relationship between an employer and a worker. If the employer is engaged in private enterprise a worker involved with him would be in private employment. If the employer is a governmental or "public" agency then the worker might be said to be in public employment. In either case employment occurs when there is work to be done and when, generally, the employer is satisfied that an applicant can do the required tasks. In neither case does an applicant have any inherent "right" to a position except as provided by law, rule or contract. The fact that public employment is supported by public funds does not alter this premise in any way.

Despite the fact that applicants for employment have no special "rights" to a position in either public or private employment there are some real differences in the respective situations. Essentially in private employment the relationship between the employer and the applicants are private ones without a competitive aspect. However, applicants in the public service are competing against others and they are entitled to assurance that their competitive position is safeguarded. In public employment, as found in the formalized civil service or merit systems at least, there are more limitations and restrictions in the selection of personnel than are found in private employment. Many of these restrictions are imposed for the purpose of maintaining equality of opportunity for the respective candidates.

Because of the criticisms noted by Stahl and other competent observers there are many who would prohibit, eliminate or restrict the use of the oral interview in the personnel selection process in law enforcement. But the use of the oral interview as an integral part of the selection procedure in the police service has produced some significant successes, imperfect though the system may be. It is the personal observation of many police officials that obvious misfits who have survived the "objective" portions of entrance examinations have, on numberless occasions, been detected and "washed out" by oral interviews. It is true there are, at present, grave limitations on the oral interview procedure. Substantial differences of opinions exist among professionals about given candidates following a series of interviews. A specially chosen oral interview board of competent police officers did approve applicants who, in the opinions of others, seem to have serious defects of psychological or psychiatric natures.

Despite the limitations of the interview techniques it has some advantages which are unique. For example there is an aspect of law enforcement which is, in a word, physical. No amount of data, no matter how precise, can convey to an employer the sense of "presence" which characterizes the applicant. In the interview this quality is identifiable rather easily. Further, the interview provides a real opportunity to tie together the separate tests and examinations which, taken together, constitute the employment process. Correctly used the interview is a device for clarifying or verifying the unanswered questions and inferences which arise in the other phases of the testing activity. This can be done in no other way. Our choice therefore does not appear to be whether or not the oral interview shall be used as a part of the selection process in the law enforcement but rather, how can it be improved so as to be a more effective instrument in the employment of potentially competent and effective peace officers.

THE ORAL INTERVIEW BOARD

In personnel management the term "oral interview" is used in a number of differing contexts. It may be used to informally screen applicants for positions exempt from civil service or a merit system or for special assignment within a class or grade. It is also used in a variety of ways in the examination of candidates for promotion from grade to grade. For the purpose of the discussion here the term "oral interview" describes the situation in which the applicant formally faces an interviewer or interviewers or when he participates as a member of a group of applicants under observation. The purpose of the interview is to provide an opportunity for the applicant to present his case and to enable the interviewer to observe and question him.

In private employment, the most common practice is to have most, if not all, applicants for technical, clerical and similar positions interviewed by a single "interviewer." In the larger companies, and in many progressive smaller ones, this interviewer is a professional personnel management employee who has special skills in this exacting work. More often than not this technician is a college graduate in psychology or personnel management. He brings to the interview situation the particular knowledge and skills which, it is hoped, will produce the best possible results.

In public employment, the situation is usually quite different. In order to eliminate or minimize the criticisms mentioned earlier every effort is directed toward making the oral interview process as "fair" as possible. The one significant development designed to make the interview more acceptable in public personnel practice is to have the applicant observed and heard by a number of interviewers. The several interviewers generally sit together and as a group constitute what is commonly known as an "Oral Board" or an "Oral Interview Board." The candidate is then presented to the group and the formal interviewing follows. It is with this form of the "oral interview" that this chapter is concerned.

It should be recognized at the outset that the meeting of an oral board to interview applicant for positions in law enforcement is but one part of a competent oral interview procedure. The interviewers on a board have key roles in the success of the system. However there is another key figure known as the "examiner" or "personnel technician." In the paragraphs that follow the term "examiner" will appear frequently and his relationship to the oral interview system and to the interviewers must be clearly understood.

Basically there are two essential parts of a competent oral interview procedure in law enforcement. The two parts are (1) a program, and (2) the interviewers. The examiner has the great responsibility of providing the program. It is his task to assure that this program is adequately prepared, competently implemented and meaningfully interpreted. Usually but not always the examiner is or should be a professional personnel man. Regardless, the responsibilities must be met if the oral interview system is to be a success.

The second part of the oral interview process is the interviewer. It is the responsibility of law enforcement officers assigned to this duty to so conduct themselves in the interview situation that the greatest possible benefit will accrue to the police service. This requires a high degree of competent and close attention. It is clear that there must be a close working relationship between examiners and interviewers if the oral interview procedure is going to improve as a personnel selection technique. It is the unanimous opinion of the civil service personnel and the law enforcement officers who worked with Dr. Blum in his studies that such a relationship could and would lead to exciting new concepts of the oral interview in law enforcement.

A successful oral board interview is the direct result of program planning. Whatever failures and lack of effectiveness we find in the oral board procedure can be traced to gross underplanning. It appears quite frequently that the person responsible for the oral interviewing of police candidates is not aware of the needs of the service. He makes no demands upon the interviewers except that they be available on the desired date. The only test for a reporting form is that it be capable of reproduction without difficulty. This kind of preparation may be relatively inexpensive but, in its application, it is not effective.

The first step in planning a program for an oral board is to identify the objectives of the interviewing procedure and commit them to writing. This will focus the attention of everyone concerned upon the basic purposes of the procedure. The goals of the test must be described in such a way that all the interviewing is directed toward the accomplishment of the desired ends. The orientation of oral interviews towards specific goals will enable us to make intelligent evaluations of the results. Not only will we see the results of a given board operation but, in addition, we will be able to determine if the long range benefits of this procedure are being achieved.

A good statement of objectives will define and limit the scope of the oral testing. It will directly affect the manner and length of time candidates are questioned and will assist in a more reliable evaluation of their responses. A clear understanding of the purpose of an oral interview will assist in the design of reports to be used in recording results. It will surely be of great assistance to the interviewers by clarifying the role they play on the board. In many ways then, statements of purpose will aid in the production, implementation and evaluations of the oral interviews so that they become more valuable instruments in police personnel selection.

After establishing his objectives the examiner must identify the specific traits which he wishes the testing to cover. Authorities almost unanimously agree that the oral interview technique should not be used to test personal qualities and attributes which can be examined in some other, more objective fashion. It is at this point that an examiner will find himself on unfamiliar ground. He will find little authoritative documentation about the personal qualities needed for successful performance in law enforcement. For example the question of how "aggressive" or how "authoritarian" a policeman must or must not be has never been resolved. Indeed all we know is there must be an enormous amount of research work done in police personnel management before this kind of question can be answered.

Despite the uncertainty about the specific traits to be sought out by the oral board there is a feeling among police executives that appropriate traits can be identified in oral interviews. In Blum's[3] study the members of an oral board commented upon the characteristics they noted in the applicants they passed or failed. In describing these characteristics the board identified successful candidates with such things as:

"Good appearance, able to speak up, forceful, able to fit into discipline, capable of being trained, sincere, flexible, uses good English, energetic, mature, sustained interest in personal advancement, genuine interest in becoming a peace officer, stability, wholesome, conscientious, good past experience in police work, good educational background, well adjusted."

Similarly a wide range of negative characteristics were noted in the candidates who were failed by the board. Admittedly these are opinions but they are considered opinions. The officers who gave them are police commanders with considerable training and many years of experience. The opinions were based upon lengthy and perceptive interviewing of the applicants. It is reasonable therefore, to assume these opinions have considerable merit. Obviously before we can positively identify a potentially successful candidate there will have to be more precise definitions of the required traits. Perhaps this will come from similar studies and other experimentation.

The examiner's next step should be to identify the topics of discussion which should be explored in the interview. The chosen areas, if properly explored by the interviewers, should cause the candidate to give responses which can be interpreted in terms of his character, his life experience, and his chances for success in police work. To some examiners this may seem to be needless preparation and to some interviewers, excessive regimentation. Nevertheless a planned effort to elicit significant responses from the candidates will be more productive than any unplanned activity. The more common areas of interviewing include education, previous work experience, military experience, civic and social activities and similar topics. This is not to say that interviewers should have no latitude for exploring avenues which open during discussions. Quite to the contrary, experienced interviewers should operate flexibly in their questioning. The course suggested here is a device for keeping the questioning within fruitful areas, keeping in mind the limited available time for each interview.

The next consideration in the program planning is how to record and report the evaluations of the interviewers. Unlike other portions of the entrance examination procedure the end product of the oral interview is not produced by the candidate. This report rather is the personal analysis of an observer about a candidate based upon what that candidate said and did in the observer's presence. The construction of any kind of a formalized report presents great difficulty to an examiner because of the amount of material which can be covered in even a short interview.

The usual report of an interview includes a listing of the personality traits or other factors which the examiner wants to know about the applicants. Opposite each factor there is usually a scale of values. These values give the interviewer a convenient way to report his opinions about the subject. At the present state of development of the oral interview procedure in police work, the traits listed will range widely. Such simple ones as "Appearance" will be frequently found together with such ones as "Ability to organize work." Even in the case of the first trait the interviewer can comment only on the basis of one meeting with the candidate. An intelligent comment about the second is almost impossible since such a characteristic is difficult to evaluate correctly even when the subject is under observation for long periods of time. As further research mentioned above is undertaken more positive assertion can be made about the traits which the interviewers should seek in an applicant. On the basis of the discussion in Blum's[3,6] studies, it appears that such positive characteristics as appearance, forcefulness, sincerity, flexibility, language usage and habits, wholesomeness, stability, and others did impress the oral board members. Conversely, board members were impressed by such negative traits as selfishness, introversion, untruthfulness, passiveness, hesitancy, egotism and more of like character. Obviously not all traits can be described in any one report and there is question that any should be listed. Until that time when a more stable and generalized listing can be provided, each examiner must identify those qualities which he and his police chief feel to be most important for their department's use.

Perhaps even more troublesome is the problem of "scoring" the results of the interview. As pointed out above there is usually a scale of values opposite each listed trait or characteristic. The scales range from simple "pass-fail" or "suitable-not suitable" to systems in which final grades are given in terms of hundredths of one per cent. An attempt has been made to avoid the "grading" aspect by the use of descriptive phrases associated with the trait under consideration. These phrases presumably give the interviewer a convenient way to identify the response of the subject.

It must be borne in mind that the human personality is so complex that it is not possible to produce any "pure," "positive" results or score from an interview. It is difficult to isolate a single trait and describe it much less to give it numeric value. It is significant that in other professions results of similar interviews are consistently reported in narrative form rather than in numbers. This is so because many physical, mental and emotional states cannot be described except by descriptive words and phrases. In such cases a continuing series of observations are recorded until the practitioner arrives at a conclusion. At this point the professional may give an opinion and this is recorded for what it is - an opinion, no more, no less. Yet for a variety of reasons it seems necessary in public employment that the observations of the interviewers be reduced to some numerical value no matter how inappropriate this action may be. Principally this is done to satisfy the need to "rank" groups of applicants. Ranking by examination is considered the "fair" way to ensure equality of opportunity in public employment. Since this is most often done by the assigning of "grades" it follows that this must be done in oral interviews in order that the grading of the respective parts of an entrance examination will be compatible. Because of this obligation and because of the limitations described there has been produced a wide variety of forms, reports, charts, listings and other instruments designed to record the opinions of the interviewer. To date no one form has demonstrated remarkable superiority over another.

The discussion of scoring raises the point of standards. It is exceedingly important that the examiner establish firm standards against which the given factor is to be graded. It is commonly observed that, in the absence of specific instructions and frequently even when instructions are quite precise, individual interviewers will judge a response of a subject quite differently. Thus a response to a question concerning intra-unit loyalty is subject to several interpretations each dependent upon the inclinations of the respective interviewers. In many of these cases the difference is attributable to the several standards existing among the interviewers. Generally the greater the homogeneity of the interviewing group the more likely that the standards used will be similar. In the final analysis however, it is the responsibility of the examiner to define the terms and set the criteria against which the candidates are to be judged.

In addition to designating the standards for the various factors in the interview the examiner must establish a pass-fail point. The examiner must also determine whether or not non-acceptability in one factor constitutes grounds for complete rejection of the applicant. The determination of a pass-fail point is never simple and requires the complex balancing of multiple criteria. In some cases the point is more easily identified. For example any untruthfulness during an interview would certainly constitute grounds for rejection. But at what point, for example, does withdrawn or taciturn behavior render a man unfit for service in a particular department? It is apparent that as the examiner prepares his oral interview program there must be many consultations with the affected law enforcement agency.

The discussion of "non-acceptability" raises several questions which indicate a need for more research in the matter of grading interviews. In a system based upon or identified with a numerical scoring system it is possible for an applicant to be rated below passing in one factor but still have an acceptable "average" score. It seems more logical and valid that non-acceptability in any one factor ought to be cause for complete rejection of the candidate. It would appear then that the scoring of individual factors is unnecessary except as a guide to the individual interviewer. In those systems where the oral interview "scores" are used to rank applicants it is usually the average or composite score which is used to compute the final entrance examination results. Perhaps in the final analysis we are wasting time attempting to isolate and score a variety of traits. Research may eventually indicate that the best that can be said of a candidate is that he is, in the opinion of a given interviewer, "Eminently Qualified," "Well Qualified," "Qualified" or "Not Qualified." There is perhaps a case for this point of view at present. Most personnel technicians are in agreement that it is impossible to grade human attributes even grossly but we do so to conform to an existing system. Perhaps we should be looking forward to changing the basis on which "fairness" is established in public employment.

Finally the examiner must make certain that all the interviewers understand the importance of using approximately the same numerical values in scoring candidates. It is possible for one oral board member to materially affect the ranking of candidates by using abnormally high or low scores or by using a range of scores substantially different than his fellow board members. This becomes a part of the preparation of the interviewing program and is essential to the maintenance of uniformity.

We come now to the other essential element in the oral interview process. It is very important that qualified interviewers be assigned to service on oral boards. It will be of little avail to carefully prepare a good interviewing program only to have it undone by incompetent interviewing. It is difficult to understand why so much inexpert employment interviewing is accepted in law enforcement hiring practice in view of the great respect held for competent interrogation and interviewing in our other police activities.

No doubt part of the difficulty is based upon a lack of understanding on the part of executives who are responsible for the assignment of police personnel to oral interview boards. All too frequently such assignments are made on the basis of "availability" of officers at a given time without much regard for their interviewing competence. It is all too frequently presumed that because an assigned officer is a policeman he is, therefore, a competent interviewer. What has not been clearly understood is that employment interviewing is an activity calling for particular skills of the highest order. In a American Management Association study Mandell[4] states:

> "The (employment) interviewer has one of the most complex of all jobs. He needs some knowledge of psychology; he should have a thorough and up-to-date knowledge of job requirements in general and those of his organization in particular; and he must be able to relate these factors to the problem at hand and so project the behavior of the applicant. And he must base his difficult task upon the inadequate information obtained in an artificial situation: the interview."

Samuel Ordway[5] also recognized the problem when he observed:

> "The effectiveness of the oral test depends in great part on the skill of the examiners (interviewers). Thus, the examiner should possess considerable aptitude for his work before he is selected to serve as a member of an examining board. Skill in the procedure of the interview, however, may be acquired and perfected through training."

It is suggested here that responsible police departments and other agencies in the field of police personnel management jointly establish minimum standards for qualification as an interviewer or as a member of a police oral board. Perhaps one of the requirements would be some minimal educational preparation in psychology and employment interviewing. Another interesting approach might be the establishment of an appropriate "apprenticeship." Thus an officer desiring to qualify as an interviewer or oral board member would be required to sit through a number of interviewing sessions solely as a student observer. He would not participate in the interviewing. He could question board members or discuss problems with them between interviews or following the close of the session. After such orientation, perhaps the student interviewer could sit on a number of boards as a "junior" member until he has demonstrated that he was properly qualified. Only then would he be considered a full fledged board member or oral interviewer. An apprenticeship such as this would substantially upgrade the performance of oral interview boards in the police service. In view of the important relationship between oral board performance and the selection of recruits in law enforcement this would be an important step forward in police personnel management.

When the examiner comes to the point of creating an oral board to interview candidates for police service he is faced with the problem of selecting board members. Two questions arise. First, should the composition of the board be limited to police officers or should it include laymen? Second, should the board be limited to members of the police agency for which the candidates are being chosen or should it include persons from other jurisdictions. Both questions avoid the basic problem.

One of the criticisms of the oral board noted earlier is that it is subject to manipulation. The examiner must therefore create an interview situation which is as objective and unbiased as possible. A close examination of this situation reveals that the solution is not where the interviewers come from but rather the degree of their competence. Thus if a police department has capable interviewers on its staff it may be more effective to use their services. Presumably they would be most competent to evaluate applicants in terms of the needs of the service. If, on the other hand, police interviewers with the necessary skills are not readily available it may be necessary to use laymen. A competent layman would be a better board member than an incompetent or possibly even just an inexperienced police officer. It can be said then that the composition of an oral interview board must logically depend on where competent interviewers can be found, within or without the law enforcement agency.

The next step following the selection of board members is the "briefing" session for the interviewing group. At this point the examiner and interviewers meet for the purpose of clarifying the "ground rules" about the forthcoming interviewing session or sessions. The briefing is held primarily to ensure that the several interviewers have a common understanding about the purpose, scope and limitations of the oral interview procedure in which they are to participate. Here too is an opportunity to clarify any misunderstandings or to resolve any questions about the content and value systems which are a part of the program. This is the time when scoring is discussed and a semblance of uniformity is reached.

Ideally, the meeting between the examiner and the interviewers should take place well in advance of the oral board session itself. In practice, it is most often done in the few minutes between the arrival of the last interviewer at the scene of the interview and the appearance of the first applicant to be interviewed. This perfunctory orientation of interviewers to the examiner's program cannot provide the kind of understanding needed to ensure a successful oral examination. Even when the program material has previously been studied by the interviewers an hour is probably the minimum time to prepare. In some cases the preparation may take even longer. Nevertheless, only this studied approach to the interviewing sessions can produce the maximum benefits which can be obtained from oral interviewing.

No attempt is made in this chapter to describe the actual interview procedure. There is ample literature describing the most appropriate physical settings for the conducting of oral boards and an extensive literature on the techniques of interviewing. A bibliography listing suitable texts in these matters will be found at the end of the chapter. There are however a number of points which merit out attention in the actual conducting of interviews involving applicants for positions in police work.

The members of the oral board described in Blum's studies[3,6] are unanimously agreed that the most valuable asset to the interviewing process were the "background investigations" which were made on each applicant who was scheduled to appear before the board. Significant leads for depth interviewing were found in other documents such as the application and test results. But more and better information upon which to base questions was found in the investigation reports. The statements of neighbors, employers, teachers, tradesmen and others provided clues to behavior of the applicants which were not to be found otherwise. The conclusion of the board members is that such investigation should be made on all applicants to be interviewed by an oral board even though such investigations are expensive and oftentimes difficult to make.

Another point concerns one aspect of the physical appearance of candidates as they faced a board. Just as interviewers become accustomed to the interview situation so too may interviewees! An oral interview is apt to be an unnerving experience for a candidate who has never been before a board. On the other hand a candidate who has appeared before several boards may display a coolness and emotional control as a result of his experience. Board members must weigh "symptoms" of distress carefully having due regard for the applicants age, background and employment experience.

Finally there is great caution which must be used in phrasing questions directed to the applicants. The use of "loaded," "leading" or "stress" questions should be avoided. Questions which by their nature elicit incorrect or invalid answers from the candidates thus giving the interviewer an opportunity to place them in a defensive position serve no useful purpose. Questions which have no acceptable answers or those which are beyond the applicants knowledge or experience are also unsuitable. And questions which call for a candidate's statement of what he "would do" under certain circumstances are not acceptable. Generally questioning of candidates should be directed toward the determination of facts. The interview is a place to enlarge upon information which is presently available about the applicant, to clarify doubtful information and to seek out new information. The board must concern itself with facts not suppositions.

At the conclusion of each oral interview session there is an opportunity to engage in some interesting and productive study of the oral interview process. This can be done by a "debriefing" or critique. It seems certain that if each oral interview session were examined critically and in depth immediately upon its completion much could be gained. Among the facets of the procedure which could be examined are: the success or failure of the session to meet the objectives, whether or not the traits sought were identified; how suitable the value systems were and how well the scoring met the needs of the program, and finally what strengths and weaknesses were disclosed in the interviewing techniques. When time is taken objectively to assess individual oral board sessions then such sessions will improve in quality.

These then are the basic ingredients for a successful oral board procedure. (1) The program material should be set down formally in writing to the greatest extent possible. It is particularly important that program materials be readily available for the oral board members. The examiner should be able to provide each board member with a written program consisting of not less than: (a) a statement of objectives of the proposed interviewing procedure; (b) an exact identification of the attitudes, traits, knowledge, skill and other characteristics which the examiner wants considered and evaluated; (c) a definition of the terms used; (d) the criteria, standard or values which will be applied in the consideration and evaluation of the qualities, and finally (e) a description of the scoring system to be used in reporting the evaluactions of the interviewer. This basic material should be distributed to the board members several days before the scheduled interviews for their study.

(2) The successful oral board procedure is a product of the interviewers. It requires a high degree of knowledge and skill in order effectively to implement the interview procedure. It is important therefore that we seek a substantial measure of competence in the members of oral boards who propose to evaluate the candidates for service in law enforcement.

The place of the oral interview generally and the oral interview board specifically in the selection of police officer candidates is assured. Experience has clearly shown that the oral interview is an important and meaningful device in screening men. It may be, in fact, the best instrument we now possess to do our selection job.

Present literature concludes that no "objective" testing process or device existing today will demonstrate the presence of certain desirable qualities in police candidates. We are confident that the value of interviewing will be more extensively developed as time goes by.

It is hoped that the foregoing discussion will have focused the attention of the reader upon the immediate necessity for further research and documentation in the use of the oral interview in law enforcement personnel selection. It will be through the orderly process of study that this useful technique will be made more valid and of greater reliability.

BIBLIOGRAPHY

1. Ordway, S. H., Jr., and O'Brien, J. C.: An Approach to More Objective Oral Tests. Pamphlet No. 2, Society for Personnel Administration, Washington D. C., 1939.
2. Stahl, O. G.: *Public Personnel Administration.* New York, Harper Brothers (4th Ed.) 1956.
3. Blum, R. H., Goggin, W., and Whitmore, E. J.: A study in deputy sheriff selection procedures. *Police, 6:2* pp. 59-63, 1961. (See also the full mimeographed report of this study) .
4. Mandell, M. M.: The Employment Interview. American Management Association, Research Study No. 47.
5. Committee on Oral Tests in Public Personnel Selection, Samuel H. Ordway, Jr. Chairman: Oral Tests in Public Personnel Selection; A Report Submitted to the Civil Service Assembly. Civil Service Assembly of the United States and Canada, Chicago, 1943.
6. Blum, R. H., *et al*: A further study of deputy sheriff selection procedures. *Police, 6:4* pp. 77-79, 1962. (See also the full mimeographed report of this study) .

Supplemental Bibliography

Batson, Eleanor R., et al: *Municipal Personnel Administration.* (6th Ed.) International City Managers' Association, Chicago, 1960.

Bingham, Walter V.: Oral Examinations in Civil Service. Pamphlet No. 13, Civil Service Assembly of the United States and Canada, Chicago, 1939.

Drake, Francis S.: Manual of Employment Interviewing. Research Report No. 9, American Management Association.

Hagerty, Phillip E.: The Placement Interview. Personnel Brief No. 18, Public Personnel Association.

Jacobs, David L. G.: Employment Interviews. *Traffic Digest and Review, 7:4,* July 59.

Kahn, Robert L., and Cannell, Charles F.: *The Dynamics of Interviewing.* New York, John Wiley and Sons, Inc., 1957.

Kephart, Newell C.: *The Employment Interview in Industry.* New York, McGraw-Hill Book Co., 1952.

Lev, J.: Validating selection procedures for interviewers and claims adjusters. *Public Personnel Review, 18:*p. 232, 1957.

Mandell, Milton M.: The Employment Interview. Research Study No. 47, American Management Association, 1961.

Mandell, Milton M.: Employment Interviewing Personnel Methods Series No. 5., U.S. Civil Service Commission, Washington, D.C., 1956.

Mosher, Wm. E., Kingsley, J. Donald, and Stahl, O. Glenn: *Public Personnel Administration.* New York, Harper and Bros, 1950.

Webster, E. C.: Decision making in employment interviews. *Personnel Administration, 22:*pg. 15, 1959.

Chapter IX

SELECTION FOR WHAT? —
THE LONG RANGE GOALS

T HE RECRUITMENT and selection of qualified personnel is not the final goal of police administration. These activities, as important as they are, constitute only the beginning step in the long movement toward the accomplishment of the total law enforcement responsibility. The principal goal of law enforcement, which is barely discernible on the horizon, is the attainment of a satisfactory level of public freedom and security through the cooperation and mutual respect of the public on the one hand and the law enforcement officers on the other hand. A civil Utopia will have been realized when the police service, by competent guidance and direction based upon fair and impartial application of the law, will be accepted by the citizen who is in turn motivated by a sincere sense of personal responsibility and judicious concern for the rights of his neighbor. This objective may seem beyond expectation yet no barrier stands in the way except the selfish indulgence of individuals within our society. The police and the public must work collectively toward an orderly transition of society by the exercise of patience, understanding and self-restraint. The individual citizen will dictate the rate of progress by his demonstration of readiness to accept his measure of personal and social responsibility that is the concomitant of his freedom.

MINIMUM STANDARDS IN SELECTION

In the meantime the police administrator must employ personnel to provide public services on the day-to-day basis. At the same time he must build an organization that will facilitate movement toward the Utopian objective. Each of the foregoing obligations require the selection of the best qualified applicants that are available to the department. The preceeding chapters contain a summation of the principal selection devices that are used by law enforcement agencies. No attempt has been made to define the minimum qualifications of an officer. It is doubtful that any single statement of basic standards would satisfy law enforcement services throughout this country due to the vast differences that exist between individual agencies with respect to size, functional responsibility, leadership, local history and customs, economic status of the community, the situation in the local labor market, etc. Hence, any specific statement of qualifications will be subject to challenge and with some degree of justification. However, to establish a base of reference the minimum standards described by Frost appears to be reasonable:[1]

> "A police officer should have at the very least an intelligence quotient of 104 if the Otis Quick Scoring Mental Ability Test is used, and 110 if the Army General Qualification Test is employed.... The prospective officer should be a high school graduate or possess the equivalent amount of education and experience.... The candidate must be endowed with a personality which will ensure a healthy mental attitude toward police situations and people of various racial, religious and cultural backgrounds.... The police departments must require that the applicants be between twenty-one and twenty-five years of age.... Police candidates must be subject to and pass rigid physical and medical examinations......These are the absolute minimum which any police agency can safely employ."

This statement of qualifications conforms to standards that are currently in effect in most progressive jurisdictions. There are a number of departments that demand more of their candidates. There are also a large number of law enforcement agencies that are hesitant in the adoption of such minimum standards in the belief that it will limit access to many potential candidates. An objective analysis of the leading law enforcement agencies in the nation will reveal that there has been a consistent and accelerating trend toward higher minimum standards in recruitment and selection.[2]

The great latitude found in entrance requirements prompts consideration of the objectives behind the employment screening process. Police applicants are screened and tested for two basic reasons: (a) to determine whether or not each of the candidates possesses the basic qualification in sufficient degree to indicate probable successful performance of police duty, and (b) to identify candidates that not only qualify for probationary assignment but also evidence a capacity for future development and application as mid-management and top level administrative appointees. The first reason satisfies the present need for manpower —the second reason guarantees future growth in service potential and administrative competence. In making these statements caution must be observed that present testing devices can only measure certain abilities and skills within a limited range of accuracy. The measurement devices are not precise. Further, the testing methods are restricted to an assessment of what the candidate *can do* not what he *will do.* Our testing and evaluation techniques are therefore more accurate with respect to present ability than they are in the forecasting of future performance. Nevertheless, the civil service structure with its recent pronouncements in support of establishing "career services" must recruit in terms of potential life tenure. In the law enforcement service skill and competence in police judgment is intimately related to actual work experience which is itself related to tenure. Thus, the police administrator must take every reasonable step to assure that the recruitment and selection procedures facilitate the induction of persons having both present ability to serve and capacity for future development.

POLICE PROFESSIONALIZATION

The progressive administrator must foster a continuing interest in individual and organizational improvement. This goal has sometimes been discussed in terms of a concerted movement toward police "professionalization." A realistic appraisal of the progress toward "professionalization" will lead to two fundamental questions: (a) What standards or qualifications must be met to justify "professional status?" and (b) What objective would be gained by the achievement of "professional status?" While this topic has been discussed within and without official law enforcement circles no specific answer to these questions has acquired general acceptance at this time. The concensus is in support of the belief that service qualifications and standards should be raised and operational procedures refined to the level that law enforcement representatives would merit and receive the degree of public acceptance that is enjoyed by persons in the established professions of law, medicine, theology, education, etc. Professionalization implies the concurrent existence of other characteristics that must be subject to study and application by law enforcement before true "professional status" will be attained. Among these latter characteristics will be found such elements as: (a) a fund of common knowledge pertinent to the field of endeavor; (b) a code of ethical conduct for the members; (c) a system of internal discipline; (d) individual accountability for professional performance, and (e) freedom of professional movement, etc.

While the authors of this book believe that the status of the individual law enforcement officer will be raised through his own efforts and the conscientious leadership of police administrators they are equally convinced that achievement of true professional identification will be reserved for a select group within law enforcement. There are many factors that point to the logic of this view. For example: the broad scope of police duty; the vast employment of separate, diverse and at times unrelated skills; the intense concentration on high frequency limited action assignments; the restrictions on mobility within the service; the high dependence upon "on-the-job" training in contrast to extensive study in academic and social disciplines; the almost universal inclination to accept a "status quo" philosophy toward current problems; the lack of opportunity to engage in basic research; these are among the more readily recognized elements that have a direct bearing upon the potential acquisition of professional standing. Each of the characteristics mentioned above militate against individual qualification as a professional. A number of these limitations are inherent in the nature of police duties as they are currently performed. The modification of established practices will not be easy and in many instances must await changes in custom, operational techniques and administrative experience. Other characteristics can and must be changed by united effort within the service, the only real barrier being the lack of will and imagination essential to the task. Vollmer, who was perhaps the first vocal advocate of police professionalization stated the case quite simply when he said:[3]

"By establishing a reasonably proficient method of selecting beginners we have made the first step. . . ." "We would most certainly not feel that a man was entitled to practice law or medicine, if he had only passed his entrance examination into college. In a more comparable analogy, you would not expect a man to become a skilled journeyman carpenter, plumber or machinist, when he had only just been selected as an apprentice. Then why should we expect a rookie officer, without required study and training and no other device for measuring his competency except a certain number of years of service, to rate as a member of a profession or even a skilled journeyman in his field?"

Among the many proponents of police professionalization there are differences of opinion as to whom the status should apply. On the one hand are those who proclaim that the label should extend to all sworn personnel employed as full time police officers. The adherents to this concept see professionalization as a socially acceptable mantle that might satisfy their need for a symbol of attainment and, more importantly, serve as a medium to secure economic remuneration in keeping with the professional image. At the opposite end of the spectrum will be found those who believe true professionalization can become a reality but only for a very few. This latter group visualizes the police professional as a person of high academic qualification who by unique circumstance has had the opportunity to engage in a number of major police experiences above and beyond those normally encountered by the average officer. This person would also demonstrate an administrative capacity beyond that required to direct routine police services. In this context police professional status would be very restricted. The advocates of this position are fearful that if less exacting standards are accepted identification as a professional will have no meaning and public recognition of the inadequacy will prove detrimental to all law enforcement. In contrast, the granting of status to a select group of highly qualified persons who can withstand any challenge as to their competence and ability will benefit all of law enforcement.

The practical approach to professionalization seems to lie somewhere between the two extremes stated above. It stands to reason that professional status will not be granted to the rank-

and-file police officer under present standards or on the basis of duties performed. In many police departments, particularly the larger agencies, a member may devote his entire career to the issuance of parking citations, driving a patrol wagon, serving as a desk clerk, performing foot patrol in a particular area, etc. He may never have had occasion to investigate a major crime, testify before the Grand Jury, serve as a training officer, participate in the preparation of a department budget, or function as a member of an examining board. Under present standards a member may only be required to produce evidence of a high school diploma or pass an equivalent test. There is no standard as to the high school subject matter or the course grades that were earned. Once a person has become a member of a law enforcement organization there are few, if any, requirements that he participate in any planned educational program except those offered sporadically by the agency as an inservice training program designed to facilitate department operations. Voluntary engagement in any plan of self-improvement is usually limited to the sterile memorizing of answers to civil service type questions as a direct means of securing promotion. The desire for promotion is stimulated more by the financial rewards than by any conscious concern for the opportunity to advance toward participation in management. Promotion is sought more as an escape from the monotony of routine patrol than it is pursued as a challenge to engage in supervision and administration. These comments may seem to be too severe; however, I suggest that an objective review of the activities of most law enforcement associations will reveal the harsh truth of these observations. The statements are not offered as a condemnation of individual officers or their associations but rather as a means of illustrating the broad chasm that must be bridged before the rank-and-file can expect consideration for professional status.

DEVELOPMENT OF MANAGEMENT PERSONNEL

Perhaps this is the time when those engaged in law enforcement service must accept the fact that all persons on the department payroll are not destined to become professional. This is not to imply that the department roster will be down-graded. Acceptance of the probability that professional status will be reserved to an upper echelon offers the opportunity to advance the concept of developing a valid semi-professional or certificated technician status within law enforcement that would include a larger number of the personnel and still justify recognition. A program based upon this principle has been sponsored by the newly formed Peace Officer Standards and Training Commission of California.[4] Establishment of standards for such a semi-professional or specialist group would not be as difficult or restrictive as those essential to full professional status. Progress in this area will hasten the day when both status groups will become a reality. As mentioned above it is illogical to assume that the lower echelon who are engaged in performing menial routine tasks requiring limited skills will receive public acceptance as qualifying for preferred status. The movement to blanket in all personnel is actually harmful in several important respects;

    (a) It will defeat any reasonable opportunity for professional recognition on the part of those highly qualified police officers who are otherwise entitled to status.

    (b) It will delay the attainment of proper recognition by the skilled technicians in the service.

    (c) It is harmful to over-all morale as it offers to every member the promise of a goal that is actually beyond reach of many of them.

One of the significant oversights associated with law enforcement is the failure of administrations to provide a program designed to develop future mid-management and top level administrators. This lack of recognition of the need actively to train selected members to fill key management positions is a mark of administrative immaturity. Under the influence of current civil service practices law enforcement has been subject to the same short-sighted and indifferent approach to the selection of management personnel as it has experienced in the selection of recruits. Failure to take a more realistic position is excused on the basis that present procedures are followed in the interest of "equal opportunity" or to preserve the "democratic principle." However, when an appointment is to be made to a key management or administrative position the appointing authority is the first to recognize that "equal opportunity" and the "democratic principle" are not adequate criteria for qualification. As a matter of fact these factors are the least important of the many criteria that should be considered. In many jurisdictions the appointing authority seeks contact with the most qualified professional that the community can afford. The public accepts this approach because the individual citizen wants the benefit of competent direction in the vital public services. Of all the branches of public service law enforcement has been the most resistant to lateral entrance into the service particularly at the administrative level. Ironically, the top administrative position in law enforcement is the exact focus of attack and criticism when a department falls into public disfavor. The corrective movement is in the form of removal and replacement of the chief of police. The stability of the rank-and-file can be measured in terms of the number of administrators that have served and passed on to other activities. The quip is sometimes heard at the appointment of a new "chief" that "He's on the way out."

It is unfortunate that some newly appointed administrators tend to accept their position purely as a financial gain that permits some modest exercise of personal privilege within the tolerance of uncertain political support and the whims of departmental cliques. Too few of the new incumbents look upon their own appointment as an opportunity to initiate effective programs that will raise law enforcement to higher prominence. The uneasy tenure of many law enforcement officials is due to the fact that the service as a whole has not developed and established an adequate base of standard operational criteria that will withstand the test of independent objective assessment. The history of the service has shown that changes in policy and procedures are more apt to occur in response to external pressures demanding correction than they are to result from the deliberate conscientious study and evaluation of critical areas initiated by the police service itself.

The development of future police administrators is an essential phase in any long range program to up-grade the service. The developmental program must be orderly and include planned assignments of such nature and duration as to assure the opportunity for the selected member to become involved in basic problems and participate in their solution. Rotation of assignments is not enough. The plan must require individual responsibility for the performance of specific tasks that are subject to measurement and evaluation. The developmental program should also require some independent study and familiarity with the major intellectual disciplines at least to the extent that the administrative trainee will be cognizant of the broad universe of human experience and be able thereby to extract from those fields the facts and postulates that might be applicable to law enforcement in the service of the public. To those who might view this suggestion as being too academic and unnecessary I ask that they carefully review the recent history of the progress in law enforcement services. Current police publications and technical literature offer abundant evidence of the close and growing relation between police skills and achievements in the major sciences. The daily operation of a police department is utterly dependent upon such devices as the radio, teletype, various physical and chemical tests, photography, medical determinations and the law of probability. In recent years a number of law enforcement agencies have found it advisable to organize special units to meet particular service demands. Such fundamental functional units as a "Community Relations Bureau," a "Juvenile Aid Bureau," a "Rehabilitation Division" and a "Public Relations Division" identify administrative attempt to fill a void in police services. The adequate operation of these new units will depend upon the availability of specific information and skills. The solution to many of the problems will rest upon knowledge to be found in such disciplines as anthropology, history, psychology, political science and sociology.

The administrative trainee must be groomed to meet the demands that will face the department tomorrow. To school the member only in reference to the problems of today will emphasize current practices and stunt imaginative growth that is essential in a constantly changing society. One of the principal failings of law enforcement in meeting the current trend in social change has been the identification with the "status quo." While both the law and local custom require the police to enforce conformity with the law as it is, law enforcement agencies have not been denied the right to seek support for proper accommodation and adjustment in the interest of peace and justice during the period of transition. There has not been any significant overt movement toward accommodation and adjustment due to the limited vision manifest by police administrators.

Just as survival and prosperity in business and industry is intimately related to the performance of the managers of tomorrow the success and adequacy of police services will be directly related to the presence and skills of those upon whom the administrator can rely. Progress and efficiency will demand the effective use of available personnel. Peter Drucker, a noted industrial consultant, states the situation in concise terms:[5]

> "It has become almost a truism in American management that the human resources is of all economic resources the one least efficiently used, and that the greatest opportunity for improved economic performance lies in the improvement of the effectiveness of people in their work."

This observation applies equally to the field of police administration. In his writings Mr. Drucker expresses concern for the development of the "responsible worker" and points out that there are four essential factors to be taken into consideration; (a) careful placement; (b) high standards of performance; (c) provide the worker with information that is essential to his needs, and (d) provide an opportunity for his participation in activities that will give him management vision. These four factors could be applied in any program of police personnel development. The same writer also makes the obvious point that:

> "To motivate the worker to peak performance, it is equally important that management set and enforce on itself high standards for its own performance of those functions that determine the workers ability to perform."

This statement directs attention to two sound administrative principles: (a) the need for the administration to set an example of effective conduct, and (b) the responsibility of administration to assure that the department personnel have the necessary direction and facilities to permit the accomplishment of their assigned tasks.

A personnel development program should be dynamic and geared to the growth and flow of public service demands. It must be broad enough in scope to provide guidance and encouragement to all department personnel especially those in the midmanagement and top administrative levels. While relatively few will actually qualify for command positions, the larger number of mid-management members will be the persons in actual direct control and supervision of major functional units and they must therefore be made a part of the administrative team. A sound personnel development program will provide a number of auxiliary benefits of appreciable value to the administration of which the following are a few examples:

(a) It will stimulate a real and lasting interest among the personnel and foster the belief that the service is a worthwhile endeavor,

(b) It will encourage assessment of the worth of each member and the department as a whole in terms of services performed rather than cost in terms of tax dollars expended,

(c) The agency will acquire a resource of management knowhow and experience that will assist the administration in the timely solution of problems,

(d) The administration will not suffer from lack of continuity in objectives or services upon the termination of a key administrator. The training program will provide a replacement who will be able to assume the responsibility without disruption in operations,

(e) The department will be in a position to provide administrative talent to an allied agency. This type of cooperative support tends to build mutual respect and co-ordination between agencies.

(f) Promotional opportunities within the department will be improved thereby stimulating morale in the lower echelons.

(g) Public recognition of the demonstrated administrative ability and effective performance of police services will lead to citizen support of other department programs essential to public service, and

(h) Public acceptance of the staff development program will

attract to the police service young men of ability who seek identification with a career activity with a professional potential.

THE NEED FOR POLICE RESEARCH

Business, industry, government and the professions have undertaken research activity in an attempt to gather a basic fund of useful knowledge that will contribute to the understanding of their primary field of interest. This gathering of knowledge is pursued in the belief that it will assist in the measurement and control of the functional environment wherein the individual organization provides its service. Research, properly conducted, has proven its worth in many areas. Whereas research activity was considered an unusual function and suffered from restricted budget and technical staff a few decades ago it is now considered the key to the future by every organization that has had the courage and foresight to participate in a planned program. Business and industry have tended to limit research activity to areas of immediate concern in relation to the economic and profit aspects of the individual company. In many essential public services the government has established its own research programs or has sought industrial participation through contract and financial grants. Research has been undertaken in such areas as; public education, highway transportation, water pollution, smog control, urban redevelopment, job training, child care, communicable disease control, and many others. The police service has not enjoyed the benefit of the general acceptance of research. Some studies have been undertaken with relation to "delinquency" and "rehabilitation" but these were prompted primarily from the view of the social adjustment of the individual.

The police service must demonstrate its interest in and acceptance of the need for basic research in the law enforcement field. In the isolated instances where research has been undertaken it is marked by its restricted scope and reflects the tendency of most police agencies to avoid direct association with the research activity. During the last fifteen years a number of major departments have moved toward research by the establishment of "research and planning" units. However, few of these operational units actually engage in or are qualified to undertake basic research in areas of immediate concern to law enforcement. Most of these "research and planning" units devote time to routine analysis of operational statistics, the preparation and issuance of department orders or the preparation of public relations releases. The lack of enthusiasm toward basic research study on the part of the law enforcement agency is in sharp contrast to the growing interest in police data manifested by outside organizations. The police service has not been able to establish proof that past and current programs and procedures are winning the battle with crime. The progress of the future lies in the imaginative use of research opportunities.

Basic research is needed in the field of police personnel selection. The selection devices mentioned in this text suggest specific study areas. In summarizing the status of personnel testing C. H. Lawshe states:[6]

> "Tests are not a cure-all for all personnel ills. They cannot be used to clear up the results of mismanagement and supervisory bungling. They will not always work in every situation; and when they do work they will not yield perfect results. The adequacy of a test or a testing program is evaluated not in terms of perfection but in terms of batting odds. A particular test should not be criticized because it resulted in the hiring of one or two bad employees but rather it should be evaluated in terms of whether or not it selected fewer bad employees that the previously used technique. And finally, it should be clearly understood that tests are not advocated as a substitute for tried and true selection and placement procedures. Instead, tests are instruments that yield facts about the applicant, which facts, in combination with other facts obtained from the application blank, from references, and from the interview, make possible a more intelligent and reliable hiring decision."

Hence, it can be readily seen that there are many avenues of important research in the matter of personnel management. Each advance in testing technique that can be developed will reduce the margin of error in the selection process which will in turn reduce the loss of funds expended in the processing and training of recruits. The savings in selection will permit more effective use of the funds in the up-grading of qualified personnel and the development of other internal programs. The urgent need for a plan of action is evident in the significant social movements of today which find the police agencies standing between the many contending forces. Quinn Tamm, Executive Director of the International Association Chiefs of Police recently stated:[7]

> "The most important lesson is that there is no status quo in law enforcement. There must be constant progress, brought about by careful scrutiny of the department structure, operations and end results, as well as continuous anticipation of changes in the community that will call for periodic evaluation of the law enforcement processes."

This observation was confirmed recently by another recognized police administrator who while participating in a seminar organized for the purpose of discussing police planning and research made the terse statement:[8]

> "The police administrator is paid to anticipate."

The research opportunities in the field of police service are many. The following excerpts taken from recent police publication is illustrative of the scope of the challenge;[9]

> "The image American law enforcement projects to the nation and the world is negative. . . . . .
>
> ". . . . the cleavage between the police and the community is no longer confined to the criminal elements, minority groups, and slum areas. It seems to have expanded to the great middle class for reasons that are not clear. This is significant because the middle class tends to set the standards for the community.
>
> "Police functions that need review and radical change are police personnel management, police control practices, organizational patterns, the concept of crime prevention and activities which have been scrutinized by every congressional and state investigating agency; namely, questionable practices in the interrogation, custody and treatment of police prisoners. . . . . .
>
> ". . . . the advancement made in police technology is not as substantial as we are led to believe, primarily because it has materially assisted the police to withdraw from the community, to become isolated. The comtemporary police officer's con-

tact with the public is distant — if it exists at all — and the friendly personal relationship is lost or obscure."

These are indicative of the rich opportunities that await the progressive police administrator. The challenge is clear; the steps are uncharted but the means of progress have been tested and proven.

Law enforcement cannot stand by any longer waiting for some other group to offer solutions to its basic problems. Answers to police administration questions, the improvement in personnel techniques, the modernization of operating procedures must generate from the police services. Existing methods of procedure must be examined objectively and retained if valid and discarded if they do not meet the demands of the service. Over the years the law enforcement service has made accommodation for the use of devices and techniques developed outside of the service. A major portion of the credit for police success can be attributed to these adopted tools. It remains for the service to analyze its basic functional concepts and philosophy in the light of modern requirements. The search for new concepts and a fresh approach to continuing problems will be facilitated immeasurably by the use of talent possessed by department personnel who have been carefully selected and are encouraged by an enlightened administration.

PERSONNEL SELECTION IS THE KEY TO THE FUTURE OF LAW ENFORCEMENT SERVICE.

BIBLIOGRAPHY

1. Frost, Thomas M.: *A Forward Look in Police Administration.* Springfield, Thomas, 1959.
2. O'Connor, George M.: Survey of selection methods. *The Police Chief.* October, November and December issues 1962, Volume XXIX, Numbers 10, 11 and 12.
3. Vollmer, August.: *Police Organization and Administration.* Sacramento, California State Department of Education, 1951.
4. See Rules and Regulations of the Commission on Peace Officer Standards and Training. Issued on October 23, 1960, and subsequent directives in compliance with Sections 13506 and 13510 of the Penal Code of California.

5. Drucker, Peter F.: *The Practice of Management.* New York, Harper and Row, 1954.
6. Lawshe, C. H.: *Principles of Personnel Testing.* New York, McGraw-Hill, 1948.
7. Tamm, Quinn: Rebuilding a scandal-torn police force. *The Police Chief,* Volume *XXIX:*Number 2, February 1962.
8. Holstrom, John D.: Paper presented before the Police Planning and Research Institute, April 24, 1963, Oakland, California.
9. Brandstatter, A. F.: New frontiers for the police. *Police,* Volume *7:* Number 2, November-December 1962.

SAMPLE PRESS RELEASE MATERIAL FOR USE IN RECRUITMENT

A CAMPAIGN TO RECRUIT deputy sheriff matrons began with the publication of a two-column photograph of a very attractive young female deputy opening a barred cell door with a big ring of shiny keys. Underneath the photograph was the caption, "Class in the Calaboose." The accompanying copy read:

> "Marilou M_____ is (insert jurisdiction)'s nomination for America's best looking turnkey. She's a matron at the county jail, and the sheriff's department is looking for two more like her. Matrons hold deputy sheriff rank and are concerned primarily with custody of female prisoners. Interested women between twenty-one and thirty-three should contact the civil service office in the Courthouse. Closing dates for application is (given date)."

A follow-up article published the following week featured the same good-looking girl, this time posed next to a shiny new patrol car. The caption stated, "Sheriff Seeks Exceptional Women," and was followed by this copy:

> "The (jurisdiction) Sheriff's Office has announced there are a limited number of openings for exceptional young women who are seeking a career in law enforcement. Sheriff _____ stated that examinations are being held (given date) to select women candidates for assignment to the Corrections Division of the Sheriff's Office. This position is open to all young women between twenty-one and thirty-three years of age who meet the physical and educational requirements. County residence requirements have been waived for this position, which pays $581 a month at the top scale."

> "Interesting and varied assignments await those selected for employment in this modern and progressive department. Rehabilitation, counselling, supervision and control of inmates, special details and transportation duties are among the many fascinating and rewarding tasks these deputies are allowed to

perform. Previous experience is not required. These job opportunities are offered to all young women who possess the important qualities of intelligence and ability, and who are interested in a challenging career. Successful candidates will be given on-the-job training as well as attendance at departmental and special training schools. Detailed information and applications may be obtained at the county civil service offices in the Courthouse in (town) . Closing date for filing is (date) ."

It is often wise to place paid advertising in the newspaper prior to the release of announcements. The newspaper is, in consequence, often willing to give free space in the form of printing the releases at the same time that it prints the advertisements for the police positions. Copy submitted for publication as a news release might read as follows:

"The (jurisdiction) Civil Service Commission announced today that they are now accepting applications for the position of deputy sheriff. Openings are currently available in this highly sought after law enforcement position.

Candidates who qualify will undergo a series of thorough written, psychological and physical agility tests, all designed to identify men qualified for the serious and rigorous responsibilities of being a deputy sheriff.

The sheriff's office has one of the best retirement programs in (name of state) , in addition to many fringe benefts. In addition to a high salary range (enter) , opportunities for advancement are more in evidence than in many area police agencies. The department has a long-standing policy of encouraging its members to engage in educational programs. The officer who is willing to work hard to reach professional status is among the first to be considered when promotional opportunities arise. Men between twenty-one and thirty-three years of age who have a desire to become a professional law enforcement officer are encouraged to file their application as soon as possible at the county civil service offices."

Appendix II

SOCIOMETRIC RATINGS

D URING ONE PHASE of the psychological testing all the applicants were divided into groups of six men each. They were told to organize themselves to conduct mock oral board examinations. The requirements for the mock examination were that three men serve on the mock board, that one man be interviewed, and that two men observed the board itself rating its members on the goodness of the questions asked. Questions were to be limited to those that a real oral board could be expected to ask; they must be decent and relevant. Each mock board was to sit for fifteen minutes and then to be rotated in such a way that each man in the six man group occupied each position: board member, applicant, and observer. They were all given paper and pencils with which to record their observations. They were not told they would later be asked to rate each other.

After the mock board sessions were completed the men were separated and warned strenuously against looking at each others' comments. They were told to take a clean sheet of paper, not to put their name on it for the ratings were anonymous, and to number from one through sixteen. After each number they were to write the word "Best" and leave a space; then write the word "Least" and leave a space. They were then instructed to choose one of the six men in their group in response to the questions to come as the "best" one, that is the one they would choose to be with or recommend, and to name another man from their group as the one they would "least" want to be with or recommend in the police work situation described by the question.

The questions were as follows:

1. Who in your group is the man you would be most likely to choose to ride in a two man patrol car in a rough and tough area? Which man is your least choice as a partner in a patrol car in a rough and tough area?

2. ...chose to ride in a two man patrol car in an upperclass

neighborhood requiring polite and diplomatic contact with citizens? Least?

3.   ...choose to organize groups of jail inmates to run discussions in the jail among the inmates in order to air their gripes and lead to better understanding by inmates about why they became criminals?

4.   ...expect to receive rapid promotion in the Sheriff's Department because of his ability to lead and direct men?

5.   . . . take a responsible assignment on under-cover work requiring him to keep his mouth shut and his eyes open?

6.   ...in giving testimony to a citizen's crime commision to impress them as a mature person with common sense and a good head on his shoulders?

7.   ...in giving testimony on the witness stand in a criminal case regarding an arrest and evidence would impress the jury as direct, not easily rattled, and a reliable observer.

8.   ...in handling a call by a family reporting their child to be lost would be able to be sympathetic and helpful with that family in distress?

9.   . . . in interrogating a suspect would do a good job?

10.   ...able to deal with minority group citizens, Negroes or Mexicans, in an unprejudiced and absolutely fair fashion?

11.   ...would you trust to be honest and moral; to refuse bribes, deny unfair favors to friends, and to refuse offers to go along with vice.

12.   ...would be prompt and well organized in writing up his reports of incidents, arrests, and daily activities?

13.   ...to be able to take unpleasant orders from superiors without rebellion, delay or griping?

14.   ...to be able to avoid being too soft or tender hearted, or being conned by an offender?

15.   ...to withstand the temptation of throwing his weight around, of being too hard on suspects, of abusing the rights of citizens, or of being "badge-happy"?

16.   Were you actually on an oral board for this examination, who would you most want to see become a fellow officer? Who least?

Appendix III

MATERIALS FOR USE IN BACKGROUND INVESTIGATION

POLICE DEPARTMENT

HALL OF JUSTICE

REFERENCE
NUMBER

Dear Sir: Re:

Birthdate:

Height: Weight:

Fingerprint class:

       The above person is an applicant for a position in this department and at one time resided or was employed in your jurisdiction.

       It will be greatly appreciated if you will cause a check to be made of your files and let us know whether or not this individual has ever come to your attention. A brief synopsis of any derogatory information will materially assist in determining his suitability for police employment. You may use the bottom or reverse side of this sheet in replying.

       Thank you for your cooperation. If we may render similar service to you at any time, please call upon us.

       Very truly yours,

S2/bbg

       Chief of Police

Identification files _____

Traffic _____

Juvenile _____

Other _____

POLICE DEPARTMENT

who attended your school from   to
                                    is an applicant for a position
as police officer in this department.

We feel it essential that the personal history of a police officer be above reproach. We are soliciting your assistance in determining his pattern of personal conduct.

It will be appreciated if you will check school records to determine if he was a disciplinary problem while attending your school. A brief statement concerning his scholastic ability and extra-curricular activities will also be helpful. The enclosed sheet is for your convenience.

Your cooperation in assisting us to select officers of unquestioned integrity is appreciated.

Very truly yours,

/bbg

Enclosure   Chief of Police

POLICE DEPARTMENT

CONFIDENTIAL INQUIRY

has applied for a position in this department. We are informed that you can furnish information of value concerning the applicant's qualifications.

Will you please assist us by expressing your opinion of this individual in answer to the questions on the attached sheets. None of your replies or comments will be seen by, or be quoted to, the person in question.

We rely upon well-informed individuals to assist us in the selection of personnel of outstanding integrity who are qualified for public service training, and who will maintain high standards of performance in the police field. Also, the information you supply may permit us to guide the unqualified candidate into a field more compatible with his personal qualifications.

Your cooperation and an early reply in this matter will be appreciated.

Very truly yours,

/bbg   Chief of Police

POLICE DEPARTMENT

REFERENCE
NUMBER

who was a tenant at
from   to   is an
applicant for a position as police officer in this department.

We feel it essential that the personal history of a police officer be above reproach. We are soliciting your assistance in determining if, while living at the address indicated, he exhibited the qualities of character, integrity, sobriety and reputation which a police officer must demonstrate.

Will you kindly give us your estimate of him in the points indicated on the enclosed sheet? None of the replies or estimates will be seen by, or quoted to, the candidate.

Your cooperation in assisting us to select men of unquestioned integrity is appreciated.

Very truly yours,

S2/bbg

1 enclosure   Chief of Police

Concerning _____
1. The applicant attended this school from _____
    to _____ .
2. His highest grade attained was _____ .
3. The type of course he took was _____ .
4. Academically speaking, his work was _____ .
    If poor or unsatisfactory, state the primary reasons:

_____
_____

5. His I.Q. is approximately _____ .
6. His extracurricular activities were: (1) _____Overindulged.
                                          (2) _____Average.
                                          (3) _____Neglected.
7. His general reputation morally was: (1) _____Excellent.
                                          (2) _____Satisfactory.
                                          (3) _____Questionable.

8. He (was) _____ (was never) _____ suspended while enrolled in this school. If so, state the reasons:_____
_____.

9. The previous school that this student attended was _____
_____.

Please state any further remarks that may effect the applicant's desirability as a police officer with the City of _____.

_____

_____

Name _____
Title _____
School _____
Date _____

Concerning the application of _____ .

1. What were the dates of his employ with your company?
   From _____ to _____ .

2. (a) What was the nature of his job at the start? _____
   _____

   (b) What was he doing when he left? _____
   _____

3. He states he was earning $_____ per _____ .
   Is that correct? Yes _____ No _____

4. Did he follow instructions satisfactorily? _____
   _____

5. Did he show an ability to learn readily? _____
   _____

6. Was his attendance record good? _____

7. Did he lose much time because of poor health? _____

8. Do you know any financial difficulties he had? _____
   _____

9. Did he have any domestic problems that interfered with his job? _____

10. How did he get along with his supervisor? _____
    _____

   With his fellow workers? _____

11. What type of safety record did he have? _____
Was he involved in any accident? _____

12. How would you describe his honesty, morals, and personal habits? _____

13. Would you re-employ him? _____
Why? _____

14. Are you convinced that he is honest, reliable and capable enough to be given a responsible job as a police officer? If not, why? _____

15. For whom did he work just before he entered your firm?
Company name: _____
Address: _____
Supervisor: _____
Nature of the applicant's job: _____

16. For whom did he work next after leaving your firm?
Company name: _____
Address: _____
Supervisor: _____
Nature of applicant's job: _____

17. If you know of other persons who may be able to furnish information concerning his character or work record, please give their names and addresses:

Signed _____
Position _____
Address _____
Date _____

CONFIDENTIAL REPORT

Applicant

1. Are you related to the applicant? _____ If so, what is the relationship? _____

2. Between what dates did the applicant rent from you?
    From _____ To _____

3. Did the applicant pay his rent regularly? _____ If he did did not pay regularly, what were the circumstances? _____

    _____

4. Why did the applicant leave your quarters? _____

    _____

5. To your knowledge, did the applicant ever use drugs or intoxicants? _____ If so, to what extent? Please explain fully. _____

6. Would you recommend the applicant for the position of Patrolman? _____

7. Is the applicant of good moral character? _____
    If not, state why. _____

8. Are you aware of any circumstances which might disqualify the applicant for public service? _____

    _____

9. Please give any additional pertinent facts which may occur to you. _____

    _____

Signed _____

Address _____

_____

Date _____

Below is a list of questions which may aid the investigator interviewing persons, involved in one way or another, with police
applicants. Aim for specific facts to back up any statement given.

1. How long has the person known the applicant, how well, and
   what has been the person's relationship with the applicant?
2. Is the applicant industrious and is his work accurate?
3. Does the applicant initiate work?
4. What is the applicant's ability to work with others?
5. Is the subject often away from work due to illness?
6. Is the applicant generally liked by persons with whom he
   comes into contact?
7. Can the applicant control his temper?
8. Does the person being interviewed know of anyone with
   whom the applicant has been quarrelsome or who dislikes
   him?
9. What is the reputation of the applicant's social associates?
10. What type of reputation does the applicant posses concerning
    credit and for taking care of his financial obligations?
11. Has the person being interviewed observed the subject when
    he has been drinking? How often and how much does the
    applicant drink? How does drink affect him?
12. Has the applicant been known to gamble? To what extent?
13. Has the applicant's home life been consistently happy? If
    not, what has been the cause of his unhappiness?
14. What is the subject's reputation with women? Is he the
    "Casanova or Don Juan" type?
15. Prior to assignment to police duty, recruits attend a recruit
    training school. Among other purposes, this is to develop
    necessary knowledges, skills, to develop desirable abilities
    and to correct any deficiencies. What are the applicant's de-
    sirable qualities? What deficiencies might need correcting?
16. Who else knows the applicant well? This question is used to
    develop other sources of information.
17. Have there been any instances where the applicant has
    shown a deviation from consistently good judgment?
18. Is there any reason to question the applicant's moral or
    physical courage?

BACKGROUND INVESTIGATION REPORTS

Below is listed a general outline for the writing of background investigation reports. The general format of this outline should be adhered to for the sake of uniformity; however, the content of the report under the main headings may be varied to fit the individual situation.

I. OPENING
   A. Brief description of the applicant.
      1. Attach picture, if any, taken at time of fingerprinting.
      2. Include age, date of birth, and where born.

II. RESIDENCES
   A. Start with present address and work back to address at time of tenth birthday.
      1. Describe house, neighborhood, atmosphere of area in general.
      2. Describe contacts with neighbors and landlord in each instance.
      3. Account for each period of time—if letters were sent out of state or area—state where letters were sent and results if available at time of report.

III. EDUCATIONAL BACKGROUND
   A. College, if any.
      1. Report on contacts made with advisors or teachers.
      2. If a graduate—check year book if practicable and report on activities listed.
      3. Obtain information concerning any student groups the applicant might have been a member of.
      4. Report on grades—compare with those claimed on Personal History Form.
      5. Report on health record—absences due to illness.
      6. Report on any indication of misconduct or behavior problems.
   B. High School
      1. Same as above for college. Best contact is usually with counsellor.
   C. Grammar School
      1. Information concerning any contacts made with Principals or teachers who might have known or taught the subject.

IV. FINANCIAL AND CREDIT HISTORY
  A. Credit Bureaus and Associations.
    1. General report on credit history.
  B. Banks
    1. Status of checking account, if any, and verification of statement of savings.
  C. Charge accounts
    1. Information concerning whether or not paid on time and any instances of delinquency.
V. MILITARY SERVICE
  A. When, where and how entered specific branch of service.
  B. Rank attained and duties.
  C. Report concerning contacts made with former members of unit if they are available for interview.
  D. Results of letter sent to Records Center.
VI. CRIMINAL AND TRAFFIC RECORD
  A. Results of local file check.
  B. Results of FBI and CII check.
  C. Results of DMV and DDL check.
  D. List and briefly describe description of any traffic accidents in which involved.
  E. Results of letters and contacts made with all PD's and SO's where lived, worked, or near location where stationed while in the service.
VII. PAST EMPLOYMENT
  A. Results of talks with employers, supervisors, and fellow employees.
  B. Information concerning specific duties performed.
  C. How much sick time was taken while employed.
  D. Evidences of whether he was an agitator, chronic griper, or trouble maker.
VIII. FAMILY RELATIONS
  A. Result of interview with wife.
  B. Result of interview with father and mother.
  C. Result of interview with in-laws, if any.
  D. Results of interview with others.
    1. Aunts, uncles, brothers and sisters, etc.
X. REFERENCES
  A. Results of interviews with references.

IX. PERSONAL RELATIONS
   A. Results from friends and sub-references.
   B. Girls applicant has dated.
   C. Report on any evidence of drinking, gambling, "chasing."
   D. Good deeds performed for others.
XI. MEDICAL HISTORY
   A. Result of interview with family physician.
XII. SUMMARY
   A. Un-investigated leads or work remaining to be done.
   B. Summary of personality of the applicant as supported by the investigation. Positive—Negative.
   C. Last paragraph to be recommendation regarding employment of the applicant.

POLICE DEPARTMENT

HALL OF JUSTICE

REFERENCE
NUMBER

**REQUEST FOR AND CONSENT
TO RELEASE OF INFORMATION**

This is to request that any information on the following matters be provided to:

, Chief of Police
, California

☐ 1. Record of any medical treatment or history of treatment for nervous or mental illness.

☐ 2. Transcript of scholastic record.

☐ 3. Record of any disciplinary action.

☐ 4. Information concerning my loyalty to this country and its institutions, or other information that would negatively affect my handling classified or confidential information.

☐ 5. Record of any credit history.
The following will serve to identify my records. My name is

--------------------------------   ----------------------------
           (Witnessed)   (Signature)

--------------------------------   ----------------------------
             (Date)   (Date)

314-1087

REQUEST FOR AND CONSENT TO RELEASE OF INFORMATION FROM CLAIMANT'S RECORDS

NOTE.—The execution of this form does not authorize the release of information other than that specifically enumerated herein.

TO	Veterans Administration,	NAME OF VETERAN (*Type or print*)
		CLAIM NO. (*If no C–No. give other identifying number*) C–

NAME AND ADDRESS OF ORGANIZATION, AGENCY, OR INDIVIDUAL TO WHOM INFORMATION IS TO BE RELEASED

VETERAN'S REQUEST

I hereby request and authorize the Veterans Administration to release the following information, from the records identified above, to the organization, agency, or individual named hereon:

INFORMATION REQUESTED (*Number each item requested and give the dates or approximate dates—period from and to—covered by each.*)

This is to request that any information on the following matters be

sent to   , Chief of Police,   .

1. Record of any history of treatment for nervous or mental illness.

2. Record of any disciplinary action, courts-marital or official reprimands.

3. Record of any derogatory information concerning my loyalty to this country and its institutions.

4. Any other information that would negatively affect my handling classifed or confidential information.

5. Date of/and Place of Birth

6. Date and Place of entry to service.

7. Date and Place of discharge from service.

PURPOSES FOR WHICH THE INFORMATION IS TO BE USED

In connection with my application for police employment.

NOTE.—Additional items of information desired may be listed on the reverse hereof.

DATE	SIGNATURE AND ADDRESS OF CLAIMANT, OR FIDUCIARY, IF CLAIMANT IS INCOMPETENT

POLICE DEPARTMENT

DATE FILED

| Month | Day | Year |

PERSONAL HISTORY QUESTIONNAIRE

INSTRUCTIONS

Fill out this questionnaire completely and accurately. If your questionnaire is made out properly it may increase your chances for employment. All statements in your questionnaire are subject to verification. Incorrect statements may bar or remove you from employment. If space provided is inadequate, add another page and identify additional information by item number.

1. YOUR NAME? (Print)

    FIRST   MIDDLE   LAST

2. Give any other names you have used
   or been known by, and attach a statement giving reasons (if none, so state)

   YOUR PHONE NUMBER

   HOME _____

3. YOUR ADDRESS? (Print)

   BUSINESS _____

   NUMBER   STREET   CITY   STATE

4. WITH WHOM DO YOU RESIDE?_____

5. WHEN WERE YOU BORN?_____ 6. WHERE WERE YOU BORN?
                        MONTH   DAY   YEAR

                                         CITY   STATE   COUNTY

7. ARE YOU SINGLE, MARRIED, SEPARATED OR DIVORCED?_____

8. IF SINGLE, DO YOU LIVE WITH YOUR PARENTS? _____ YES OR NO _____

9. GIVE FOLLOWING INFORMATION REGARDING MARRIAGE, OR MARRIAGES:

WHEN	WHERE	BY WHOM	WIFE'S MAIDEN NAME

10. GIVE FOLLOWING INFORMATION CONCERNING YOUR PARENTS AND YOUR SPOUSES' PARENTS:

NAME	ADDRESS	LIVING?	WHERE BORN
FATHER			
MOTHER'S MAIDEN			
FATHER-IN-LAW			
MOTHER-IN-LAW			

11. ARE YOU LIVING WITH YOUR WIFE? _____YES OR NO_____

12. IF NOT, STATE REASONS _____

13. WERE YOU EVER LEGALLY OR VOLUNTARILY SEPARATED? _____YES or NO _____
    HOW MANY TIMES? _____

14. WERE YOU EVER DIVORCED OR HAD A MARRIAGE ANNULLED?_____ YES or NO _____
    HOW MANY TIMES? _____

15. IF A MARRIAGE TO WHICH YOU WERE A PARTY WAS EVER DISSOLVED, FILL OUT THE FOLLOWING:

HOW	TO WHOM WAS DIVORCE GRANTED
SEPARATED	
DIVORCED	
ANNULLED	

16. LIST BELOW EVERY CHILD BORN TO YOU:

NAME	DATE OF BIRTH	PLACE OF BIRTH	WITH WHOM AND WHERE RESIDES?

17. ARE YOU NOW SUPPORTING ALL CHILDREN BORN TO YOU, ADOPTED BY YOU AND STEPCHILDREN?
    _____ YES OR NO_____
    IF NOT, GIVE FULL DETAILS _____
    _____
    _____
    _____

18. HAVE YOU EVER BEEN INVOLVED AS DEFENDANT IN A PATERNITY PROCEEDING ____YES, NO____
    IF YES, STATE FULL DETAILS _____
    _____
    _____
    _____

19. HAS ANY MEMBER OF YOUR IMMEDIATE FAMILY EVER BEEN ARRESTED FOR OR CONVICTED OF A
    FELONY CRIME? _____ YES NO:____   IF YES, GIVE PARTICULARS BELOW

NAME	RELATIONSHIP	CRIME COMMITTED	WHERE ARRESTED

20. GIVE THE NAMES OF EVERY MEMBER OF YOUR IMMEDIATE FAMILY WHO IS STILL LIVING : INCLUDE
FATHER, MOTHER, SISTERS, BROTHERS, UNCLES, AUNTS.

NAME	RELATIONSHIP	ADDRESS	OCCUPATION

21. HAS ANY MEMBER OF YOUR IMMEDIATE FAMILY EVER BEEN TREATED FOR A NERVOUS OR MENTAL
DISORDER? _____ YES OR NO _____ : IF YES, GIVE PARTICULARS BELOW

NAME	RELATIONSHIP	NATURE OF ILLNESS	WHERE & BY WHOM TRT'D

22. ARE YOU A CITIZEN OF THE UNITED STATES? _____YES NO _____: (Only U.S. Citizens are eligible
to apply: If not a native born
NATURAL BORN : ____ NATURALIZED ____ DERIVATIVE _____   citizen, present naturalization
papers.)

23. HAVE YOU EVER BY WORD OF MOUTH OR IN WRITING ADVOCATED, ADVISED, OR TAUGHT THE
DOCTRINE THAT THE GOVERNMENT OF THE UNITED STATES OF AMERICA OR OF ANY STATE
OR ANY POLITICAL SUBDIVISION THEREOF SHOULD BE OVERTHROWN OR OVERTURNED BY
FORCE, VIOLENCE, OR ANY UNLAWFUL MEANS? _____ YES OR NO_____

24. ARE YOU NOW OR HAVE YOU EVER BEEN A MEMBER OF ANY SUBVERSIVE ORGANIZATION ?
_____ YES NO _____

25. HAVE YOU EVER BEEN CONNECTED OR AFFILIATED IN ANY MANNER WITH OR HAVE YOU EVER
ATTENDED ANY MEETINGS OF ANY SUBVERSIVE ORGANIZATION ? _____YES NO____   IF
YES, DESCRIBE THE CIRCUMSTANCES AND REASONS FOR ATTENDANCE.

_____

_____

_____

-3-

RESIDENCES

26. LIST ADDRESSES SINCE YOUR TENTH BIRTHDAY, STARTING WITH PRESENT ADDRESS AT TOP

FROM MO. YR.	TO MO. YR.	ADDRESS OF RESIDENCE	CITY AND STATE	FROM WHOM RENTED INCLUDE ADDRESS

EMPLOYMENT

27. WHAT IS YOUR OCCUPATION OR CALLING? _____

28. ARE YOU NOW OR HAVE YOU EVER BEEN ENGAGED IN ANY BUSINESS AS AN OWNER, PARTNER, OR CORPORATE MEMBER? _____YES OR NO _____: IF YES, GIVE DETAILS BELOW:

_____
_____
_____

29. WHAT IS YOUR SOCIAL SECURITY NUMBER? _____

30. WERE YOU EVER DISCHARGED OR FORCED TO RESIGN BECAUSE OF MISCONDUCT OR UNSATISFACTORY SERVICE? _____YES OR NO _____: IF YES, GIVE DETAILS BELOW:

_____

31. HAVE YOUR EMPLOYERS ALWAYS TREATED YOU FAIRLY? _____YES OR NO_____: IF NOT, EXPLAIN

_____

32. DO YOU OBJECT TO WEARING A UNIFORM? _____YES OR NO _____

33. DO YOU OBJECT TO WORKING NIGHTS? _____ YES OR NO _____

34. HAVE YOU HAD EXPERIENCE WITH SHIFT WORK? _____YES OR NO _____

35. HAVE YOU EVER FILED A CLAIM FOR WORKMAN'S COMPENSATION? _____YES   NO_____: IF YES, GIVE DETAILS BELOW:

_____
_____
_____
_____
_____

36. List all jobs you have held in the last ten years. Put your present or most recent job first. By being complete you may improve your chances for employment. If you need more space, you may attach additional sheets. Include military service in proper time sequence and temporary part-time jobs.

FROM_____TO _____   EXACT TITLE OF POSITION_____.
　　　Month and Year　　　Month and Year

NAME AND ADDRESS OF EMPLOYER   YOUR DUTIES ARE:

NAME & TITLE OF YOUR SUPERVISOR

REASON FOR LEAVING   NUMBER SUPERVISED   SALARY PER
                                                        MONTH:

FROM_____TO _____   EXACT TITLE OF POSITION_____
　　　Month and Year　　　Month and Year

NAME AND ADDRESS OF EMPLOYER   YOUR DUTIES WERE:

NAME & TITLE OF YOUR SUPERVISOR

REASON FOR LEAVING   NUMBER SUPERVISED   SALARY PER
                                                        MONTH:

FROM_____TO _____   EXACT TITLE OF POSITION_____
　　　Month and Year　　　Month and Year

NAME AND ADDRESS OF EMPLOYER   YOUR DUTIES WERE:

NAME & TITLE OF YOUR SUPERVISOR

REASON FOR LEAVING   NUMBER SUPERVISED   SALARY PER
                                                        MONTH:

FROM_____TO _____   EXACT TITLE OF POSITION_____
　　　Month and Year　　　Month and Year

NAME AND ADDRESS OF EMPLOYER   YOUR DUTIES WERE:

NAME & TITLE OF YOUR SUPERVISOR

REASON FOR LEAVING   NUMBER SUPERVISED   SALARY PER
                                                        MONTH:

FROM_____TO _____   EXACT TITLE OF POSITION_____
　　　Month and Year　　　Month and Year

NAME AND ADDRESS OF EMPLOYER   YOUR DUTIES WERE:

NAME & TITLE OF YOUR SUPERVISOR

REASON FOR LEAVING   NUMBER SUPERVISED   SALARY PER
                                                        MONTH:

. 36. CONTINUED ....

List all jobs you have held in the last ten years. Put your present or most recent job first. By being complete you may improve your chances for employment. If you need more space, you may attach additional sheets. Include military service in proper time sequence and temporary part-time jobs.

FROM_____TO _____   EXACT TITLE OF POSITION_____
　　　Month and Year　　　Month and Year

NAME AND ADDRESS OF EMPLOYER   YOUR DUTIES ARE:

NAME & TITLE OF YOUR SUPERVISOR

REASON FOR LEAVING   NUMBER SUPERVISED   SALARY PER
　　　　　　　　　　　　　　　　　　　　　　MONTH:

FROM_____TO _____   EXACT TITLE OF POSITION_____
　　　Month and Year　　　Month and Year

NAME AND ADDRESS OF EMPLOYER   YOUR DUTIES WERE:

NAME & TITLE OF YOUR SUPERVISOR

REASON FOR LEAVING   NUMBER SUPERVISED   SALARY PER
　　　　　　　　　　　　　　　　　　　　　　MONTH:

FROM_____TO _____   EXACT TITLE OF POSITION_____
　　　Month and Year　　　Month and Year

NAME AND ADDRESS OF EMPLOYER   YOUR DUTIES WERE:

NAME & TITLE OF YOUR SUPERVISOR

REASON FOR LEAVING   NUMBER SUPERVISED   SALARY PER
　　　　　　　　　　　　　　　　　　　　　　MONTH:

FROM _____TO _____   EXACT TITLE OF POSITION_____
　　　Month and Year　　　Month and Year

NAME AND ADDRESS OF EMPLOYER   YOUR DUTIES WERE:

NAME & TITLE OF YOUR SUPERVISOR

REASON FOR LEAVING   NUMBER SUPERVISED   SALARY PER
　　　　　　　　　　　　　　　　　　　　　　MONTH:

FROM_____TO _____   EXACT TITLE OF POSITION_____
　　　Month and Year　　　Month and Year

NAME AND ADDRESS OF EMPLOYER   YOUR DUTIES WERE:

NAME & TITLE OF YOUR SUPERVISOR

REASON FOR LEAVING   NUMBER SUPERVISED   SALARY PER
　　　　　　　　　　　　　　　　　　　　　　MONTH:

37. DO YOU HAVE ANY PHYSICAL DISABILITIES AT THIS TIME OR HAVE YOU EVER HAD ANY?
_____YES OR NO_____ : IF YES, GIVE DETAILS BELOW:

_____
_____
_____

38. LIST BELOW ANY EXTENDED ABSENCES FROM WORK YOU HAVE HAD BECAUSE OF PERSONAL ILLNESS AND DESCRIBE THE CAUSES: _____

_____
_____
_____
_____

39. LIST BELOW EVERY CIVIL SERVICE COMPETITIVE EXAMINATION YOU HAVE TAKEN. IF NONE, SO STATE.

AGENCY	APPROXIMATE DATE OF EXAM.	POSITION ON LIST	STATUS

40. ARE YOU NOW ON ANY ELIGIBILITY LIST? _____ YES   NO _____ : IF YES, LIST BELOW:

_____
_____
_____

41. IF YOU WERE EVER PLACED ON AN ELIGIBILITY LIST AND WERE NOT HIRED, STATE WHY:

_____
_____
_____
_____

42. WERE YOU EVER REJECTED FOR ANY CIVIL SERVICE POSITION? _____YES   NO_____ : IF YES, WHY? _____

_____
_____
_____

43. HAVE YOU EVER PREVIOUSLY SUBMITTED AN APPLICATION FOR APPOINTMENT TO THIS POLICE DEPARTMENT? _____YES   NO_____ : APPROXIMATE DATE: _____

44. HAVE YOU EVER RECEIVED UNEMPLOYMENT INSURANCE OR OTHER FEDERAL, STATE OR LOCAL BENEFITS OR ASSISTANCE? _____ YES   NO _____.

KIND	LOCAL OFFICE	ADDRESS	FOR HOW LONG?

45. IN THE SPACE PROVIDED BELOW LIST YOUR REASONS FOR APPLYING FOR THIS POSITION:

MILITARY STATUS

If you have served with the Armed Forces during the past five (5) years, Veterans Preference may be given if honorably discharged.

46. HAVE YOU EVER SERVED IN A MILITARY OR NAVAL ORGANIZATION OF THE UNITED STATES? _____ YES   NO _____

47. GIVE BRANCH OF SERVICE _____ COMPANY _____ REGIMENT _____ DIVISION _____ SHIP _____

48. WHAT IS YOUR SERVICE NUMBER? _____

49. HIGHEST RANK HELD _____

50. HOW MANY PERIODS OF ACTIVE MILITARY SERVICE HAVE YOU HAD? _____

51. LIST ALL MEDALS AND DECORATIONS AWARDED YOU AS A MEMBER OF THE ARMED FORCES:

52. WHAT IS THE TYPE OF YOUR DISCHARGE? HONORABLE, DISHONORABLE, MEDICAL, HONORABLE CONDITIONS, ETC.? BE EXACT _____

53. GIVE DATE AND LOCATION OF ENTRANCE TO ACTIVE DUTY _____

54. GIVE DATE AND LOCATION OF DISCHARGE _____

55. IF YOU HAVE HAD NO MILITARY SERVICE, GIVE REASONS _____

56. WERE YOU EVER COURT-MARTIALED, TRIED ON CHARGES, OR WERE YOU THE SUBJECT OF A SUMMARY COURT, DECK COURT, CAPTAIN'S MAST OR COMPANY PUNISHMENT, OR ANY OTHER DISCIPLINARY ACTION WHILE A MEMBER OF THE ARMED FORCES? _____ YES   NO _____; IF YES, EXPLAIN BELOW: _____

57. GIVE PERIOD OR PERIODS OF ACTIVE MILITARY SERVICE:

From _____ To _____ From _____ To _____

From _____ To _____ From _____ To _____

From _____ To _____ From _____ To _____

58. ARE YOU NOW OR WERE YOU EVER AN ACTIVE OR INACTIVE MEMBER OF ANY BRANCH OF THE UNITED STATES RESERVE FORCES? _____YES NO_____ STATE WHICH: ACTIVE OR INACTIVE _____

59. BRANCH _____ UNIT _____ RANK_____

ADDRESS _____ FROM _____ TO _____

60. ARE YOU NOW, OR WERE YOU EVER, A MEMBER OF THE NATIONAL GUARD? _____YES NO_____

61. STATE _____ REGIMENT _____ UNIT _____RANK_____

FROM_____ TO _____ TYPE OF DISCHARGE_____

62. LIST ANY DISCIPLINARY ACTION TAKEN AGAINST YOU IN THE NATIONAL GUARD OR OTHER RESERVE UNIT. _____
_____
_____

EDUCATION

63. INDICATE ON FORM BELOW, THE VARIOUS SCHOOLS YOU HAVE ATTENDED AND OTHER INFOR - MATION REQUESTED. IF YOU CANNOT REMEMBER, SAY SO. DO NOT TROUBLE TO WRITE THE SCHOOL FOR INFORMATION.

NAME ADDRESS (CITY AND STATE)	NO. FULL YRS. WORK COMPLETED	WHEN ATTENDED	GRADUATE	PRINCIPAL OR DEAN
GRAMMAR SCHOOLS_____				
JUNIOR HIGH _____ SCHOOLS				
HIGH _____ SCHOOLS				
UNIVERSITY _____ OR _____ COLLEGES _____				

63. SCHOOLS **(Continued)**

NAME ADDRESS (CITY AND STATE)	NO. FULL YEARS WORK COMPLETED	WHEN ATTENDED	GRADUATED	PRINCIPAL OR DEAN
BUSINESS COLLEGES				
EXTENSION OR CORRESPONDENCE COURSES				

HIGH SCHOOL	SUBJECTS TAKEN	GRADES

JUNIOR COLLEGE COLLEGE OR UNIVERSITY	SUBJECTS TAKEN	GRADES

64. WHAT SCHOOL SUBJECTS WERE MOST DIFFICULT FOR YOU?

_____

_____

65. WHAT SCHOOL SUBJECTS DID YOU LIKE BEST?

_____

_____

66. WERE YOU EVER EXPELLED OR SUSPENDED FROM ANY SCHOOL OR WERE YOU EVER DISCIPLINED
BY ANY SCHOOL OFFICIAL? _____ YES   NO _____ : IF YES, GIVE PARTICULARS BELOW.

_____

_____

_____

FINANCIAL HISTORY

67. IS YOUR LIFE INSURED? _____ YES NO _____
    VALUE OR AMOUNT _____ COMPANY _____ CITY & STATE_____

68. HAVE YOU A SAVINGS ACCOUNT? _____ YES NO _____
    AMOUNT _____ BANK _____ CITY & STATE_____

69. HAVE YOU A CHECKING ACCOUNT? _____YES NO _____
    AMOUNT _____ BANK _____ CITY & STATE_____

70. DO YOU HAVE ANY INVESTMENTS? _____YES NO _____
    (stocks, bonds, etc.)

    AMOUNT _____ COMPANY _____ CITY & STATE_____

71. DO YOU OWN OR ARE YOU BUYING YOUR OWN HOME? _____ YES NO _____
    AMOUNT INVESTED _____ BANK OR COMPANY _____
    CITY & STATE_____

72. DO YOU OWN OR ARE YOU BUYING OTHER REAL ESTATE? _____YES NO _____
    AMOUNT INVESTED _____ BANK OR COMPANY_____
    CITY & STATE_____

73. DO YOU OWN OR ARE YOU BUYING AN AUTOMOBILE? _____YES NO _____
    AMOUNT INVESTED_____ AMOUNT OWING_____ MAKE_____ YEAR_____LICENSE_____

74. WHAT INCOME OTHER THAN SALARY DO YOU HAVE AT PRESENT? INCLUDE WIFE'S SALARY.
    _____
    _____

75. HOW MANY PERSONS ARE DEPENDENT UPON YOU FOR SUPPORT?_____

CREDIT HISTORY

76. LIST FIRMS WITH WHICH YOU HAVE, OR HAVE HAD, CHARGE ACCOUNTS. LIST FIRMS FROM WHOM
    YOU HAVE BORROWED MONEY FOR ANY PURPOSE.

    TYPE OF BUSINESS:

    _____
    NAME of FIRM   AMOUNT :

    _____   _____
    Street Address   City & State   Date Opened   Date Closed

    PURPOSE:

CREDIT HISTORY (**Continued**)   TYPE OF BUSINESS:

_____   AMOUNT :
         NAME of FIRM
_____   _____
Street Address   City & State   Date Opened   Date Closed
PURPOSE :

....

                                          TYPE OF BUSINESS:

_____   AMOUNT :
         NAME of FIRM
_____   _____
Street Address   City & State   Date Opened   Date Closed

PURPOSE :
....

                                          TYPE OF BUSINESS:

_____   AMOUNT:
         NAME of FIRM
_____   _____
Street Address   City & State   Date Opened   Date Closed
PURPOSE :
....

                                          TYPE OF BUSINESS:

_____   AMOUNT:
         NAME of FIRM
_____   _____
Street Address   City & State   Date Opened   Date Closed
PURPOSE :
....

                                          TYPE OF BUSINESS:

_____   AMOUNT:
         NAME of FIRM
_____   _____
Street Address   City & State   Date Opened   Date Closed
PURPOSE :
....

76. CREDIT HISTORY (Continued)

WHAT IS YOUR TOTAL INDEBTEDNESS AT PRESENT ? _____
WHAT DOES THIS COVER ?_____

HAVE YOUR CREDITORS TREATED YOU FAIRLY ? _____ . IF NOT, EXPLAIN _____
_____

HAVE YOU EVER BEEN SUED ? _____ YES NO _____ . IF YES, GIVE DETAILS _____
_____
_____

CRIMINAL HISTORY

Answer all of the following questions completely and accurately. Any falsifications or misstatements of fact will be sufficient to disqualify you summarily. (Exclude Traffic Citations)

77. HAVE YOU EVER BEEN ARRESTED OR DETAINED BY POLICE ? _____YES NO_____ - IF YES, GIVE DETAILS BELOW :

CRIME CHARGED _____   POLICE AGENCY _____

DATE _____ DISPOSITION OF CASE _____

CRIME CHARGED _____   POLICE AGENCY _____

DATE _____ DISPOSITION OF CASE _____

CRIME CHARGED _____   POLICE AGENCY _____

DATE _____ DISPOSITION OF CASE _____

78. HAVE YOU EVER BEEN PLACED ON PROBATION ? _____YES NO_____. IF YES, GIVE DETAILS BELOW:
_____
_____
_____

79. HAVE YOU EVER BEEN REQUIRED TO PAY A FINE IN EXCESS OF $25.00 ? _____YES NO _____
IF ANSWER IS YES, GIVE DETAILS BELOW. _____
_____
_____

80. HAVE YOU EVER BEEN REPORTED AS A MISSING PERSON OR AS A RUNAWAY ?_____ YES NO_____
IF ANSWER IS YES, GIVE COMPLETE DETAILS, INCLUDING JURISDICTION, DATES AND OUTCOME.
_____
_____
_____

- 13 -

CRIMINAL HISTORY (Continued)

81. IF YOU HAVE EVER BEEN FINGERPRINTED BY A POLICE AGENCY OTHER THAN FOR AN ARREST, GIVE DETAILS BELOW. YOUR ANSWERS WILL BE CHECKED WITH THE FBI AND OTHER AGENCIES.

AGENCY _____ DATE _____ PURPOSE _____

AGENCY _____ DATE _____ PURPOSE _____

AGENCY _____ DATE _____ PURPOSE _____

DRIVING HISTORY

82. CAN YOU OPERATE A MOTOR VEHICLE? _____YES   NO _____

83. DO YOU POSSESS A VALID OPERATOR'S LICENSE FROM STATE OF CALIFORNIA? ____ YES NO ____
OPERATOR'S LICENSE NUMBER _____ YEAR ISSUED _____

84. DID YOU EVER POSSESS AN OPERATOR'S LICENSE ISSUED BY ANY STATE OTHER THAN CALIFORNIA _____ YES NO _____ . IF YES, GIVE STATE AND NUMBER _____

85. WAS YOUR LICENSE EVER SUSPENDED OR REVOKED? _____YES   NO _____ . IF YES, STATE WHICH AND GIVE REASONS_____

_____

86. WAS YOUR LICENSE EVER RESTORED? _____ YES NO _____ WHEN _____

87. HAVE YOU EVER BEEN REFUSED AN OPERATOR'S LICENSE BY ANY STATE? _____YES NO _____
IF YES, GIVE DETAILS _____

88. HAS YOUR LICENSE EVER BEEN PLACED ON NEGLIGENT OPERATOR'S PROBATION?
_____ YES   NO _____ . IF YES, GIVE DETAILS _____

_____

89. HAVE YOU EVER BEEN INVOLVED IN A MOTOR VEHICLE ACCIDENT? _____ YES NO _____ .
IF ANSWER IS YES, GIVE COMPLETE DETAILS FOR EACH ACCIDENT WHETHER COLLISION OR NON-COLLISION:

Date _____   Police Investigation? _____ Yes   No _____

Location: _____   Cause of Accident: _____

Injury or Non-Injury _____   Who Legally at Fault? _____

Date _____   Police Investigation? _____ Yes   No _____

Location: _____   Cause of Accident: _____

Injury or Non-Injury _____   Who Legally at Fault? _____

Date _____   Police Investigation? _____ Yes   No _____

Location: _____   Cause of Accident: _____

Injury or Non-Injury _____   Who Legally at Fault? _____

CRIMINAL HISTORY (Continued)

90. LIST BELOW ALL TRAFFIC CITATIONS YOU HAVE RECEIVED:

LOCATION (CITY)	APPROX. DATE	NATURE OF VIOLATION	PENALTY OR DISPOSITION

91 WHAT CHURCH DO YOU ATTEND? _____ ADDRESS _____

92. NAME OF RABBI, PASTOR OR PRIEST _____

93. DO YOU TYPE? _____ YES   NO _____ How many words per minute? _____

ACQUAINTANCES

94.

Fill in below the names of five persons not related to you, and not former employers or references, who are friends, fellow students, or fellow workers. Names listed should be those of persons who have seen you frequently during the past year.

NAME _____

ADDRESS _____ RESIDENCE PHONE _____

BUSINESS ADDRESS _____ BUSINESS PHONE _____

BUSINESS, OCCUPATION OR PROFESSION _____

IN WHAT CAPACITY IS THE ABOVE KNOWN TO YOU _____

NAME _____

ADDRESS _____ RESIDENCE PHONE _____

BUSINESS ADDRESS _____ BUSINESS PHONE _____

BUSINESS, OCCUPATION OR PROFESSION _____

IN WHAT CAPACITY IS THE ABOVE KNOWN TO YOU _____

NAME _____

ADDRESS _____ RESIDENCE PHONE _____

BUSINESS ADDRESS _____ BUSINESS PHONE _____

BUSINESS, OCCUPATION OR PROFESSION _____

IN WHAT CAPACITY IS THE ABOVE KNOWN TO YOU _____

REFERENCES (Continued)

NAME _____

ADDRESS _____ RESIDENCE PHONE _____

BUSINESS ADDRESS _____ BUSINESS PHONE _____

BUSINESS, OCCUPATION OR PROFESSION _____

IN WHAT CAPACITY IS THE ABOVE KNOWN TO YOU _____

NAME _____

ADDRESS _____ RESIDENCE PHONE _____

BUSINESS ADDRESS _____ BUSINESS PHONE _____

BUSINESS, OCCUPATION OR PROFESSION _____

IN WHAT CAPACITY IS THE ABOVE KNOWN TO YOU _____

REFERENCES

95. Fill in below the names of six persons not related to you, and not former employers, who have known you intimately for a substantial period, perferably more than 5 years. All persons to whom you refer will be asked to appraise your character, ability, experience, personality and other qualities.

NAME _____ ADDRESS _____

BUSINESS, OCCUPATION OR PROFESSION _____ YEARS KNOWN _____

BUSINESS ADDRESS _____ BUS. PHONE _____ RES. PHONE_____

NAME _____ ADDRESS _____

BUSINESS, OCCUPATION OR PROFESSION _____ YEARS KNOWN _____

BUSINESS ADDRESS _____ BUS. PHONE _____ RES. PHONE _____

NAME _____ ADDRESS _____

BUSINESS, OCCUPATION OR PROFESSION _____ YEARS KNOWN _____

BUSINESS ADDRESS _____ BUS. PHONE _____ RES. PHONE _____

NAME _____ ADDRESS _____

BUSINESS, OCCUPATION OR PROFESSION _____ YEARS KNOWN _____

BUSINESS ADDRESS _____ BUS. PHONE_____ RES. PHONE_____

NAME _____ ADDRESS _____

BUSINESS, OCCUPATION OR PROFESSION _____ YEARS KNOWN_____

BUSINESS ADDRESS _____ BUS. PHONE _____ RES. PHONE _____

NAME _____ ADDRESS _____

BUSINESS, OCCUPATION OR PROFESSION _____ YEARS KNOWN _____

BUSINESS ADDRESS _____ BUS. PHONE_____ RES. PHONE _____

96. I HEREBY CERTIFY THAT ALL STATEMENTS MADE IN THIS QUESTIONNAIRE ARE TRUE AND
COMPLETE, AND UNDERSTAND THAT ANY MISSTATEMENTS OF MATERIAL FACTS WILL SUB-
JECT ME TO DISQUALIFICATION OR DISMISSAL.

_____
(Signature in Full)

_____
(Date and Time Completed)

97. This questionnaire, together with as many of the following as are available, should be delivered to the Chief
of Police,   for the attention of the Personnel Office. If any are not immediately available, they should be mailed in as soon as possible. No appointments will be made until all have been supplied.

1. ABOVE MATERIAL COMPLETED
2. COPY OF BIRTH CERTIFICATE
3. COPY OF HIGH SCHOOL DIPLOMA
4. COPIES OF HONORABLE DISCHARGE
   AND SERVICE RECORD

NAME INDEX

Beall, Wm.: 85
Berger, P.: 85
Blum, Richard: 151, 186, 187, 189, 194
Blumer, Herbert: 85
Brown, C. W.: 86, 102

Cahill, T.: 85
Chope, H.: 85
Comber, E.: 85

Downing, J. J.: 85
Drucker, Peter: 208
Dudycha, G. J.: 99

Fording, A. H.: 85
Frost, T. M.: 56, 200
Fuld, L. F.: 60
Funkhauser, Mary Lou: 85

Germann, A. C.: 52, 58, 104
Ghiselli, E. E.: 86, 100, 101, 102
Gibbons, J.: 85
Gilman, Kay, 85
Goggin, Wm.: 85
Gorer, G.:
Gough, H.: 96, 107, 108
Guidici, J.: 85

Hagen, Elizabeth: 103
Hanman, B.: 61
Holmes, B.: 99
Humm, D.: 106

Jackson, President Andrew: 6

Kahneman, D.: 100, 101

Kendall, W. E.: 67, 68
Kole, D. M.: 105

Lawshe, C. H.: 211
Lewis, B. Earl: 85
Libert, R.: 136

Macrae, D.: 85
Madigan, F.: 85
Mandell, M. M.: 192
Martin, E. M.: 104
Meehan, J.: 85
Meredith, Wm.: 85
Mullineaux, J. E.: 104

Newman, J.: 85

O'Brien, J. C.: 182
O'Connor, G. W.: 99, 109, 110
Oglesby, T. W.: 99
Ordway, S. H.: 182, 192
Osterloh, Wm.: 85

Pomeroy, W.: 85

Rokeach, M.: 96
Ross, J.: 85
Routt, F. V.: 85

Sanford, N.: 96
Smith, Bruce: 161
Stahl, O. Glenn: 7, 182
Sterne, D. M.: 104
Stewart, G.: 85
Stewart, N.: 102
Stone, C. H.: 67, 68

SUBJECT INDEX